# DICTIONARY OF ALCHEMY

BY

MARK HAEFFNER

**A E O N**

Originally published by Aquarian Press
under the title The Dictionary of Alchemy
by Mark Haeffner © 1991

this edition published 2004
by Aeon Books
www.aeonbooks.co.uk

British Library Cataloguing in Publication Data
A C.I.P. is available for this book from the British Library

ISBN 1 904 658 12 1

Printed and bound in Great Britain

# Contents

# Acknowledgements

The help I have found in writing this book has been so complex and varied, that it is difficult to give appropriate thanks here.

The Bible of medieval alchemy was *The Emerald Tablet* (*Tabula Smaragdina*), and this work suggests the vital importance of meditation in the alchemical opus. I was introduced to the meditative approach to philosophy by teachers of Tibetan Buddhism, and have gained immense inspiration for my work from talks by Tibetan lamas. Their inspiring faith and courage in their spiritual practice has given me the confidence to tackle world views far from the realm of rationalist science, and to retain a conviction that our modern outlook is merely a relative and impermanent form of conditioning.

My studies commenced with work on John Dee and his Elizabethan library collection, and over a number of years I have been deeply grateful to the staff of the Duke Humphrey Library, and of the Bodleian Library in general. Without their patient help this work could never have arisen. I also owe thanks to the public library in Oxford, and to the staff of the Warburg Library in London, with its invaluable collection of photographs.

Illustrative material in this work was provided by the Bodleian Library in Oxford, by the Warburg Institute Library in London, and by the British Library, and I am most grateful for their permission to publish these pictures.

Without stalwart personal support from friends and family, this book would not have come to fruition. Faithful friends have helped in so many ways. Sarah Boss provided me with working space, and with tea and inspiration in times of despondency, and I cannot sufficiently thank her. John and Barbara Wankly played a vital role in encouraging me to continue, and they introduced me to experts who gave advice on publishing.

Barbara also introduced me to Mrs Willmott, a lifelong student of alchemy and of wisdom traditions, who provided books and advice.

My long-suffering family have helped to nurse me through a period of ill health whilst I was writing, above all my sister Kate. My sisters Kate and Janey, as well as my parents, offered strong support.

Mike Hookham has given many inspirational talks on mystical philosophy, and I have enjoyed conversations with him on eastern and Tibetan alchemy in the Buddhist tradition. The Tibetan tradition of medical alchemy is, however, as yet too poorly documented to provide an entry here.

On the academic side, I could never have felt confidence in this project without the timely support of Dr Charles Webster, whose work on the Paracelsian physicians provided the basis for my studies. Dr Webster was then at the Wellcome Unit for the History of Medicine in Oxford, and is now Fellow of All Soul's College in Oxford.

The late Dr Charles Schmidt of the Warburg Institute encouraged my early ventures into this area of study.

My friend David Brooks has offered useful perspectives on magical traditions relevant to alchemy.

At an early stage in writing, I approached Eileen Campbell, and she nursed the book through a series of problems, providing support and encouragement to finish this complex task. Without her kind support, the book would never have seen the light of day.

In a work which ranges through Chinese and Indian alchemy, Paracelsian, medieval, Islamic and Hellenistic traditions, it is inevitable that I have relied on a tremendous range of literature, and I apologise in advance if there is any book or source which I have not sufficiently acknowledged. I have made much use of the collected works of C.G. Jung, published by Routledge and Kegan Paul, and I am extremely grateful to Oxford University Press for permission to quote from their edition of the works of Thomas Vaughan, edited by Professor Alan Rudrum (see Bibliography). I have used the Methuen edition of Ben Jonson's marvellous play, *The Alchemist*, and am grateful for permission to quote extracts.

# Introduction

## The Extent and Scope of the Subject of Alchemy

In offering readers *The Dictionary of Alchemy*, it is not easy to justify or to explain the fascination and the range and diversity of this subject without launching into a fresh volume. The very definition of the word 'alchemy' requires rather extensive discussion, and recent studies of the subject reveal that the old view of alchemists as seekers after the elixir or touchstone for transmuting metals into gold is totally inadequate. In his brilliant study of the primitive roots and structure of alchemical thought, *The Forge and the Crucible: The Origins and Structure of Alchemy*, Mircea Eliade traces alchemical concepts back to primitive mythology, and he discusses traditions of alchemy in Chinese Taoist and Indian Sanskrit sources, and also refers to a Burmese tradition. Professor Joseph Needham devotes several substantial volumes of his *History of Science and Civilization in China* to the study of Chinese Taoist alchemy, with prolific illustrations and quotations. Professor Needham also makes references to Indian alchemy, not only in Sanskrit texts, but also in Tamil works; he also refers to alchemy as existing all over South-east Asia, including Japan, Korea and Vietnam. This opens up exciting new vistas in the study of this subject, and my hope is that my *Dictionary of Alchemy* will encourage a more enthusiastic approach to this much neglected area.

Having regard for the vast scope of my subject, the *Dictionary* offers a series of entries which, it is hoped, will illuminate the meaning of alchemy for the many practitioners and philosophers in various cultures who have regarded this as a 'divine art'. The book includes entries on Indian and Chinese alchemy, and I have tried to make some cross-cultural references in other key entries.

The initial inspiration to compose such a dictionary came from the study of the publications of C.G. Jung on this subject. The Jungian approach is brilliantly illuminating in dealing with the multifarious symbolism and myth which surrounded the *opus alchymicum*, but in his enthusiasm for psychological explanation Jung tended to ignore the historical background. He is also rather dismissive about the chemical labours of the alchemists, many of whom had well-equipped laboratories. My book seeks to redress this balance by providing a series of entries which deal with the main personalities of the tradition, as well as illustrating the conceptual structure of alchemical thought. Amidst the wealth of quotations and explanations provided by Jung, there is little help in explaining the basic concepts of the origin and nature of metals and minerals, or the fundamental ideas of the elixir and the Philosophers' Stone. My *Dictionary* is designed to provide a representative selection of the main philosophers of the alchemical tradition, including some who are more 'scientific' in their approach, like Georgius Agricola, the father of metallurgy, and others who are more legendary, like Maria Prophetissa.

The scope of this work means that it is designed to be illustrative rather than comprehensive. The time scale covered is daunting, and the focus is upon the origins and evolution of our western tradition. Although Chinese Taoist alchemy was probably much more ancient, the western tradition is traced back to the Egyptians of Hellenistic times. The historical time limits which I have set for the *Dictionary* cover the period from the Hellenistic mother of the tradition, Maria Prophetissa, or Maria the Jewess, chosen because she is the first identifiable historical personality in early alchemy, to the time of Sir Isaac Newton, whom Maynard Keynes described as being 'the last of the Babylonian and Sumerian magi'. There is now extensive published research on Newton's alchemy, and no biographer can ignore the subject. It seemed appropriate to close my historical period with Newton, since he is the last alchemist who could be said to belong to the ancient adept tradition. In his now famous lecture, Keynes claimed that Newton was the last man to hold a truly Renaissance view of the cosmos, a view in which Creation was seen as a kind of treasure hunt of mystic clues and occult hints.

In general, it is fair to say that alchemy was eclipsed during the eighteenth century, but enjoyed a revival during the nineteenth century with the Theosophical movement and with the creation of the Hermetic Society of the Golden Dawn. The overall shape of the alchemical tradition after the time of Newton has been brilliantly sketched in by Christopher McIntosh in his book *The Rosicrucians*, and it would seem unwise and unnecessary to trespass upon his territory. He shows how the great Rosicrucian movement of the seventeenth century continued to exert its influence during the eighteenth and nineteenth centuries, and how its effects still reverberated in the twentieth century, when it was outlawed by the Nazis. There are a number of publications which deal admirably with the Hermetic Society of the Golden Dawn, which was very important to the intellectual and poetic development of W.B. Yeats. When Yeats joined the society of Hermetic students in 1887, he encountered an old man who practised alchemy, boasting some success in discovering the elixir of life, 'but the first effect of the elixir is that your nails fall out and your hair falls off'. This nineteenth-century adept hoped to drink the elixir when he grew old, but the potion dried up too quickly! (W.B. Yeats, *Selected Criticism and Prose*, p.330)

To extract a clear definition of alchemy from the wealth of material which I have used might be likened to the task of seeking to extract metals from their ores through a laborious process of smelting. The historical sources on alchemy, including its experimental practitioners and its philosophers, are very extensive indeed, and they are not easily accessible. The texts which are available are notorious for the obscurities, the arcane symbolism, and the obsession with secrecy in the art. Most people who are interested in alchemy recognize it as a richly pictorial subject, with its fire-breathing mercurial dragons, its serpents and lions, its unicorns and phoenixes. But there are few people who have sought to initiate themselves into the arcane, mythic texts.

Prior to the plethora of modern research on the subject, writers on alchemy had a fairly easy task. Much work on the western tradition was undertaken by A.E. Waite (a founder member of the Golden Dawn), who composed a number of useful papers discussing the meaning of alchemy and the significance of occult traditions, such as the Cabala, which were so closely associated with alchemy. However, the advance in research on Chinese and Indian alchemy has coincided with a fresh and vigorous investigation of the Paracelsian movement of the sixteenth and seventeenth centuries, and the literature concerned with the subject fills a rather vast bibliography. (Much invaluable material is published in the volumes of the journal *Ambix*, which is devoted to the history of alchemy and early chemistry.) Paracelsian alchemy is now recognized as a key factor in the history of medicine, for Paracelsus, the rebellious Swiss physician, introduced a whole system of alchemical medicine whose impact upon the benighted world of Renaissance medical scholarship was electrifying. Walter Pagel has provided us with a deep insight into the intellectual and spiritual world of Paracelsus himself, and Dr Charles Webster and Professor Allen Debus have done much to reveal the significance of the Paracelsian movement. My *Dictionary* includes entries on the remarkable personality of Theophrastus Paracelsus himself, as upon several of his leading disciples who made original contributions to the alchemical tradition, notably Oswald Croll, Heinrich Khunrath, Petrus Severinus and Jacob Boehme. The

Rosicrucian movement of the seventeenth century was profoundly influenced by Paracelsian alchemy.

In seeking a working definition of alchemy, it seems fair to start with the popular image of alchemy, as the arcane art of transmuting base metals into gold. This image is perhaps best conveyed by an engraving of a picture by Peter Brueghel, which presents the conventional satire of the alchemist amidst the total chaos of his makeshift laboratory, littered with implements and vessels of the art. There is an inset in the top right-hand corner depicting the unfortunate family of the alchemist reduced to seeking alms, after the delusion of this most dangerous art has wrought their undoing. Two literary classics reinforce the image of the charlatan or deluded alchemist, seeking the Stone of the Philosophers, the mysterious elixir or medicine which will heal metals, transmuting them into gold: Chaucer's Canones Yeomans Tale in *The Canterbury Tales* conveys the perils of the fourteenth-century craze for alchemy, and Ben Jonson's brilliant play *The Alchemist* shows that popular practitioners of his time were still loyal to the alchemical myths of the Middle Ages. (Serious students of Shakespeare will also realize at once that his drama is full of allusions to the occult, astrological beliefs of his time, inherited directly from medieval magic and science. Although Shakespeare alludes only rarely to alchemy itself, his world view is permeated by all of the influences which made up the tradition.)

The works of Chaucer and Ben Jonson, in portraying the arts of the alchemist as little better than common deception, involving witchcraft and disreputable magical tricks, represent a tradition which is hostile to alchemy. In 1317, Pope John XXII passed an edict condemning alchemy, which began with the words;

> Poor themselves, the alchemists promise riches which are not forthcoming; wise also in their own conceit, they fall into the ditch which they themselves have digged.
>
> Cited in E.J. Holmyard, *Alchemy*, p.149

This papal bull had been made necessary because the alchemy of transmuting metals had by this time become a demented craze. There is an excellent portrait of this debased form of popular alchemy in an Elizabethan work on magic, *The Discoverie of Witchcraft*, by Reginald Scot (1586), a work which throws light on the anthropology of magic in the age of Shakespeare. Scot includes alchemy amidst his condemnation of magical trickery and fraud. He mocks the alchemists for their terminology: 'For what plaine man would not beleeve that they are learned and jollie fellowes, that have in readinesse so many mysticall termes of art: as (for a tast) their subliming, amalgaming, engluting, imbibing . . .'

In popular folklore, the aim and intention of the alchemist was quite simply to discover a means of transmuting base metals into fabled wealth:

> Now you must understand that the end and drift of all their worke, is, to atteine unto the composition of the philosophers stone, called Alixer [ = Elixir], and to the stone called Titanus, and to Magnatia [Magnesia], which is a water made of the four elements, which the philosophers are sworne neither to discover nor to write of.
>
> Reginald Scot, *The Discoverie of Witchcraft*, Book xiii, Chapter 2

My *Dictionary* offers entries on the concepts of the elixir, the Philosophers' Stone, or the medicine which was supposed to heal defects in corrupt metals. Yet the true meaning of alchemical concepts lies hidden within a complex structure of archetypal images and symbols.

It was this secrecy of the alchemical tradition which led to its condemnation as a spurious occult form of trickery involving forgery of precious metals, and the task of the interpreter is to disentangle the more genuine aspects of alchemy as a spiritual tradition which preserves a fantastic wealth of symbolism and poetic or mystical ideas about the world. The conventional definition, then, relegates the alchemists to the ranks of an extinct species of proto-scientists who dealt in delusion. Medieval scholars were already familiar with attacks upon the validity of the pseudo-scientific theory of transmutation of metals. Reginald Scot cites a well-known passage of the Arab philosopher Avicenna in which he dismisses this theory as delusion: 'Let the dealers in Alcumystrie understand that the verie nature and kind of things cannot be changed, but rather made by art to resemble the same in shew and likenesses; so that they are not the verie things indeed, but seeme so to be in appearance: as castels and towers doo seeme to be built in the clouds.' Such apparitions are nothing else but some 'bright cleere cloud'.

It seems right to start then by admitting the strength of the case against alchemy before seeking to justify the value of studying it. The symbolism and poetry of the tradition have attracted tremendous attention from Jungians since the publication of C.G. Jung's *Psychology and Alchemy* in 1944. But many other studies now throw light upon the cultural significance of the subject. Our understanding of the primitive roots of alchemical thought and philosophy has been enhanced by Mircea Eliade in his fascinating study, *The Forge and the*

*Crucible.* His view is that alchemy may be traced into the mists of prehistory, where primitive, animistic theories of the birth of metals within the womb of the Earth gave rise to notions of transmutation:

> In our view one of the principle sources of alchemy is to be sought in those conceptions dealing with the Earth-Mother, with ores and metals, and, above all, with the experience of primitive man engaged in mining, fusion and smithcraft. The 'conquest of matter' began very early, perhaps in the palaeolithic age, that is as soon as man had succeeded in making tools from silex and using fire to change the states of matter.
>
> *The Forge and the Crucible*, p.142

Alchemy emerges from Eliade's study as an adept tradition which preserves some very primitive, mythological notions of the nature of mines, minerals and metals, and it is impossible to understand the later philosophy of the alchemists without appreciating its roots in prehistoric magical conceptions of nature. Myths and theories about the origin of metals and minerals, about their gestation in the dark depths of the earth, created the basis for later alchemical theories. In this way mineral substances shared in the sacredness attached to Mother Earth. Very early on we are confronted with the notion that ores 'grow' in the belly of the earth 'after the manner of embryos'.

Eliade shows that as a result of this theory smiths and metal-workers were always regarded as carrying out a sacred task. It was believed that metallurgy involved bringing metals to birth from their embryonic form within the womb of Mother Earth, then universally regarded as a goddess. He argues that the smelter, the smith and the alchemist share a common involvement in a task which is both magical and religious, for all three groups are concerned with the pursuit of the 'transformation of matter, its perfection and transmutation'. From earliest times, the crafts and skills of smelting and working metals were sacred, and religious initiation was vital. It thus becomes easier to view the alchemist as natural successor to this primeval work. Alchemists always guarded the sacredness and secrecy of their mystic opus with the greatest strictness. They called themselves 'philosophers' and traced the origins of their tradition back to the great age of Moses and Hermes Trismegistus, even to Adam and Eve.

Some idea of the ancient dignity attributed to the art is given by Edward Kelley in the sixteenth century:

> All sages agree that knowledge of this art was first imparted to Adam by the Holy Spirit, and He prophesied, both before and after the Fall, that the world must be renewed, or, rather, purged with water.

Kelley was employed by Dr John Dee (1527 - 1608) and both men were supposed to have actually discovered a red powder which would transmute metals.

Few writers on the subject have really understood the complexity of true alchemical philosophy. Many who believed in the scientific theory of the transmutation of metals were imbued with the mystical philosophy of nature, which sees man as a microcosm, a small world with an inner heaven corresponding to the greater world, the macrocosm. Men like Dee and Kelley sought understanding of nature from divine sources, by séances in which they spoke with angels, and they regarded the true wisdom of alchemy as a prophetic tradition. Thus the philosophical alchemist might seek gold, but he must always live a life of prayer and meditation, using the texts of the ancient wise men to inspire his study of the natural world, the wonders of divine Creation.

My own researches into early alchemical ideas and beliefs about the natural world, especially its mineral and metallic realms, has been inspired by a faith in the value of what I might call pre-Newtonian philosophies or world views. Many academic studies focus simply upon the objective historical significance of occult traditions, and alchemy may be characterized as a Hermetic tradition. However, it is today becoming increasingly clear that the ruthless exploitation of our mechanistic scientific world view has had devastating consequences for the whole of the natural world around us. Although modern science, with its atomistic and molecular conceptions, seems to speak the truth about the phenomenal world, it certainly does not speak the whole truth, and it yields a very paradoxical vision: most scientists with whom I discuss alchemy are quick to point out the profound mystery of the 'wave particle duality' of matter. The Schrödinger wave mechanics which formed the backbone of quantum physics after the 1920s hardly portrays matter as very solid and tangible. In fact Fritjof Capra in his widely read book *The Tao of Physics*, argues that modern science has emerged with a view of the world which is rather mystical.

Of the major traditions of alchemy, the Chinese Taoist tradition is at least as significant as that of the West, and Taoism provided fertile ground for the flourishing of alchemical notions and symbolism. Although Taoist alchemy is almost certainly far more ancient, there seems no evidence of direct contact or influence from China in Hellenistic alchemy. However, there are remarkable parallels between East and West, and I believe that in both traditions there is a similar atmosphere of veneration and respect for the forces of nature, which belongs to the magical world view.

Egypt, where western alchemy seems to originate, was the legendary home of the prophet Hermes Trismegistus, who was a source of much inspiration to study magic during the Renaissance, and alchemy is often designated as the Hermetic tradition. The great Florentine Platonist Marsilio Ficino was asked by his patron Cosimo dei Medici to translate the Greek texts of the Hermetic tradition, before embarking on Plato's works. This is an indication of the profound veneration for Egypt as the supposed home of theological and magical wisdom, and the excitement of Renaissance scholars was fired by their belief that natural magic and Christian theology could be easily reconciled in the context of the supposedly ancient philosophy of Hermes. The myth of the extreme antiquity of Hermetic works helped the case for alchemy, as did the passion for Christian interpretation of the Cabala during the Renaissance – the Cabala and alchemy have always been strangely close mystic companions, though their exact relationship is a secret preserved by initiates throughout the ages.

Thus the alchemy of the Renaissance generated powerful interest, as adepts realized its potential as both a scientific, experimental tradition and a mystic wisdom tradition in which there was a confluence of gnostic ideas about man and nature. In writing his works on alchemy, Jung was inspired by the idea that alchemy was essentially gnostic, and there has been much recent interest in the nebulous relations of Gnosticism with Hermeticism as religious influences in the West. What are we to make of this whole complex area of study? There is certainly a danger that the whole area of alchemy, gnostic and Hermetic wisdom will disintegrate into impossibly obscure backwaters. However, there remain many people who draw comfort from more ancient and lasting views of the world, reacting with some horror at the materialism of our foolish and destructive technological culture.

Craft traditions in Hellenistic Egypt are generally considered to be the source of alchemy as almost a mystery religion in itself. Most scholars of the subject are rather perfunctory about this problem of origins, dating alchemy back to the dyeing and metallurgical crafts of Egypt in the time of Alexander the Great. However, in my view the emphasis upon craft traditions is not entirely helpful, and it is the mystical and magical nature of alchemy which constantly needs emphasis in our age which is so condescending and hostile towards such beliefs. One of the oldest surviving alchemical texts is a work entitled *Phusika kai mustika*, generally wrongly translated as 'physical and mystical things'. The title in fact refers to the 'things of nature'

(Greek *phusis* means 'nature') and to 'initiatory things' (*mustes* actually means an initiate of the ancient Greek mysteries of Orpheus or Demeter). It thus becomes clear that the true alchemist, the philosopher *par excellence*, seeks a mystical insight into the divine secrets of nature through a rigorous course of study involving both practical chemistry and religious meditation. Thousands of practitioners failed to understand the secrecy of the adept tradition, and they ended up on the rocks!

Modern studies have illuminated the way in which alchemy flourished in many different cultures, being nourished by many and varied magico-religious systems. It is no longer worthwhile to study alchemy as an isolated and eccentric pursuit of medieval gold-makers. The tradition might best be likened to a river which winds its way through history, flowing through a bewildering variety of landscapes.

Hellenistic alchemy was involved with magical initiations, with magicians like the Persian Ostanes, and fell increasingly under the influence of Gnosticism. The two founders of the Hellenistic tradition are Maria Prophetissa, who was supposed in legend to be Miriam, sister of Moses, and Zosimos of Panoplis (third century AD). Maria was called 'the Jewess', and throughout its history in the West, alchemy has had strong associations with the profound mystical system of the Cabala. Since she is also called a 'prophetess', we may presume that she was a mystical religious teacher as well as an alchemist. Zosimos quotes her with reverence in his accounts of laboratory equipment, showing the familiar confusing synthesis of mystical and chemical interests. Jung has provided a classic account of Zosimos' famous disturbing visions, which may be shamanistic, and we know that he was a member of the Poimandres sect of the gnostics. He calls alchemists the 'sons of the golden head', and there can be no doubt that a fully established adept tradition, mystical as well as experimental, existed in his time.

Our own western tradition stems directly from the Arabs, who diligently translated a range of texts from Hellenistic sources. The word 'alchemy', frequently rendered as *alchymia* in Latin, is derived from Arabic *al kimiya*, which refers not only to the art of alchemy, but also to the substance which renders transmutation possible. The word *elixir* is also Arabic, referring both to the 'medicine of metals', and to the elixir of life. (These concepts are more fully explained under their relevant entries.) Islamic alchemy was both strongly practical, as evidenced by the chemistry of Rhazes, and imbued with mystical numerology of the Pythagoreans, as we see in the case of Jabir ibn Hayyan. Jabir was certainly a mystic, his school of alchemy being closely involved with Sufi and Shi'ite Islamic mysticism. Alchemy spread throughout the Islamic world before flowing into medieval Christendom, causing great perplexity and confusion. The texts of Arabic alchemists have as yet been little investigated, however, and all we know is that there was a strong Hermetic element in Islamic science, which awaits further research.

Medieval Christian alchemy presents us with a rich variety of material. There are few texts which are really helpful in explaining the philosophy which lies at the roots of the tradition, although a Bible of medieval alchemy was *The Emerald Tablet*, found also in Arabic versions. Medieval adepts throughout Christendom were often hopelessly confused, and writers like Thomas Norton (*see* his *Ordinall of Alchemy*) attest the universal popularity of alchemy amongst artisans, merchants, noblemen and churchmen of every rank. Major texts were attributed to Plato or Aristotle or Thomas Aquinas as alchemists battled for respectability against dangerous charges of heresy or witchcraft. Alchemy became increasingly part of a subculture, associated with magic and astrology. A revealing text in this context is *The Secret of Secrets*, which was edited by the famous philosopher Roger Bacon, who was also a keen alchemist. This purports to contain advice on the subject of kingship from the philosopher Aristotle to his pupil Alexander the Great. The work provides a mixture of astrology, alchemy, and even phrenology, in a typically medieval synthesis. The wealth of symbolism in the art guided alchemists into the stormy waters of the unconscious psyche, as we may see in the strange and disturbed poems of George Ripley, who was Canon of Bridlington Priory in Yorkshire. There was certainly an esoteric teaching of alchemy, an oral tradition of interpreting the texts which seems to have been strongly millennarian, concerning the material nature of the world, the Creation and the Last Judgement (*see* **Petrus Bonus**).

To provide anything like a full account of the rich world of medieval Hermetic occultism would be impossible within a brief scope, and I hope that some entries in my *Dictionary* may suggest how vital this area of study is, and also how little explored.

Moving from the medieval world to the Renaissance upheaval which affected every area of science and philosophy, we find that 'natural magic' then became far more acceptable. The liberating atmosphere of this period had a tremendous impact upon alchemy, which could now be interpreted in the light of a new world view, which regarded Hermes as an ancient Egyptian prophet, perhaps of the time of Moses – many alchemical texts were attributed to Hermes from the outset of the tradition. Men like John Dee indulged their fascination with cabalist numerology, to produce a form of esoteric alchemy which greatly influenced the rise of the Rosicrucian movement: Dee's *Monas hieroglyphica* (Antwerp, 1564) seems to have created virtually a new alchemical movement. The combined effects of the works of Pico della Mirandola, of Ficino and of Henry Cornelius Agrippa von Nettesheim was to create a truly revolutionary tradition of suppressed wisdom and gnostic enlightenment. Frances Yates has argued that Copernicus and other great Renaissance scientists were deeply influenced by religious Hermetism, and there can be no doubt that alchemy still inspired many deeply religious men to a philosophical study of nature.

The greatest of the reforming Renaissance alchemical philosophers was Theophrastus Paracelsus, who rose to fame as a physician. His voluminous works were edited and published mainly after his death and they inspired a movement of medical alchemy. Recent scholarship on the Paracelsian movement has shown the extent of the 'Paracelsian revolution' in medicine and occult theories of the world. Above all, Paracelsian philosophy involved a view of man as the microcosm, the lesser world, with inner heavens within his psychic constitution. Health and sickness were governed by these inner heavens. Thus man could never be viewed in isolation from the universe, nor could the universe ever be considered as an abstract system, divorced from human experience and human values. It is easy to argue that the havoc wrought by modern scientific technology arises partly from the loss of this dignified world view, in which man and nature are inseparable spiritually. Modern physics has only reluctantly accepted that the observer in experimental science is crucial. In general environmentalists argue that the mechanistic world view created by Descartes drove a wedge between man and nature, leading to the rejection of the ancient tradition of Hermetic wisdom, with its spiritual philosophy (*see especially* Carolyn Merchant, *The Death of Nature*, Wildwood House, 1982). The Paracelsian revolution offered new hope to those who languished amidst the impractical abstractions of Aristotelian logic and philosophy:

> When the *Mysterium Magnum* in its essence and divinity was full of the highest eternity, *separatio* started at the beginning of all Creation. And when this took place, every creature was created in its majesty, power and free will. And so it will remain until the end, until the great harvest when all things will bear fruit, and will be ready for gathering. For the harvest is the end of all growth . . . .. And just as the *Mysterium Magnum* is the wonderful beginning, so the harvest is the wonderful end of all things.

Surveying the wisdom of ancient philosophies, one begins to feel that

if modern cosmologists dropped all of their discourse on the subject
of Black Holes, and spoke merely of the 'Great Mystery' of Creation,
the public might be less deceived as to the explanatory powers of
modern cosmic concepts. In the sixteenth century, Paracelsus drew
upon the oral tradition of alchemical speculation to formulate an
overall alchemical interpretation of Genesis, of the Creation of the
world and of man, through a Trinity of alchemical principles – salt,
sulphur and mercury – which are envisaged not as material elements,
but as spiritual animating principles. With him, we take leave of the
deluded world of the medieval dabbler in Arabic transmutation
theory. His writings bring to birth a new tradition which respects the
deep, divine mystery of Creation in man and nature, yet which
provides a chemical basis for future theories. Man is a microcosm, a
complete world in himself: 'For the sun and the moon and the planets,
as well as stars and the whole chaos, are in man.' Disease and healing
can only be understood in terms of this deep mystery.

The Paracelsians of the sixteenth and seventeenth centuries are an
interesting group, and constitute a major category in my *Dictionary*.
They include Oswald Croll, Petrus Severinus of Denmark, the
Frenchman Duchesne, the German Heinrich Khunrath and the
Englishmen Robert Fludd and John Dee. No alchemist or chemist
worth his salt could ignore Paracelsus during this period, and even
Robert Boyle makes respectful reference to him. Overall, the
Paracelsian view of man as the 'lesser world', whose psyche mirrors
the vastness of the starry cosmos, influenced poets, philosophers,
mystics and theologians. Jacob Boehme inaugurated a tradition of
spiritualized alchemy, free of laboratory work, which was immensely
influential in seventeenth-century mysticism, and the poet Thomas
Traherne in his devotional *Centuries* shows the depth of spiritual
inspiration from Paracelsus:

> You'll never enjoy the world aright, till the sea itself floweth in your veins,
> till you are clothed with the heavens and crowned with the stars.

Alchemical influence permeates the metaphysical poetry of the
seventeenth century, and there are many allusions to the art in Donne.
His poem 'A Nocturnall upon St Lucies Day, Being the shortest day',
is a fine example of the spiritualizing of alchemical ideas:

> Study me then, you who shall lovers bee,
> At the next world, that is at the next Spring,
> For I am every dead thing
> In whom love wrought new Alchimie.

The depth of archetypal mythology of death and rebirth, which the alchemists experienced in the course of their labours in the laboratory, has been shown in the twentieth century by Jung. His argument that adepts were involved in a sort of 'participation mystique', in which the archetypal psyche projected dream-like visions into the world of nature, is confirmed in many texts. There was a popular Middle English poetry of alchemy, which drew upon the myths of 'greene lyons', dragons, serpents, toads and the whole alchemical menagerie (*see* **Beasts and Birds; Dragon; Thomas Norton; George Ripley**).

The cultural impact of alchemy has scarcely been conceded by historians of literature and society; however, a service to this cause has been done by Frances Yates and by Christopher McIntosh in his book *The Rosicrucians*. But as poetry and mysticism were inspired by alchemy, so experimental science also owes its debt to this strange tradition. These areas of interest interweave in the complex Rosicrucian movement. It should never be forgotten that alchemy was experimental in a sense which is deeper than our external meaning: experiment for the alchemist demanded the whole man – *ars totum requirit hominem*. The depth of emotional and religious energy involved, and the interweaving of science and piety, is revealed in a passage from Thomas Vaughan, a passionate Rosicrucian, who was the brother of the metaphysical poet Henry Vaughan:

> On the same Day my deare wife sickened, being a Friday, and at the same time of the day, namely in the Evening, my gracious God did put into my head the Secret of extracting Oyle of Halcali, which I had once, accidentally found at the Pinner in Wakefield, in the dayes of my most deare wife. But it was againe taken from me by a wonderful judgement of God, for I could never remember how I did it, but made a hundred Attempts in vain. And now my glorious God (whose name be praysed for ever) hath brought it againe into my mind, and on the same day my deare wife sickened; and on the Saturday following, which was the day she dyed on, I extracted it by the former practice.

Thus amidst the deepest sorrow and grief, 'God was pleased to conferre upon mee, the greatest Joy I can ever have in this world, after her Death'. The simplest secrets of chemistry were for the alchemist often seen as miracles, as divine revelations of the deepest truths of Creation. Here we are far from the world of the charlatan, the gold-seeking alchemist, the man who indulged only in what Vaughan calls the 'torture of metals'.

The best overall summary and account of the aims of the true adept, as opposed to the dabbler in alchemical chemistry, is that given by Jung in a recorded interview with Mircea Eliade:

> The alchemical operations were real, only this reality was not physical but psychological. Alchemy represents the projection of a drama both cosmic and spiritual in laboratory terms. The *opus magnum* had two aims: the rescue of the human soul and the salvation of the cosmos. What the alchemists called 'matter' was in reality [the unconscious self]. The 'soul of the world', the *anima mundi*, which was identified with the spirit *mercurius*, was imprisonned in matter. It is for this reason that the alchemists believed in the truth of 'matter', because 'matter' was actually their own psychic life. But it was a question of freeing this 'matter', of saving it – in a word, of finding the philosophers' stone, the *corpus glorificationis*.
>
> William McGuire and R.F.C. Hull (eds), C.G. *Jung Speaking*, interview with
> Mircea Eliade, pp.221 – 2

In the modern quest for the true nature of matter, physicists have emerged with a vision of reality which is ever more paradoxical and strange, and it would seem far too soon to pronounce any modern judgement on ancient views of the spiritual nature of matter. Probably the strongest case for a spiritual interpretation of the cosmos is that of Pierre Teilhard de Chardin. Another interesting recent account of modern ideas is provided by David Bohm, himself a brilliant physicist, in *Wholeness and the Implicate Order.*

Chief exponents of the Hermetic tradition in England in the sixteenth and seventeenth centuries were John Dee and the Rosicrucians Thomas Vaughan and Robert Fludd. John Dee is a representative figure of this movement, in which mathematical, experimental science was closely entwined with cabalist and magical speculation. Dee's synthesis of the Renaissance tradition of cabalist alchemy is to be found in his fabulously obscure book, *Monas hieroglyphica*. This work, according to the researches of Frances Yates, was of immense importance in encouraging the Rosicrucian alchemical movement (*see* F.A. Yates, *The Rosicrucian Enlightenment*). Dr Yates does not include alchemy in her study of the Hermetic tradition, but she does recognize it in her survey of the Rosicrucians:

> Another element in the Renaissance Hermetic tradition was the revival of alchemy. Alchemy was always called a Hermetic science; many of the early alchemical treatises were attributed to 'Hermes Trismegistus', including the famous *Emerald Tablet*, the bible of the alchemists, which gives the Hermetic philosophy of nature in a mysteriously compact form. Though we connect alchemy with the specific aim of making gold, it was

concerned with the scientific problem of the transmutation of substances as a whole and this included, for the pious alchemist, spiritual and moral transformation.

'Thrice Great Hermes' was generally regarded as an ancient Egyptian prophet, of the time of Moses, and a body of magical and philosophical writings was attributed to him. These writings were very popular in Hellenistic times, and also influenced the Islamic world view, but it was not until the Renaissance that the *Corpus Hermeticum* reached the West. Containing as it did a whole range of treatises which presented an astrological form of nature mysticism, it provided a fresh view of the Creation. The texts were enthusiastically received, and works like the *Asclepius* exerted a tremendous influence on the Renaissance of the Cabala and natural magic during the sixteenth century. Alchemists during this period tended to study such texts of occult philosophy closely, for they sought a new magical world view.

In wrestling with the deep problems of interpreting the alchemical tradition, I have found the most profound insight in the works of Thomas Vaughan, who provided eloquent English translations of the Rosicrucian manifestos. In his work, alchemy rises to the dignity of a fully elaborated philosophy of Creation. He embraced wholeheartedly the magical philosophy of the Renaissance which involved a new Hermetic interpretation of the Genesis myth. Here is his account of the Hermetic vision of Creation:

Trismegistus in his Vision of the Creation, did first see a pleasing gladsome Light, but interminated. Afterwards appeared a horrible sad Darknesse, and this moved downewards, descending from the Eye of the Light, as if a Cloud should come from the Sunne. This darknesse (saith he) was condens'd into a certaine water, but not without a mournfull inexpressible voyce or Sound, as the vapours of the Elements are resolved by Thunder. After this (saith that great philosopher), the holy word came out of the Light, and did get upon the water, and out of the water he made all Things.

Thomas Vaughan was a dedicated experimenter, a practitioner of alchemy, and we see here how he uses the Hermetic philosophy of Creation to supplement the Genesis view, which as a Christian he wholeheartedly embraced. Like so many of the more serious, more learned alchemists, Vaughan rejects the idea of the art as a means of transmuting metals, of gaining wealth and power. Rather he makes clear that for him alchemy involves penetrating the magical secrets of nature, as divine Creation. He makes this explicit in *Euphrates* (1655):

I have, Reader, in several little Tractats delivered my judgement of philosophie, for Alchymie in the common acceptation, as it is a torture of Metalls, I did never believe, much less did I study it. In this point, my Bookes being perused will give thee Evidence, for there I referre thee to a subject that is universall, that is the foundation of all Nature, that is the Matter whereof all things are made, and wherewith being made are nourished. This I presume can be no metall . . .(p.513)

[I ever conceived that in *metalls* there were great Secrets provided they be first reduced by a proper Dissolvent, but to seek that Dissolvent, or the matter whereof it is made, in Metalls, is not only Error but Madness.]

The works of Thomas Vaughan indicate that for centuries alchemists handed on their philosophy of nature through an oral tradition, and all of the earlier texts which come down to us, notably that Bible of alchemy *The Emerald Tablet*, are too obscure for literal interpretation.

Many readers of this *Dictionary of Alchemy* will have formed the impression that the subject really is concerned only with the problem of seeking a means to transmute baser metals into gold and silver, and there are many texts which prepetuated this myth. However, it is to be hoped that my sketches of the lives of some of the alchemical philosophers will reveal that they were just that: philosophers of nature who sought a harmonic vision of man and nature.

## Alchemy as a Cultural Phenomenon

It is to be hoped too that this book will help to sort out some of the confusion which now arises from the immense cultural diversity of alchemical traditions. Modern research knows of an Indo-Tibetan, as well as a Chinese Taoist, tradition of elixir alchemy, and reference has already been made to the complex roots of western Christian alchemy. Thus 'alchemy' becomes a word whose definition eludes us, and yet there are remarkable common features between the alchemical traditions in the most diverse cultures. All forms of alchemy include both a concept of metallic transmutation and an idea of a mystic elixir of life: in western alchemy the Philosopher's Stone of transmutation is also called an elixir or medicine of metals, and western alchemists knew of an elixir as a medicinal panacea for human ailments. In general it is true to say though that Indo-Tibetan and Chinese alchemy were more concerned with elixirs for providing longevity and immortality, whilst western alchemists concentrated upon the theory and mythology of metals.

When Jung embarked upon his interpretation of alchemy, there was little information available to him on the vast realm of Taoist elixir alchemy. However, Jung was most deeply influenced by a Chinese text for which he provided an introduction. This was *The Secret of the Golden Flower*, translated and edited by his friend Richard Willhelm. This text, Jung tells us, provided the first inspiration for his monumental labours in studying alchemy, its symbolism and psychic meaning. Jung also provided an introduction for Willhelm's edition of the Chinese oracle, the *I Ching*, and this work provided the framework for many Chinese alchemical texts, as is evident from the rich variety of illustrations provided by Professor Joseph Needham in his studies of Chinese alchemy. One text which makes possible a comparison between eastern and western alchemy is the work of Ko Hung, entitled *Nei P'ien*. Just as Paracelsus and other western alchemists base their work on a philosophy of Creation, so the Taoists operate within the framework of their cosmic view:

> Tao enwombed Primal Unity and cast in their mold the two symbols (Yin and Yang). Tao breathed forth Grand Beginning and forged the 1,000 genera. Tao turns the 28 lunar mansions and fashions the beginning of things. Tao is the reins and whip for the whole complex of spiritual powers and blows the breaths characterising the four seasons. Tao holds in subtle embrace all vast, silent space, enfolding in relaxed embrace all that is brilliant.
>
> Nei P'ien, tr. J.R. Ware, *Alchemy, Medicine and Religion in the China of 320 AD*

My own feeling is that modern science lacks the spacious feeling of cosmic vision, being imprisonned within the labyrinth of ever more complex mathematical speculation on an apparently infinite range of subatomic particles – although many will perhaps feel that modern science is more real than that of the ancient occult traditions. The philosophical alchemy, whether of the East or of the West, provides us with an imaginative and profound account of nature, a mythic vision of Creation as a sacred mystery, not to be penetrated by the uninitiated. Ko Hung castigates the ignorance of people who refuse to believe in the transmutation of metals, affirming that such a belief is totally obvious:

> They claim crystal is a substance found only in nature, like jade. And so, since gold also happens to be found in nature, why should people believe that there is a system for manufacturing it? The ignorant do not believe that minium and white lead are the products of a transformation in lead, nor do they believe that the mule . . .is born of a donkey and a mare, for they insist that each thing has a unique seed.

The Chinese alchemists worked with gold and cinnabar preparations, believing that the longer they were heated, the more marvellous were the changes they would undergo. There was an abundance of legends about the mystic elixir of life: for instance the Yellow Emperor is supposed to have risen into the sky to join the Immortals (*Hsien*) after taking the divine elixir. It was believed that gold and cinnabar could enter the blood and breath circulatory system, thus conferring immortality. Ko Hung tells us that by taking reverted cinnabar, we will cause vermilion birds and phoenixes to hover above us. Myth and symbolism, dreams and visions combine in Chinese alchemy, as they do in the western tradition, to create a fresh, animated vision of man and nature.

Alchemy of the Chinese type was practised throughout Asia and Japan, though no adequate study of it yet exists. It is well known, however, that Indo-Tibetan alchemy was involved with yoga and magic. The ability to transmute metals was one of the *siddhis* or magical powers associated with high attainment in yogic practice. As in China itself, strict yogic exercises and practices, involving breath control, were part of the quest for the mystic elixir of longevity or immortality. In the course of studying and practising Tibetan Buddhist meditation, I have often heard mention of an esoteric tradition of Tibetan alchemy deriving from Sanskrit origins. Tibetans use the image of transmutation of metals as a metaphor for the meditative life, which seeks to transmute the iron elements of life, death and the constantly flowing rebirth or karmic process into the gold or purity of enlightenment. It is also well known to Tibetan scholars, that the mining of gold was strictly regulated by the Dalai Lamas: it was believed that removal of gold from the earth would actually weaken its structure. There are stories of men who have found huge gold nuggets, only to be instructed by the Dalai Lama to bury them again! A highly respected teacher of Tibetan language and grammar has told me that this was indeed the view of traditional Tibet. Here we see how original alchemy is rooted in an ecological view of the world, a religious attitude of the deepest respect for nature, of fear that to exploit the resources of Mother Earth will bring ruin to mankind.

In publishing this collection of entries on alchemists and their philosophy, my own hope is that they may contribute to a more imaginative vision of man and nature, and that the future will bring an account of the cosmos which is more harmonious and integrated. Modern culture has inevitably fragmented thousands of specialist disciplines in a way which would never have been imaginable in the age prior to Newton. Alchemy gives us the opportunity to reassess our contemporary world view in the light of more ancient wisdom. It would be foolish to pronounce the ancient mystical gnostic and

Hermetic traditions dead. The Jungian account of alchemy has brought the subject to life, suggesting that the dream world of the unconscious mind is profoundly alchemical in its character. My own contribution is to seek to provide a reference work which will guide the reader into the labyrinth of pre-Newtonian science and philosophy of nature. The view of alchemists was deeply religious in its genuine expression, and there are many modern thinkers who lament the fierce attempts to establish the tyranny of scientific materialism – Teilhard de Chardin has led the way in 'spiritualizing' our concept of the material world, and many others have followed. In the light of this modern movement to see through the more superficial interpretations of science, a study of alchemical mystical philosophy may prove profoundly helpful and enlightening.

# Abraham Eleazar
## Abraham the Jew; uncertain dates

All that is known of this shadowy figure comes from **Nicholas Flamel** (1330 – 1417) who was inspired to take up the alchemical quest when he purchased Abraham's mysterious book for two florins, engraved on leaves of bark. On the first page gilded letters read: 'Abraham the Jew, Prince, Priest, Levite, Astrologer and Philosopher, to the Jewish People, Dispersed Through God's Wrath into Gaul, Greetings.' In the text Abraham advocates **transmutation** to help pay taxes to the Roman Emperor, an early call to **alchemy**. This shows the importance of Judaic alchemy in the craze of Flamel's time, with the **Cabala** as a major influence. Flamel was puzzled by the letters of Abraham's text, which were neither Greek nor Latin: perhaps they were Hebrew or Syriac.

An illustrated sixteenth-century **manuscript** supposedly written by Abraham, *Livre des figures hieroglyphiques* (Book of Hieroglyphics), is now in the Bibliothèque Nationale, Paris, while a book published in Leipzig in 1760, *Uraltes chymisches Werk* (Ancient Chemical Work), also purports to be Abraham's work, although it shows clear Paracelsian influence (*see* **Paracelsus**).

*See* Titus Burckhardt, *Alchemy*, chapter 14.

# Acid and Alkali

The concept of this basic chemical antithesis emerges clearly in the seventeenth century with the work of **van Helmont** and **Robert Boyle**. Early alchemists worked with lists of *aquae* (waters) (*see* **Aqua**), and a familiar acid was *aqua fortis* or nitric acid, whose preparation is described in **Geber**, *De inventione veritatis* (On the discovery of the truth) (fourteenth century). Holmyard traces preparation of nitric acid back to the tenth-century Jabirian corpus (*see* **Jabir ibn Hayyan**). During the thirteenth century, it was prepared by distilling nitrate with alum and ferrous sulphate. Alum and nitrate were also known to Ko Hung in fourth-century China (*see* **Chinese Alchemy**), but no nitrate reagents were known in the early medieval West. Sulphuric acid from 'oil of vitriol' was familiar in the sixteenth century, however, and was popular with the Paracelsian iatrochemists. Hydrochloric acid was known from 1640.

Acids were very important for purifying, separating and cleaning **metals**, and **myth** portrayed them as *devouring* metals. Nitric acid was used to separate silver from **gold**, dissolving the former and not the latter, while sulphuric acid was known from pseudo-Geber, prepared from vitriol, as dissolving all metals except gold. Precipitation of silver from nitric acid solution baffled and fascinated alchemists, especially van Helmont. **Newton** wrote a tract, *De natura acidorum* (On the nature of acids), in which he uses his theory of particles, and experiments with nitric acid deeply impressed him: he dissolved many metals and obtained precipitates from solution. *Aqua regia* was famous as the only 'water' or acid which would dissolve gold: this was prepared by adding sal ammoniac to nitric acid. In the mixture of hydrochloric and nitric acid, gold dissolves to a soluble chloride, silver to an insoluble one, thus *aqua regia* was ideal for separating gold from silver.

'Alkali' belongs to the class of scientific words derived from Arabic: *al-qaliy* denotes calcined ashes of the plants 'salsola' and 'salicorna'; *qualay* = to fry, or to roast. 'Alcalay' was originally a saline substance from calcined ashes of marine plants, soda-ash. **Chaucer** lists together 'sal tartre, alcalay, and salt preparat', **Ripley** in *Compound of Alchemy* lists 'Sal Alkaly, Sal Alembroke, Sal Attinckan', and Ben Jonson gives 'Alkaly' in company with 'sal tartre', arsenic and vitriol as regular alchemical substances. The English Paracelsian surgeon John Woodall explains that **Paracelsus** 'termeth every vegetable salt Alkaly'.

*See* C. Singer, E.J. Holmyard, A.R. Hall and T.I. Williams, *A History of Technology*.

# Adam and Eve

The **myth** of **Creation** as told in Genesis naturally became the focus for alchemical speculation, but alchemists also drew upon traditions such as the **Cabala** or the **Hermetic texts**. Adam and Eve are important in the alchemical mythology of William Blake, and his well-known painting 'Eve and the Serpent' shows a very alchemical serpent. It is vital to realize that the Hermetic alchemical tradition flows through literature into modern times.

**Edward Kelley** tells us that secrets of the art were actually imparted to Adam by the Holy Spirit, 'and He prophesied both before and after the Fall, that the world must be renewed, or, rather, purged with water'. Adam is the primordial man, the **microcosm** or lesser world, living at first in perfect **harmony** with **nature** and with his own nature. Dame Frances Yates explains in *Giordano Bruno and the Hermetic Tradition* that Adam in the Hermetic tradition is more than human, belonging to the class of 'star demons', the seven Governors who rule the Cosmos. The Fall is interpreted as Adam's exercise of free will in involving himself with nature in the bodily, elemental world, yet still preserving his spiritual nature.

**Zosimos**, belonging to the gnostic tradition of **Hellenistic alchemy**, also refers to this esoteric Adam, giving a meaning to each letter of his name, and Jung explains that the cabalist figure of Adam Cadmon was identified with the 'son of the philosophers', the 'man of light' imprisoned in man's mortal body. Thus Adam is prominent both in gnostic religious **alchemy**, where he is equivalent to *Anthropos* and in the Hebrew Cabala, where he symbolizes man's contradictory physical-spiritual nature.

### The Cabalist Adam

Alchemy is so intertwined with the Hebrew Cabala in its speculative form that the theology of Adam becomes vital to understanding the esoteric tradition of alchemy, which is chiefly concerned with the **redemption** of the Adamic nature of man. Already, Zosimos (third century AD) shows the baffling syncretism in alchemy. He equates Adam with Thoth **Hermes**, as giver of names to worldly things, says that the Chaldean and Hebrew word *Adam* means 'blood red earth', and reads into the letters of the name secret meanings in thoroughly cabalist **spirit**: A = ascent, D = descent, A = North, M = meridian, South, fire burning in fourth region. Zosimos says that only the Hebrews and Hermetic texts hold this doctrine about 'the Man of Light and his guide the Son of God'. (*See* Jung, *Psychology and Alchemy*, p.350.)

The esoteric doctrine of Adam Cadmon is vital to the Cabala, and came to influence Renaissance **Neoplatonism** and the whole Paracelsian world view. The God of the ten Sefiroth, or emanations, is directly identified in his purest spiritual form, for man prior to the Fall is nothing other than a pure, untainted being. When cabalist **numerology** (the technique called *Gematria*) is used on his name, he is found to possess the very name of God in his creative manifestation in the world. The cabalist doctrine of Adam as **microcosm** clearly emerges in the *Zohar*, one of the principle cabalist texts.

Cabalists interpret Adam's sin as one of refusal to grasp the greatness and the **unity** of the Sefiroth in God, i.e. a failure of comprehension and understanding. His insight is restricted to the first Sefirah or emanation of God. This lack of all-embracing understanding leads to the split between the sexes and to the creation of Eve – in esoteric, alchemical myth Eve is equated with Pandora.

The division in the primal unity is the theme of most Creation myths: the Cabala contrasts the **Tree** of Life and the Tree of Knowledge. The Genesis myth involves tearing the fruit from the tree, that is, man's disrupting of the natural order, or the unity of tree and fruit. There is also the image of the moon losing her own light, and being forced to reflect the borrowed light of the sun. (*See* Gershom Scholem's illuminating studies on the Cabala in the manuscript work 'Rising Dawn' or Marie-Louise von Franz's edition of Aquinas' *Aurora consurgens*.)

## Adam in Medieval Alchemy

At first, cabalist doctrines remained in the penumbra of medieval alchemy, and it was not until the burgeoning of the Renaissance Christian Cabala that they became central. Adam is vital to alchemical myth, because the esoteric core of the tradition concerns the redemption of man by the healing power of the *Lapis* or '**Stone** of the Philosophers', which Jung has shown to be equated with the figure of Christ, Saviour and Redeemer of the world (*see also* **Jungian Theory of Alchemy**). We find this in the sixth parable of the thirteenth-century *Aurora consurgens*, attributed to St Thomas Aquinas. Here, the writer uses the Pauline concept of Christ as the second Adam: the first Adam by his sin brought death into the material world, but the second Adam is Christ the redeemer, who liberates man from death by his resurrection. The idea of redemption is the key to gnostic and Christian alchemy.

As a spiritual tradition alchemy involves transformation of the inner man and realization of man's microcosmic nature. God moulds the body of Adam from the four corruptible **elements**, from mortal clay, and in this he has within himself the elements of Creation; he also resembles the *Lapis* itself, for he has within himself the capacity for redemption, for spiritual transformation and renewal. **Paracelsus**, who breathed new life into alchemical tradition and who drew upon a wealth of cabalist interpretation, explains that God creates Adam from the **Prime Matter** of the black earth, often called Adamic Earth (*terra Adamica*) and he has within himself the bodily clay from which Eve is created. Thus he has in his being the hermaphroditic character of **Mercury** (see **Hermaphrodite; Mercury**). But to the earthly elements is added the soul, or **quintessence** which is the principle of redemption, or of what Jung calls 'individuation'.

A dramatic illustration in a fourteenth-century Italian **manuscript** shows Adam as Prime Matter, or 'Adamic Earth', pierced by a mercurial arrow. The Philosopher's Tree sprouts from his genitals; the moon looks on, a symbol of *nigredo*. The corresponding picture of Eve shows her with the tree rising from her head: Jung interprets this as the contrast between the *anima* function in the man, and the *animus* in female psychology. (This picture is reproduced in Jung, *Collected Works*, Vol. 12, and in Stanislas Klossowski de Rola, *The Secret Art of Alchemy*. It comes from the *Miscellania d'alchimia* (Miscellaneous Alchemy) manuscript in the Lorenzo Medici Library, Florence.)

For Adam and Eve as primal pair, see **Conjunctio**, or mystic marriage. For Zosimos and the alchemical concept of Adam see Jung, *Psychology and Alchemy*.

# Agricola, Georgius
**Latin for Georg Baur; metallurgist and mining technologist; born Glachau, Saxony, 24 March 1494, died 1555**

This great scientist is the father of European metallurgy and his work *De re metallica* (On Metallurgy) is a source of abundant information on mining, **metals** and minerals.

Agricola studied at Leipzig, graduating BA, then became a classics teacher at the town school of Zwickau, becoming Principal in 1520. He lectured at Leipzig University from 1522, then went to Bologna to study **medicine**; he also studied in Venice and Padua, and seems to have gained his MD in Italy. In 1526 he settled in Joachimstal, a mining district of Bohemia, as town physician, and studied mineralogy. He became town physician of Chemnitz in 1533, and Burgomeister in 1546, dying there in 1555. He obtained strong patronage and tax exemption from Duke Maurice, Elector of Saxony.

German mining handbooks like the *Bergbuchlein* (Little Book on Mining in the Mountains) were predecessors of his works, which are listed here.

**Publications:**

*Bermannus sive de re metallica* (1530) (Bermannus) (octavo, Froben Press, Basle). This is a dialogue between a miner and two Italian doctors concerning miners and minerals. Its glossary of German mining terms gives Latin meanings, thus providing a unique reference work.

*Libri quinque de mensuris et ponderibus* (Five books on weights and measures) (1533) (octavo, Paris, enlarged edition 1550). This book is a study of classical weights and measures.

A collection of Agricola's writings issued by Frobenius of Basle (1546), with dedication to his patron, Duke Maurice of Saxony, containing the following works:

1) *De ortu et causis subterraneorum, libri V* (Five books on the origin and cause of subterranean things). This covers the origin of ores and mineral deposits.

2) *De natura eorum qui effluent ex terra, libri 3* (On the nature of things flow from the earth), dealing with subterranean water, mine gases, volcanic eruptions and exhalations.

3) *De natura fossilium, libri 10* (On the nature of fossils, book 10). This discusses rocks and minerals, which are divided into six classes: earths (including clays and chalks), solidified 'juices' (including salt, alum and vitriol); stone (gems, etc.); rocks; metals; compounds. (*See* John Stillman, *The Story of Early Alchemy and Chemistry*.) J.R. Partington praises the account of crystal formations with the comments on hardness, weight, colour and lustre which provide the basis also for modern scientific description.

4) *De veteribus et novis metallis, libri 2* (On old and new metals). This is a history of mining and metallurgy, including the story of the discovery of German mines.

*De animantibus subterraneis* (On subterranean living things) (1549) (one book, octavo, Froben Press, Basle). This contains fascinating accounts of salamanders dwelling in flames, of good and bad mining **spirits**, and of spirits who kill men with their breath (an animistic way of describing poison gases in mines). The author also believed in 'Kobolds' which are probably distorted reflections, optical illusions seeming to mimic men, perhaps derived from Greek word *Cabali*.

*De re metallica* (1556), in 12 books, dedicated to Duke Maurice of Saxony. This posthumously-published work was Agricola's crowning achievement, laying firm foundations for the rapidly growing science of metallurgy. It covers 'mining geology, mining engineering and working, as it existed in Germany . . . with very full descriptions of the smelting of ores and of the assaying and analysis of ores and alloys' (Stillman, op. cit.) The work contains a remarkable series of woodcuts of mines and their machinery, dispelling any idea that this was an age of primitive technology, and Book 9 describes processes and machinery.

# Agrippa, Henry Cornelius
## 1486–1535; native of Cologne

Dame Frances Yates says of Agrippa: 'His *De occulta philosophia*
[Occult Philosophy] is now seen as the indispensable handbook of
Renaissance Magia and Cabala, combining the natural magic of
Ficino with the Cabalist magic of Pico', and it was a key work for
disseminating Renaissance **Neoplatonism**. He dismissed
alchemists as 'either physicians or soap-boilers', but his study of
occult philosophy was vital to men like **John Dee** who sought a
synthesis of natural **magic** and scientific philosophy.

Agrippa studied with Abbot **Trithemius** of Sponheim from 1509 to
1510, and in 1510 visited England, meeting humanist scholars. He met
Erasmus, and studied in Italy and France. Although his 'occult
philosophy' was cited in witchcraft trials, he was a respected humanist
philosopher: a revival of Hebrew studies was linked with the growth
of learned magic of the **Cabala**. In 1526 his work 'On the vanity of
sciences', *De vanitate scientiarum*, was likened to Erasmus' *Praise of
Folly* as an indictment of all learning, both academic and occult.

His *Occulta philosophia* of 1533 presents the Hermetic vision of the
universe, in which there are three worlds, the lowest world of the
**elements** being manipulated by natural magic. Book Two concerns
astral magic, involving mathematics. Book Three concerns **angel
magic**, used by philosophers like Dee to contact divine intelligences
in order to discover deeper secrets of the universe. Hebrew letters with
numerical values are vital to transcending popular magic and,
according to Agrippa, the 'Name of Jesus is now all-powerful,
containing all the powers of the Tetragrammaton'. This, then, was the
world of the Renaissance Hermetic magi.

*See also* **Magic**; Frances Yates, *The Occult Philosophy in the
Elizabethan Age*.

# Aion/Aeon

This word appears in Herakleitos (floruit 500 BC), who calls the aion
a child at play. The Stoics, who evolved the doctrine of the cosmic
year, defined the aion as the period between the **Creation** of the world
from fire and its destruction. This concept must be a key to early
**alchemy**, for the **uroboros**, the serpent devouring itself, is the main
emblem of Hellenistic adepts, with its inscription 'All is One'. The
great serpent was called *Agathos Daimon*, (Good Spirit) and in Orphic
cosmology this is the symbol for Helios, the Sun, which also

represents the cosmic year. In magical papyri the magical word *abraxas* is used to mean aion. It is clear that this doctrine of periodic creation and destruction of the cosmos was crucial to the esoteric doctrines which gave rise to the cult of alchemy.

### The Gnostic Concept of Aion

Alchemists like **Zosimos** were gnostics, gnostic ideas permeate early alchemy, and the aion formed part of gnostic speculation. There is much evidence that alchemical ideas of birth, death and resurrection originated in gnostic Hellenistic philosophy, being later adapted to Christian doctrines of the death and resurrection of Christ. (*See* **Adam**; **Redemption**; Jung, *Collected Works*, Vol. entitled *Aion*).

The gnostic **myth** of aion may provide a link between alchemical myth and various cults and mysteries of the ancient world. The Orphic god Phanes is portrayed in the cosmic **egg** with a serpent twined around him, for example, and there are similar pictures of Mithras as 'The Invincible Sun' (*Sol Invictus*). Orphic and Mithraic mysteries seem to have worshipped the serpent as a solar, spiritual energy symbol, and Hellenistic alchemists seem to have drawn upon such mystery cults.

# Air

*See* **Elements**.

# Albertus Magnus
## or **Albrecht**; *c.*1193–1280

As alchemists traced their pedigree back to **Adam**, **Hermes**, Moses and other prophets, they had no problem in attributing texts to great scholastic theologians like Aquinas or Albertus Magnus. The background of rampant alchemical research in monasteries, penalized in successive Church decrees, together with the Church's official ban on alchemical **manuscripts**, led to them being ascribed to such infallible authorities.

Abbot **Trithemius** said of Albertus that he was 'great in necromancy, greater in philosophy, but greatest in theology'. Perhaps, like **Roger Bacon** or **John Dee**, his scientific interests led him into unorthodox experiments. He devoted his life to paraphrasing **Aristotle**, and his important book *De animalibus* (On animals) is a compendium of Aristotelian life science. It is admirably clear and concise, as is his *De mineralibus* (On minerals), a substantial scientific survey, even if derivative.

Albertus was born at Lauingen in Swabia of noble family: he held the title 'Count of Bollstadt'. After joining the Dominicans during his studies at Padua in 1223, he enjoyed a meteoric rise, gaining the title 'Doctor Universalis'. From 1228 he lectured in the German universities of Freiburg, Ratisbon, Strasburg and Cologne. It was during his Paris sojourn (1245 - 8) that he began his philosophical writings, which are to Aristotle as the moon is to the sun, shining with a borrowed light. He rose to become Provincial of the Dominicans in Saxony and he was Bishop of Ratisbon from 1260 to 1262. In 1262 he retired to the cloisters of Cologne, where he died.

Tradition has it that Albertus, like Roger Bacon, owned a magical talking head of brass; his pupil Thomas Aquinas is said to have smashed the head for disturbing his studies. In his *Religio Medici*, Sir Thomas Browne claimed to have solved the riddle of the head, saying that it was the bubbling head of an alchemical still. Stories of talking heads were also a feature of **Hermetic texts**, and they were actually constructed by mechanical means.

Another legend says that Albertus caused a garden to bloom in winter for Duke Wilhelm II of Holland - possibly an allusion to the alchemical garden.

Many alchemical manuscripts were attributed to him, and the *Libellus de alchimia* (Little Book of Alchemy), which survives in an early fourteenth-century manuscript, is sometimes said to be his. The Preface quotes Ecclesiastes: 'All wisdom is from the Lord God, and hath been always with Him, and is before all time.' The author boasts of travels throughout Christendom, and also the Middle East, consulting Jews and Arabs, as well as nobles, ecclesiastics and philosophers who have lost their money. He has watched 'decoctions, sublimations, solutions and distillations'. The work presents the standard **mercury-sulphur theory of generation of metals**, with **gold** resulting from the combination of red **sulphur** and **mercury**. (A red sulphur is needed for gold, a white one for **silver**.) (*See also* **Elixir**.)

In *Studies in Medieval Science*, Pearl Kibre discusses the authenticity and quality of various alchemical manuscripts attributed to Albertus Magnus, thus giving sound insight into the chemical and alchemical learning of the period.

*See also* J.R. Partington's article 'Albertus Magnus on Alchemy', *Ambix*, 1937, pp.3 - 20.

# Alchemy

A central theme of this *Dictionary* is the cultural range of alchemy. Our word is derived directly from the Arabic *al kimiya*, used in the Islamic world to denote not only the art of producing the **elixir** or the Philosopher's **Stone**, but also the substance or medium of **transmutation**. Western alchemy was derived from **Islamic alchemy**, but also from the Judaic traditions, and from the start involved theories of transmutation using elixirs or the mythic Philosopher's Stone. Our tradition is generally divided between esoteric or mystical and exoteric or practical: *alchimia speculativa* was philosophical or mystical, distinct from *alchimia practica*, which was experimental and chemical.

The true origins of alchemy are related to etymology: *al kimiya* is generally traced back to the Greek words *chemia* or *chemeia*, whose origin is far from certain. The Coptic word *khem* was used to denote the fertile Nile Delta, and this may be the root for *chemeia*: the black soil may have the significance of *prima materia* (*see* **Prime Matter**). The fertile Delta was a stark contrast to surrounding arid desert, and Egypt was the home of every imaginable form of sorcery and mysticism, and of multifarious crafts and trades of varying honesty, while **Hermes Trismegistus** was always treated as the Egyptian father of alchemical tradition. However, early **Hellenistic alchemy**, with its gnostic affinities, is a profound mystery. The word *chemeia* for alchemy was common in the time of Diocletian, whose decree of *c.* 300 AD attacks 'the old writings of the Egyptians which treat of the *chemeia* of gold and silver'. Here *chemeia* seems equivalent to transmutation – but the obscurity of the word to alchemists themselves is shown by **Zosimos** (third century AD) who believed that the mythic figure Chemes founded the tradition.

An Indian scholar, Dr S. Mahdihassan, has provided a convincing case that the Chinese word *Chin-I* or *Chin-je* may be the root of *chemeia* and or of *kimiya*: the Chinese word means literally 'gold juice', used to denote elixirs, and in southern Chinese dialect it sounds much more like *kimiya*. He suggests that Chinese traders may have brought stories of their alchemy to the bustling port of Alexandria, although most sources suggest a powerful Egyptian religious element in early alchemy.

The suggestion that **Chinese alchemy** may have provided inspiration for the Egyptian tradition raises the unsolved problem of relating alchemy as a cultural phenomenon, which was discussed in the Introduction. Alchemy exists throughout Asia, including China, India, Tibet, Burma and Japan. Most of these cultures seem to have become interested in possible magical or physical transmutation of **metals**, but **gold** seems to function more as a magical ingredient of elixirs of life. Dr Mahdihassan argues that the earliest alchemical traditions of China and India were essentially concerned with juices or potions of immortality. Chinese alchemy is probably the earliest form, dating from the third century BC or even earlier, and involving both transmutation theory and elixir **magic**. Everywhere there is confusion and apparent contradiction in the aims of adepts. Alchemy always has a strong element of magic and of mysticism, the experimental, physical aspect seeming more of an introduction to mystic, magical secrets of transformation of **spirit** than a form of experiment.

Above all, alchemy should be regarded as a popular tradition, giving an outlet for heretical modes of religious and magical thought amongst a whole range of people: the texts all bear witness to involvement of priests, from highest prelates to humblest friars. The wealth of alchemical literature, still untapped, includes thousands of popular poems in many languages.

Recent research on alchemy has uncovered the vitality of the Paracelsian tradition of medical alchemy, comprising a scientific revolution in **medicine** and pharmacy (*see* **Paracelsus**). Men like **Oswald Croll** and **Andreas Libavius** evolved a form of chemistry which was immensely indebted to alchemy, and **Robert Boyle** and **Joan Battista van Helmont** show similar ambivalence. Alchemy and **astrology** were thriving in the late seventeenth century, contemporary with the founding of the Royal Society, and we now know that **Newton** was a remarkable Hermetic adept. **Elias Ashmole**, founding member of the Royal Society, combined deep faith in alchemy with devotion to astrology both as a means of practical divination and as a world view.

Alchemy involves a world view, with most adepts believing that the elemental world is bathed in influences from stars and planets. Man is interpreted as microcosm, and the great secret of the elixir or Philosophers' Stone is often said to be within man himself, the treasure of spiritual realization. Whereas the link between chemistry and alchemy was dissolved during the eighteenth century, this spiritual, mystical aspect of the tradition persisted to exert strong influence on poets like William Blake and W.B. Yeats. The 'modern' tradition of alchemy is beyond the scope of this survey, but there are many who still believe in a form of alchemical philosophy.

The following quotation conveys the dignity and nobility of the medieval alchemical philosophy:

The adept kneels before his master. The scroll says: 'I will preserve in secrecy the secrets of the science of alchemy.'

The master replies: 'Receive the gift of God under the consecrated seal.'

From the earliest times, alchemy was known as the 'sacred science'; its initiatory secrets to be guarded from the greed of the vulgar populace.

The bird at the top represents the Holy Spirit, with two angels as guardians of divine revelation in the opus.

From Elias Ashmole, Theatrum chemicum Britannicum (London, 1652).

By kind permission of The Bodleian Library, Oxford.

RR. W. 29 (9) p.12.

Know, O Alexander, that the first thing created by God, glorified by his name, was a simple spiritual essence in exceeding perfection and excellence, in which were the forms of all things. This He named Reason. Out of this essence there was created another, next to it in rank, which was called the Universal Soul.

Out of the latter he brought into being a third essence named Matter (*hyle, hayula*). Matter on receiving dimensions, i.e. length, breadth, and thickness, became pure body. Then this body adopted a spherical form, which is the best of all forms, and greatest in space and continuation. Out of this spherical form there were created the heavens, planets, and all other ethereal bodies, the purest of them being the first and the coarsest last.

So, beginning from the first, or the all-comprehending sphere, to the last sphere which is the sphere of the fixed stars, then follow the spheres of the planets: Saturn, Jupiter, Mars, Sun, Venus, Mercury, the sphere of the moon and then the sphere of the four elements. So the earth is the centre of all the spheres, and it is the coarsest of all bodies in essence and thickest and most solid of them in substance.

Man is the noblest of all animals, in construction, and the preponderating element in him is fire. In the composition of man there are united all the essences of creation – whether elemental or composite, because man is composed of body which is coarse and material, and of the soul which is a pure, heavenly and spiritual essence.

Therefore for it is necessary for thee, O Alexander, if thou intendest to acquire the knowledge of the realities of all beings, that thou shouldst begin with the knowledge of thine own soul as it is the thing nearest to thyself. Then thou shouldst try to know other things.

*Secretum Secretorum: Discours IV, Vol. 5 – 6, ed. Steele, p.229*

# Alembic

**John Donne** uses the metaphor of 'loves Limbecke' in his alchemical poem 'A Nocturnall uppon Saint Lucies day' and **Chaucer** lists amongst the alchemical equipment used by the Canon and his Yeoman 'Curcurbites and alembykes eek'. The word belongs to the important class of Arabic scientific words adopted in Europe: Arabic *al anbiq* means a still, and this comes from the Greek *ambix* which is applied to the head of the still. The alembic was a glass or copper **vessel** used for **distillation**, like the modern retort. The lower part of the **apparatus** containing the liquid to be distilled was called the *curcurbit*, the word found in Chaucer in company with alembic. In fact alembic is more properly applied just to the head of the still, the capital. The alembic is familiar from classical times with a spout or *solem* to deliver the liquid into a receiver. **Maria Prophetissa** evolved the alembic by adding three funnels or beaks to form the well-known *tribikos* which is familiar from early illustrations of Greek apparatus. The alembic is regularly shown on top of the **furnace**; a pan of hot ashes or water bath was used to heat the distillation vessel (*see* **Baths**).

Distillation naturally forms a pivot of alchemical mythology and imagery, hence the vital significance of the alembic, not just as a piece of equipment, but as a symbolic vessel.

# Alkahest

Despite its Arabic ring, this is a word coined by **Paracelsus**, derived from the German *Allgeist* = all **spirit**. Paracelsians believed that water was the matrix of the world, the source of life, of the **elements** and of man (*see* **Aqua**), and they sought a universal solvent which they called 'alkahest'.

The significance of this alchemical **myth** becomes clear in records of Sir **Isaac Newton**'s experiments in dissolving various **metals** including **mercury**. *Aqua regia* and *aqua fortis* (*see* **Acid and Alkali**) were known for their power to dissolve metals. Unlike the acids, the idea of alkahest was that it should be non-corrosive. The **mercury-sulphur theory of the generation of metals** regarded metals as composed of a mercuric essence which rendered them fluid; **sulphur** gave the liquid metal solidity. Newton dissolved metals in nitric acid, believing that thereby he was releasing the mercuric constituent of metals.

The significance of a universal solvent in the quest for **transmutation** emerges from Professor Walter Pagel's study of the natural philosophy of **van Helmont** (1579 - 1644) who sought the mystic alkahest:

> In Gnosticism's descendent, alchemy, water symbolized prime matter, the origin of all body, a chaotic abyss of darkness, the residence of Behemoth or Dragon, the prince of evil, antagonist of light. It was in water that all transmutation and changes were brought about through the offices of the soul.
>
> Walter Pagel, *Joan Baptista van Helmont: Reformer of science and medicine*,
> pp.49 - 60

Water is the womb which contains the seeds, the potential for producing all metals. Experiments in which dissolved metals were precipitated from solution helped to confirm the superstitious belief that some solvent might produce **gold**.

The alkahest myth is alive in the scientific *Metallographia* (History of Metals, 1671) of John Webster, where it is discussed along with mercury and *aurum potabile*. Also, **Philalethes** was credited with a tract 'The Secret of the Immortal Liquor called Alkahest'.

# Alpha and Omega

Christ declares himself to be alpha and omega, the first and the last, in the book of Revelations, which has provided vast scope for esoteric prophetic interpretation. There are many signs that **alchemy** was also a prophetic tradition, linked in with apocalyptic and Joachimite traditions (*see* **Prophecy**). **Arnald of Villanova** and John Rupescissa both followed **Joachim of Fiore** in searching for prophetic meaning in the Scriptures, while Jung has shown that the *Lapis-Christus* parallel in alchemy is everywhere apparent, and the **Stone** of **transmutation** was a symbol of the redemptive power of Christ, the alpha and omega.

An interesting passage confirming the apocalyptic aspect of esoteric alchemy is found in the final Theorem, Number 24, of **John Dee's** *Monas Hieroglyphica* (Hieroglyphic Monad) (1564).

For the interpretation of Christ as first and last man, *see* **Adam**.

# Aludel

This is a pear-shaped **vessel**, aludel being an Arabic word for the Latin *sublimatorium* described by **Geber** and others. It is the vessel of chemical sublimation (*sublimatio = elevatio, conversio, nobilitatio, perfectio*). In a work of Robertus Vallensis (*De veritate et antiquitate artis* in Lazarus Zetzner's compilation *Theatrum Chemicum*, 1602), there is an allusion to the pure Word of God being burnt to earth in the aludel, and processed seven times: this is typical of the mystical allusion always present in the true esoteric tradition.

# Andreae, Johann Valentin
## 1586 – 1654; native of Württemberg

The Rosicrucian manifestos appeared in 1614 and 1615, and the next year *The Chemical Wedding of Christian Rosencreutz* [*Chymische Hochzeit Christiani Rosencreutz*] was published in German. Its author was not named, but was certainly Andreae. He was a citizen of

Protestant Württemberg and he studied at Tübingen from 1601, where he composed a comedy called *The Chemical Wedding*, apparently the precursor of the anonymously-published work. The book of 1616 presents Christian Rosencreutz, legendary founder of the **Rosicrucians**, as its hero, and refers to the Rosicrucian manifestos which were causing such a stir at that time. Frances Yates describes this romantic story as 'an alchemical fantasia, using the fundamental image of elemental fusion, the marriage, the uniting of *sponsus* and *sponsa*, touching also the theme of death, the *nigredo* through which the elements pass in the process of transmutation'. The alchemical allegory of the **conjunctio** is in most **manuscripts** a vital **stage** in progressing towards **transmutation**.

*The Chemical Wedding* was published anonymously, but Frances Yates argues strongly for Andreae as its author – he was famous as author of the Utopian *Christianopolis*, which is strongly influenced by cabalist and Hermetic wisdom. The story of the festivities in the *Wedding* is divided into seven days, and on the sixth, alchemists appear creating an alchemical bird, typical as symbol of the **spirit** of transmutation. Dr Yates also attributes inspiration for the drama to the splendid investiture of the Duke of Württemberg as Knight of the Garter, with festivities involving English players. She suggests that Christian Rosencreutz, putative founder of Rosicrucianism, was modelled on the Duke, using symbols of the red cross and red rose of St George.

*See* F.A. Yates, *The Rosicrucian Enlightenment*.

# Angel Magic

*Angelos* is the Greek word for messenger, so *angeloi* communicate between God and man. True alchemists seek divine wisdom, not empirical knowledge, hence those practising angel magic sought to penetrate divine secrets in **nature**: this was a vital aspect of the Hermetic tradition which inspired **John Dee**, **Isaac Newton**, and most alchemists. Dee was famous for his strange séances with **Edward Kelley**, seeking angelic communications, and angel magic was a sophisticated science in the Renaissance **Cabala** of Pico della Mirandola and **H.C. Agrippa**.

An account of the 'Hierarchies of Angels' was provided by pseudo-Dionysius the Areopagite as part of his mystical theology, much respected by Dean Colet. Countless diagrams of the Hermetic cosmos show hierachies of angels rising through the concentric celestial spheres. These were given names and domains in esoteric works like

the vast *Steganographia* of Abbot **Trithemius**, a work crucial to John
Dee and Renaissance **magic**.

In séances with his friend the alchemist Kelley, Dee used a crystal
stone which he earnestly believed had been given to him by the angel
Uriel, who appeared to him in his library window at Mortlake. The
crystal was later acquired by **Nicholas Culpeper**, the herbalist, who
believed he witnessed therein a lewd **spirit** cavorting.

**Elias Ashmole** makes the interesting suggestion of a connection
between the Philosophers' **Stone** and the scryer's crystal. Introducing
his *Theatrum chemicum Britannicum* (1651), he speaks of an invisible
angelic stone:

> The voyce of Man (which bears some proportion to these subtil
> properties) comes short in comparison; nay the Air it selfe is not so
> penetrable, and yet (Oh mysterious wonder!) a Stone, that will lodge in
> the Fire to Eternity without being prejudiced. It hath a Divine Power,
> Celestiall and Invisible, above the rest; and endowes the possessor with
> Divine Gifts. It affords the Apparition of Angells, and gives the power of
> conversing with them, by Dreams and Revelations: nor dare any Evill
> Spirit approach the Place where it lodgeth.

Ashmole believed his angelic 'stone' to be the most ancient vehicle
of **prophecy** and he claims that **Hermes**, Moses, and Solomon were
the only philosophers really to have understood the powers of the
Stone.

A belief in hierarchies of angelic intelligences was entirely orthodox
theology, but many Renaissance scholars indulged their faith in the
possibility of actually contacting angels. In fact belief in the power of
supernatural beings to aid the alchemical quest is universal: Chinese
alchemists believed their task aided and inspired by immortal beings,
*Hsiens*, who had themselves been adepts (*see* **Chinese Alchemy**).
Divine messengers were also familiar in **Islamic**, **Hellenistic** and
Judaic **alchemy**.

# Anthony, Francis
### English alchemical doctor; 1550 – 1623

The writings of this alchemical physician throw much light upon the
world of Ben Jonson's play *The Alchemist*, for he belongs to the class
of Paracelsian medical alchemists who were persecuted by the
monopolistic organization of professional doctors, the Royal College
of Physicians (founded in 1518 by Dr Thomas Linacre to restrict

medical practice in London to a handful of graduates qualified in **medicine**) (*see* **Paracelsus**). Anthony held a Cambridge MA and may have graduated MD, but he was summoned before the Royal College in 1600 for illegal practice of medicine, was fined £5 and imprisoned. He gained his freedom partly through the intercession of his wife.

He grew rich on the proceeds of his simple panacea, his *aurum potabile* or 'potable gold', and he met **Michael Maier** who approved of his theory of **gold** as the noblest of **metals** and therefore as the perfect panacea or 'cure-all'. In his polemic writings in defence of his cure he cites **Ramon Lull**, **Arnald of Villanova** and Dr Conradt Gessner, whose book on medicine has the title *Treasure of Euonymus*. Anthony published *Panacea aurea* (Panacea of gold) (Hamburg, 1598) and in 1610, *Medicinae chymicae et veri potabilis auri assertio* (The truth of chemical medicines and potable gold asserted) – the latter work came under fire from the Royal College's spokesman, Matthew Gwinne, in his *Aurum non aurum* (Gold not gold) of 1611, which inveighed against Anthony as 'asserting chemistry, but deserting true medicine'.

A contemporary of Shakespeare and Ben Jonson, Anthony belongs to the same class as Simon Forman, and he typifies the **spirit** of an age perched between advanced science, as advocated by **Francis Bacon**, and magical **alchemy**, which powerfully affected **Ashmole** and **Newton**.

*See* A.G. Debus, *The English Paracelsians.*

# Antimony

Antimony is a **metal** derived from stibnite (its sulphide), and it acquired tremendous significance with alchemists, partly because of its use in purifying **gold**. Antimony bronzes from very early times have been discovered, antimony being a substitute for tin in the alloy, but John Stillman says the metal was known only in its ore: stibnite was used in **medicines**, but the metal derived from it was regarded as a form of lead.

A work attributed to Artephius concerns antimony, and it is named amongst the materials listed by **Thomas Norton** in the fifteenth century, but antimony as a metal only became really known in the sixteenth century. The sixteenth-century metallurgist Biringuccio includes it amongst his minor minerals, saying that it shows all the signs of arrested maturation. The natural perfection of all metals being gold, antimony showed instead a shining silvery whiteness, being more brittle than glass. Biringuccio says that alchemists claim that a **tincture** of antimony can turn silver permanently into gold, but he is sceptical.

In 1598 the Paracelsian physician Dr Alexander von Suchten published *De secretis antimonii* (On the secrets of antimony), but more famous was **Basil Valentine**'s *Triumphal Charriot of Antimony*: he tells us that antimony purges gold, but also the human body, and a tiny portion fed to swine improves their appetite. He provides a full recipe for creating the 'Star Regulus', a crystalline star formation of antimony which profoundly stirred **Newton**'s imagination, but he denies that this really contains the **Stone** as many alchemists had thought. Betty Jo Dobbs explains the apparent miracle:

> The crystals of antimony are long and slender and sometimes arrange themselves in patterns on a sort of stem and so resemble the fronds of ferns. If certain very special conditions prevail in the purification and cooling of the metal, the crystalline 'branches' may appear to be arranged around a central point and so take on the appearance of a star.

Antimony is a classic example of the mythification of matter: Basil Valentine, though having denied that the star is the stone, says mysteriously that it may be 'carried through the fire with a stone serpent', until it consumes itself and merges with the serpent – this is the passage that attracted Newton. According to Basil, a wonderful curing **elixir** may be drawn from this, and magnetic properties were regarded as significant by Newton. Oh wonderful alchemical imagination!

Antimony is mined in Italy and Germany, being used in bell-making, glass mirrors and pewter; there are a number of mines near Siena. Surgeons used it for abscesses and ulcers.

*See* John Stillman, *The Story of Alchemy and Early Chemistry*; B.J. Dobbs, *The Foundations of Newton's Alchemy*.

# Apparatus

The endless symbolism of the alchemical opus uses a variety of mysterious implements and **vessels** – **pelican** or **alembic**, to name just two examples. Chaucer enumerates the best-known items in the Canones Yeomans tale:

> Sondry vessels maad of erthe and glas,
> Our urinales and our descensories,

Violes, croslets, and sublymatories,
Cucurbites and alembikes eek . . . '

Alchemical **processes** like **distillation**, sublimation or calcination are relevant to metallurgy, pharmacy (*see* **Paracelsus**), and the manufacture of cosmetics and dyes, as well as generally delving into the secrets of 'The Book of Nature', but what distinguishes **alchemy** is the mythic, esoteric meaning of the vessels and processes. Alembics, ambix or stills are used for distillation, for example, to separate the subtle **spirit** from the gross matter (hence the immense symbolic meaning of alcohol as mystic **quintessence**).

The alchemist's laboratory is depicted in an engraving after a painting of Peter Brueghel, in the illustrations of a **Thomas Norton manuscript** and in the famous picture of **Heinrich Khunrath**'s Hermetic equipment in his *Amphitheatrum* (Amphitheatre) of 1609. The former is a chaotic profusion of vessels and implements, while Norton or **Oswald Croll** were superbly equipped for performing sophisticated chemical operations, and for generating fierce heat using elaborate **furnaces**.

Pioneering work on developing apparatus was done by **Maria Prophetissa**, the Jewish and perhaps Hellinistic adept who invented the *Balneum Mariae* (*see* **Baths**) and the *tribikos* (*see* **Alembic**).

The *kerotakis* was perhaps best known of the early Greek devices. This apparatus was used to vaporize acidic liquids which would attack **metals**. It takes the form of a tube with a furnace at the bottom, and a condensing dome at the top. The heat vaporizes the liquid, which then attacks the metal, placed on a palette.

Other key items are the crucible (Chaucer's 'croslet'), and the **aludel**, a pear-shaped glass or earthen pot used for sublimation.

Aludel, alembic, **athanor** bear Arabic names and European alchemists drew much upon **Geber** (*see also* **Jabir**) for practical instructions on experiment.

## Chinese Apparatus

**Chinese alchemy** was strongly Taoist in its quest for the **elixir** to prolong life, and the Taoist patrology contains many alchemical texts with picturesque titles attesting the lengthy cyclical processes involved, for example, 'The Explanation of the Yellow Emperor's Manual of the Nine-Vessel Magical Elixir'. There was a general belief in the nine-fold process of cyclical transformation needed to purify and prepare the golden elixir. Sublimation and distillation were as important in China as in the West, with **cinnabar** and **mercury** assuming vital importance.

*An alchemist's vaulted laboratory.*
*This woodcut is copied from a medieval manuscript picture from the 'Ordinall of Alchemy' by Thomas Norton of Bristol. It shows the alchemist with a laboratory balance. Two kneeling assistants tend furnaces. This seems to be Norton's own finely equipped fifteenth-century laboratory.*
*From Elias Ashmole, Theatrum chemicum Britannicum (London, 1652).*
*By kind permission of The Bodleian Library, Oxford.*
*RR. W. 29 (9) p.51.*

Needham comments that Chinese equipment seems to have evolved naturally from cooking utensils: he enumerates a kitchen type stove, the *tsao* or *lu* (there are many types, as in the West, *see* **Furnaces**); the *ting* or reaction vessel with a lid, originally a cauldron as in the *I Ching* hexagram (sometimes called a 'suspended womb'); steaming apparatus, water-baths, condensation vessels, cooling jackets, various forms of still, a tripod vessel, a sublimatory vessel including a 'rainbow vessel' (*kung teng*).

Chinese alchemists were concerned with similar processes and substances as alchemists in the West, and used well-tried equipment suitable for long, complex reactions: as in the West, there seems to have been a strong belief that transformation was a very long process.

*See* J. Needham and Ho Ping-Yu, 'Laboratory Equipment of Chinese Alchemy' *Ambix*, 1959.

# Aqua
## Water

Water plays a vital part in **alchemy**, first as one of the four **elements**. The early Greek philosopher Thales posited water as the archetypal element, the *hyle* or first matter of the world (*see* **Prime Matter**). Adepts always related their work to the mystery of the divine **Creation**, to the Genesis passage where the **spirit** of God moves upon the waters: the primal waters of creation were given an alchemical interpretation, for the microcosmic events in the alchemical **vessel** symbolized the creation of the macrocosm.

There are many liquids used in alchemy, but solvents and **acids** are of especial importance, and there was the quest for the **alkahest**, the universal solvent. Key **processes** involve liquids, notably **distillation**, where liquid becomes spirit. Solution or dissolution is associated with the initial *nigredo* stage. This initial dissolving brings on the mortification or putrefaction, shown with dark symbols of death. But just as water belongs to the stage of death, so also there is the baptism and purification of *albedo*. The *albedo* (whitening) is so often described as a baptism, a renewal through cleansing and purification.

There was a tendency to regard all liquids as forms of **mercury**, and the mysterious **elixir** of life and **transmutation** is always treated as ambivalent, as both healing and poisonous, like mercury. The moon is associated with mercury, and with liquidity, moisture, dew and when Luna and Mercurius sprinkle the dismembered **dragon** with dew, it is fully revived, changing its hue to blood red:

As the water of ablution, the dew falls from heaven, purifies the body, and makes it ready to receive the soul; in other words, it brings about the *albedo*, the white state of innocence, which like the moon and a bride awaits the bridegroom.

Jung, *Mysterium Conjunctionis*, p.132

Mercury is the *aqua permanens*, the permanent water, to which Jung constantly refers in his writings.

Jung includes a long discussion of the 'Red Sea' as a symbol in alchemy (op. cit., p.199ff):

The Red Sea is a water of death for those that are 'unconscious', but for those that are 'conscious' it is a baptismal water of rebirth and transcendence.

The Red Sea is an ideal symbol or arcane name for the elixir or the **tincture** of transformation. Sea water, being *aqua pontica*, or *aqua permanens* (*see* **Mercury**), is regarded as the baptismal water, which purifies and cleanses, preparing the stage of *albedo* or whitening. Jung quotes *Gloria mundi* (The Glory of the World):

The mystery of everything is life, which is water; for water dissolves the body into spirit and summons a spirit from the dead.

**Transmutation** is achieved sometimes by a powder of projection, but more often there are the mysterious allusions to the **medicine** of metals, to the panacea or **elixir**, which is identified with the universal spirit Mercurius.

*Aqua permanens*, identified with Mercurius, is a mystic water. *Gloria mundi* describes *aqua permanens* as bitter, undrinkable:

A water of bitter taste, that preservest the elements! O nature of propinquity that dissolvest nature! O best of natures, which overcomest nature herself! . . .Thou art crowned with light and art born . . .and the quintessence ariseth from thee.

*See also* **Spirit**.

# Arcanum

This word is strongly magical, the Tarot pack consisting of *arcana*: it means 'magical secrets'. **Paracelsus** uses the word in his philosophy of alchemical **medicine**. In contrast with our bodily being, *arcana* are immortal and eternal, 'they have the power of transmuting, altering and restoring us', and are to be compared to the secrets of God, being vital in human health (*Archidoxies*, Bk V, trans. A.E. Waite).

# Aristotle
**born 384 BC at Stageiros, in Chalkidice, Macedonia; died 322 BC**

Although Aristotle wrote before the known emergence of **Hellenistic alchemy**, his writings on cosmology and the philosophy of **nature** completely dominated European and Islamic thought. Like Plato and Aquinas, he was credited with spurious works on **magic**, notably the *Secretum secretorum* (***The Secret of Secrets***), one of the outstandingly popular medieval **manuscripts** translated in many versions from Arabic originals. The *Secretum secretorum* purports to be a treatise on kingship, addressed by the philosopher to his pupil Alexander the Great, and has some advice on **elixirs** for prolonging life.

The teaching of Aristotle provides the basis for the theory of **elements** and qualities which dominated every aspect of science, **medicine** and magic for centuries. He believed the earth to be the realm of corruption and mortality, of the transformations of the four elements; but this is only the *sublunar* sphere. Above the sphere of the moon, the heavens are incorruptible, immortal, composed of the mystic fifth essence. The very perfection of immortal **astral bodies** suggests their dominant influence in this dark world of imperfection, hence Aristotle was often quoted in support of **astrology**, even though he predates the advent of astrology and magic in the Greek world.

Aristotle taught at the Platonic Academy in Athens from 368 to 367 BC. This had the motto 'let no ungeometrical person enter here', and propagated Pythagorean influence. In 343 BC he travelled to Macedonia to tutor Alexander from his thirteenth to sixteenth years. He returned to Athens but left on the death of Alexander, and died in his native Chalkis, leaving the most influential (although badly written) body of philosophy probably of any philosopher of any time.

*See* **Albertus Magnus** for Aristotle's influence on theories of mineralogy, geology and **metals**.

*See* J.R. Partington, *History of Chemistry*, Vol. I.

# Arnald of Villanova
**Physician and alchemist; born near Valencia, 1235, died in 1311 at sea on a voyage from Naples to Genoa**

Arnald qualifies as one of the great medieval scientists, above all as a professor of **medicine**, and his reputation as an alchemist was unparalleled, however spurious most of the **manuscripts** in his name may be. Born a Catalan, he was educated at a Dominican convent, then studied medicine at Naples. In his restless travels and his passion for reform he has been compared to **Paracelsus**, and it is vital to realize the strength of the medieval connection of **alchemy** with medicine long before the birth of the 'new' Paracelsian chemical medicine.

Arnald was personal physician to Peter III of Arragon who bequeathed to him his castle at Tarragon and he lectured at Montpellier, aside from Salerno the greatest medical school in Europe at that time. He was a scholastic writer on medicine, being fully versed in classical and Arabic works. He was completely trusted by Pope Clement V and he treated Pope Boniface VIII after his release from papal custody. His approach was strongly magical, despite his conventional scholastic learning, and he was renowned for his **elixir**, said to be a panacea for illness and for rejuvenation. Arnald was a cabalist and in 1299 was arrested by the Inquisition in Paris for his work on the *Tetragrammaton*, issued in 1292 in Hebrew and Latin, which presented his view of the Trinity.

He is said to have used chemical and metallic alchemical remedies long before the Paracelsians, and was very interested in the **sulphur** baths near Montpellier, also studied by Michael Scot. Verrier says he used **mercury** and **antimony** in the form of stibnite as part of metallic remedies.

Arnald was a prolific writer, mostly on academic medicine. His alchemical treatises are difficult to verify, but some seem consistent with his life story: *A Treatise on the Preservation of Youth*, for the benefit of Robert of Naples (d.1311), may be genuine.

A manuscript entitled *Rosarius* (The Rose Garden of the Philosophers), or *Thesaurus* (Treasure of Treasures) is also said to be genuine. This well-known work is divided into *Rosarius minor*, The Lesser Rose Garden, which deals with theoretical alchemy, and *Rosarius major*, The Greater Rose Garden, which is concerned with the practical art. The Preface says only that this is a collection from the ancient philosophers, and it is based upon the Arabic **mercury-sulphur theory of the generation of metals**. Like so many medieval tracts, it adduces mercury as the medicine of **metals** (elixir), while sulphur is regarded as the impurity causing imperfection. It also affirms the common theory that silver and **gold** can be made from mercury alone (*see* similar ideas of **Bernard of Trevisa**).

Of the other works ascribed to Arnald, a work called *Flos florum*

(Flower of Flowers), or the *Perfectum magisterium* (Perfect Mastery) contains a brief address to the King of Arragon, while the *Flos regis* (Flowers of the King) is dedicated to the King of Naples.

The *Novum lumen* (New Light) also gives priority to mercury in **transmutation** and enumerates the usual **processes**, citing the *Turba philosophorm* (The Crowd of Philosophers), the *Semita semitae* (The Seed of the Seed) was a popular work, and there is a letter to Pope Boniface VIII on alchemy.

*See* René Verrier, *Etudes sur Arnaud de Villeneuve 1240 – 1311* (Studies on Arnaud of Villanova 1240 – 1311).

# Ashmole, Elias
## 1617 – 92

Ashmole is best known today as the founder of the Ashmolean Museum in Oxford, which arose from the collection of the Cornish explorer John Tradescant. He rose to immense prestige as official historian of the Order of the Garter. The son of a Lichfield saddler, he trained in law, serving as a staunch Royalist in the Civil War. His lavish volume *The Institutions, Laws and Ceremonies of the most noble Order of the Garter* appeared in London in 1672. He was notable amongst the founding fellows of the Royal Society, being elected Fellow of the Royal Society in 1673, but he always remained true to astrological, Hermetic beliefs, never losing faith in the 'true Magick' of **alchemy** and **astrology**.

His great contribution to the study of alchemy was his *Theatrum Chemicum Britannicum* (London, 1652), the text being 486 pages, with *Prologomena*. Here he gives a passionate affirmation of deep faith in Hermetic **magic** and the Neoplatonist vision of the cosmos. C.H. Josten praises the erudite, meticulous scholarship of this work, collating Old English alchemical texts; his versions of **Thomas Norton** and **George Ripley** are truly standard.

Ashmole also translated *Fasciculus chemicus* by **Arthur Dee** (8o, London, 1650), a work designed for adepts, presenting 'choisest flowers' from Hermetic gardens, and Ashmole refers to the 'aenigmas, Metaphors, Parabols and Figures' of the art. He used an anagram of his own name, James Hasolle, for the book.

Ashmole's adoptive father was the alchemist **William Backhouse**, who in a period of sickness summoned Ashmole to confide to him 'in Silables', the secret of the 'true Matter of the Philosopher's Stone'.

For his interest in **angel magic** and Hermetic philosophy, *see* **Angel Magic** and **Hermetic Texts**; for his cosmic view, *see*

Harmony and Symmetry in Hermetic Philsophy.
The standard biography of Ashmole, with an edition of letters and documents is C.H. Josten's *Elias Ashmole.*

# *Astra*, Astral Body

**Astrology** was the province of what **John Dee** (1527 - 1608) called the 'vulgar Astrologien' (although he himself cast many horoscopes for the high and mighty), while doctrines of inner stars (*astra*) or an astral body belong to esoteric **alchemy**, expounded in many of **Paracelsus'** works. This postulates that man was created from heaven and earth, that he is part of the divine **Creation**, and that he has inner stars, a heaven within, because of his microcosmic nature (*see* **Microcosm-Macrocosm**). The sun, moon, all the planets and indeed primal chaos itself are actually within man, thus giving him a truly astral body or nature. The Greater World (macrocosm) was the maternal womb from which man was born, and he is thus composed of the four **elements**, but he possesses both an animal life and a sidereal (astral) life. The sidereal or astral body is composed of fire and air, which animate and move the animal body.

Such Paracelsian notions were not typical of early alchemists, although most had some form of doctrine of the spiritual man, bound within this mortal cave or prison.

*See also* **Adam**, who is the archetypal symbol for the astral or microcosmic man.

# Astrology

Astrology is one of the cornerstone concepts of **alchemy**: Dee calls alchemy 'astronomia inferior', and every aspect of the opus was governed by astrology, for the stars are the measure of time and the opus is a microcosmic process.

The basic tenets of astrological thought were to some extent implicit in the Greek philosophy of **Aristotle** and Plato. Plato's *Timaeus* depicts man as **microcosm** and the heavens were considered immortal, unchanging, while Aristotle created the world view which ruled medieval science: immutable celestial spheres were the abode of angelic intelligences while the world of the **elements**, contained within the sphere of the moon, was subject to corruption and change.

Astrology swept through Hellenistic culture, gaining increasing notoriety under the Roman Empire. However, its deeper origins lay in

Babylonian civilization, and oriental **magic** was heavily astrological. The earliest Greco-Egyptian alchemists were much influenced by Zoroastrian astral magic from Persia (*see* **Ostanes**). Early **alchemy** is entwined with the rise of the Hermetic tradition of astral magic, which is supposed to have its roots in ancient Egypt of Biblical times: the **Hermetic texts** suggest that the soul must mount through the spheres of the planets to reach freedom from this dark world.

European astrology came from the Islamic world, and the *Quadripartite* of Ptolemy (Greek *Tetrabiblos* = four books) was translated from Arabic versions very early on as the standard medieval textbook of basic astrology. This was the key text in medical astrology and countless medical books reproduce the famous zodiacal man. Since the heavens were not composed of the corruptible four elements, but of a mystic **quintessence** or fifth essence, the celestial bodies held a superior power or 'virtue' to the gross, elemental sublunar world, and this makes superior celestial influence logically inevitable within the Aristotelian world view. **John Dee**'s *Mathematicall Praeface* (1570) admirably sums up the doctrine of medieval and Renaissance cosmology:

> This world is of necessity, almost, next adjoining, to the heavenly motions: That, from thence, all his vertue and force may be governed. For that is to be thought the first Cause unto all: from which, the beginning of motion, is.

The heavens governed the growth, incubation and maturation of **metals** within the earth; the **mercury-sulphur theory of the generation of metals** meant that metals were born of the union, often considered a sexual union, of **sulphur** and **mercury**. The most perfect, harmonious union would yield **gold** under the influence of the sun (Sol); the moon (Luna) generated silver: Sol corresponds to sulphur, Luna to mercury (*see* **Sol and Luna**). The qualities of the other planets predominate in creating the less pure metals.

Just as the metals were seen as elemental embodiments of the planets and their virtues, so **herbs** and stones had an astral nature: the innate virtue of each herb, stone, mineral or gem was regarded as a sort of signature, arising from the radiating influence of the stars. Medieval **herbals** often present 'virtues of seven herbs' corresponding, like the metals, to the seven planets; lapidaries often present marvellous properties of twelve or seven stones or gems. The numerology of seven and twelve is vital to alchemy. (*See* **Metals and Planets** for the equation of the seven planets with the seven **metals**). In fact the entire medieval-Renaissance cosmos is pervaded by astral influence and literally nothing is exempt.

There were dissenting voices: St Augustine and other theologians were distressed by the idea of astral determinism negating free will, although the divinatory aspect of astrology is only one aspect: there is the horoscope-casting of natal astrology, or the horary astrology often used in decision-making by men as prominent as **Elias Ashmole**. The Renaissance cabalist Pico della Mirandola attacked astrology, and so did the Elizabethan John Fulke in his severe *Antiprognosticon* of 1570, dedicated to the Earl of Leicester, the case being argued on the basis of theology. However, Sir Phillip Sidney composed a sonnet beginning 'Though dusty wites dare scorn Astrologie', and he studied alchemy with John Dee, who was the Earl of Leicester's astrologer.

Dee held a mathematical theory of astral influence which he derived from **Roger Bacon**, who drew his theory of universal radiation of stellar influence from Al-Kindi and Al-Hazen:

> Astrologie is an Arte Mathematicall, which reasonably demonstrateth the operations and effectes, of the naturall beames, of light, and secrete influence; of the Stars and Planets: in every element . . .
>
> *Mathematicall Praeface*

The earth is bathed in celestial radiation, a conclusion consistent with the modern cosmology. Dee again:

> Whole Dispositions, vertues, and naturall motions, depend on the Activitie of the heavenly motions and Influences. Whereby, beside the specificall order and forme due to every seede: and beside the Nature, proper to the Individual Matrix, of the thing produced: What shall be the heavenly Impression, the perfect and circumspect Astrologien hath to Conclude.

Man as microcosm has within him stars or *astra*, as **Paracelsus** shows, and the ebb and flow of the four bodily humours are governed by the stars. Medieval alchemists like Johannes Rupescissa and **Ramon Lull** evolved the idea of quintessence, conceiving a subtle astral **spirit** pervading **nature**, working wonders and transformations in matter. For them, the elements of the world – earth, air, fire and water – are gross and without animating power; it is the spiritual, subtle, penetrative influence of stellar virtues which animates, moves and nourishes growth. The **harmony** of the spheres is ever-present, part of the unifying Pythagorean cosmic theory.

This is a vast subject and the cross-cultural diffusion of astrological ideas has yet to be studied. The doctrines of yoga, whether in its

Chinese or Indian manifestation, are much influenced by astral doctrines: thus the left and right channels of the body are ruled by sun and moon. Alchemists of India and China were yogic in their approach, and their traditions show that astrology is not confined to Hellenistic or European alchemy.

Of the vast literature, *see especially* Lynn Thorndike's *A History of Magic and Experimental Science up to the Seventeenth Century* for the herbals, lapidaries and astrological manuals.

# Athanor

The Arabic word *at-tannur* means simply an oven, but the alchemical version was a very special **furnace** or oven pictured in the form of a tower with turret or dome roof, and its purpose was to 'incubate' the egg-shaped Hermetic **vessel** (*vas hermeticum*), used for preparation of the **elixir**, whether of **metals** or of life. It was supposed to preserve a constant heat over long periods, which was required to warm the alchemical **egg** of the philosophers, which nested in sand or ashes.

*See also* **Apparatus**.

# Aurum Potabile

*Aurum potabile*, or potable **gold** was used as a **medicine** in eastern and western traditions.

**Thomas Vaughan** quotes the story of Moses and the golden calf, as suggesting that *aurum potabile* had its origin in biblical antiquity. Moses burns the idol of the golden calf, then grinds it to powder and sprinkles it upon the water, asking the children of Israel to drink therefrom.

> I am sure here was *aurum potabile*, and Moses could never have brought the Calf to this passe, had he not plowed with our Heyfer.
> *Magia Adamica* (Adamic Magic), ed. Rudrum, p.177

In **Chinese alchemy, elixirs** of long life included **mercury** and gold. In the West, Paracelsian alchemists tended to concoct panaceas (*see* **Paracelsus**), and there was a famous controversy over *aurum potabile* as used by the Elizabethan **Francis Anthony**. It is also featured in Ben Jonson's *The Alchemist*.

# Avicenna, Ibn Sina
## Arabic philosopher and physician; AD 980–1037

Avicenna is best known as 'Prince of Physicians' and he rose to highest prominence both as administrator and as philosopher-physician. His contributions to philosophy and **medicine** were immense, including his famous *Canon* which became the Bible of medical students through medieval and Renaissance times. Its mainly Galenist synthesis of classical medicine was reviled, however, by the revolutionary **Paracelsus** who felt that **alchemy** and astral philosophy were the basis for medicine, for understanding and treating the body and soul of man.

Avicenna's great contribution to alchemy was his *Kitab al-Shifa*, or 'Book of the Remedy', a study of minerals, chemistry and geology. It deals with the congealing and hardening of stones, the cause of mountains arising, the four kinds of minerals, and so forth. Following the great **Jabir ibn Hayyan**, he accepts completely the **mercury-sulphur theory of the generation of metals**, arguing that solid silver may be created by the virtue of white **sulphur** with the addition of **mercury**, and a super-pure, fiery and subtle sulphur combined with mercury may solidify into **gold** – this was the basis of the medieval 'vulgar alchemist's' theory of physical **transmutation** of **metals**. However, Avicenna is emphatic that this is a geological and not an alchemical theory. E.J. Holmyard shows that in the *Kitab al-Shifa* Avicenna launches a powerful critique of transmutatory alchemy: he states unequivocally that alchemists are only able to produce imitations – for instance applying a white **tincture** to a red metal produces fake silver, but the 'true metallic species' does not change. Using the Aristotelian distinction between 'accidental' properties, i.e. appearance and real nature, he argues that alchemist's gold or silver may fool the expert, but they are only imitations.

A deeper study of Avicenna's philosophy shows a deep Pythagorean and Neoplatonist mystical strain (*see* **Neoplatonism**). He believes in a hierarchical universe, in the great Chain of Being, a cosmos (*see* **Creation**) created by God whose influence is mediated through the hierarchies of angels.

*See* Nasr, *Islamic Cosmological Doctrines*; E.J. Holmyard, *Alchemy*.

# Azoth

This is one of the arcane names for the **mercury** of the philosophers, as the universal **spirit** of the world. In a text attributed to **Artephius**,

Azoth is said to be 'our second and living water', or the soul of dissolved bodies'. Azoth is also identified with the mercurial **fountain** in which the **King and Queen** take their **bath**. Thus it is one of the names for mercury as the **Prime Matter** or principle, the *aqua permanens* (permanent water) in which sun and moon are united in *conjunctio*.

Jung quotes the *Aurelia Occulta*, which features Azoth as meaning the **alpha and omega** which are everywhere present. The A and Z in the word correspond to Greek alpha and omega, as well as to the *aleph* and *tau* in Hebrew.

# B

## Backhouse, William
### born 1593

William Backhouse was the son of Samuel Backhouse who bought the manor of Swallowfield, near Reading, Berkshire, in 1582. His family was originally from Lancashire. William's grandfather was Alderman, then Sherrif, of the City of London and his father became High Sherrif of Berkshire and served as MP for Windsor. William himself was born on 17 January 1593. His main claim to fame is that he was **Elias Ashmole**'s adoptive alchemical father, and Ashmole kept his horoscope (to be found in the Bodleian Library, Ashmole Manuscript 332). He was a friend of John Blagrave, the astrologer and mathematical author of *The Mathematician's Jewel*, and also met **Robert Fludd**.

Backhouse's fascinating poem 'The Magistery' is dated December 1633:

**Verse 4:**
Son and Moone in Hermes Vessel,
  Learne how the Collours shew,
The nature of the Elements,
  And how the daisies grow.

Great Python how Apollo slew,
  Cadmus his hollow Oake:
His new rais'd army, and Iason how
  The fiery steeres did yoke.

The Eagle which aloft doth fly
  See that thou bring to ground;
And give unto the snake some wings
  Which in the Earth is found.

Then in one Roome sure bind them both,
  To fight till they be dead;
And that a Prince of kingdomes three
  Of them shalbe bred.

*See* C.H. Josten, 'William Backhouse of Swallowfield', *Ambix* 1949.

# Bacon, Francis
**English philosopher of the scientific revolution of the early seventeenth century; 1561 – 1626**

Francis Bacon exerted a tremendous influence upon the movement for experimental science which led to the founding of the Royal Society. His output of writings was immense, his most famous work being *The Advancement of Learning* (1605). He studied at Trinity College, Cambridge, and rose to office as Lord Chancellor, only to face ruin on charges of corruption. He retired to his estate of Verulam House, near St Albans, to construct a new edifice of scientific, empirical philosophy, under the general title of *Instauratio magna* (The Great Restoration of Science).

Bacon carried out chemical experiments, but was not an alchemist. However, his philosophical works encouraged a critical re-examination of the occult traditions of **alchemy** and **magic**. He observed:

> . . . the study of nature with a view to works as engaged in by the mechanic, the mathematician, the physician, the alchemist and the magician: but by all (as things are) with slight endeavour and scanty success.

# Bacon, Roger
**English natural philosopher; 1214 – 94**

Born at Ilchester in Somerset at the height of the Islamic-inspired Renaissance in European sciences, Roger Bacon joined the Franciscan friars and attained the highest esteem as a philosopher. His teacher was Robert Grosseteste, Bishop of Lincoln and Chancellor of Oxford University. Their school of philosophy was much influenced by mathematics, optics, and by Neoplatonist 'light metaphysics' (*see* **Neoplatonism**). The overall world view was strongly theological, with hierarchies of angels mediating divine influence to this inferior, elemental world (*see* **Angel Magic**).

Bacon joined the Franciscans in Oxford and his laboratory tower stood on Folly Bridge. He migrated to Paris in 1240. His *Opus maius* (Greater Work) was a powerful and coherent synthesis of natural philosophy, with especial emphasis on mathematics as the 'gateway and key to the sciences'. Bacon's theory of optics obeys geometric laws and he presents an Arabic theory of astrological influence: **John Dee** seems to have derived his special theory of astral influences from Bacon, Grosseteste and Alkindi. Theology remains as *regina scientiarum* (queen of the sciences).

In general, medieval scholastic science and theology was hostile to **alchemy**, which was relegated to the areas of popular superstition and heresy. However, Bacon strongly espoused the causes of alchemy and of 'Natural Magic'. In this respect, he gave powerful support to the Elizabethan alchemist John Dee, who composed a treatise defending Bacon against charges of using demonic **magic**: Dee affirmed that Bacon used only natural, Christian magic. The magical reputation of Bacon was embodied in the Elizabethan play by Robert Greene entitled *Friar Bacon and Friar Bungay*, and in the legends of a speaking brazen head, a plan to surround England with a wall of brass, the idea of giant burning mirrors to destroy enemy fleets, and even the invention of the telescope and the submarine.

In 1267 Bacon looked back on 20 years of study which had cost him 2,000 libra for instruments and 'secret books'. As an alchemist, he is difficult to assess, for his supposed alchemical works are probably spurious. However he definitely saw alchemy as a pillar of **medicine**, vital for separating helpful from harmful ingredients in medicines, and in this he anticipates the medical revolution of **Paracelsus** in the sixteenth century. He listed ignorance of alchemy in preparing medicines as one of the cardinal errors made by physicians of his day (*see* his *De erroribus medicorum* (Medical Errors)). In his *Opus tertium* (Third Work), he shows his awareness of the distinction between 'speculative' and 'practical' alchemy. The speculative he explains as dealing with the generation of things from **elements** and humours – this includes geology: gems, marble, **metals**, **salts** and pigments.

Bacon is impressive amongst medieval scholars as being a highly-disciplined scholastic philosopher, who was nevertheless keenly interested in magic and experimental science, which were closely related at this time. He was most deeply influenced by the *Secretum secretorum* (*see* **The Secret of Secrets**), a work which enjoyed tremendous popularity in the Middle Ages, with its occult and Hermetic elements. Most of his own works, however, were not published until the sixteenth and seventeenth centuries.

**Publications:**

*De mirabili potestate artis et naturae* (On the miraculous power of art and nature) (1542). This book was a contribution to the Renaissance tradition of Natural Magic and Hermeticism.

*Libellus . . . de retardandis senectutis accidentibus et de sensibus conservandis* (Book . . . on retarding the onset of old age and on preserving the senses) (1590). Edited by John Williams, the work is dedicated to Sir Christopher Hatton. It contains an account of the theory of retarding old age and conserving the senses. This was the aim of the **elixir** alchemy of the Chinese, but medieval alchemists rarely show an interest in methods of prolonging life.

*The Mirror of Alchemy*, translated by Ralph Rabbards from the medieval **manuscript** *Speculum alchimiae* (1597). The work contains little more than a simplistic account of the Arabic theory of the **mercury-sulphur theory of the generation of metals**.

*Epistolae de secretis operibus artis et naturae, et de nullitate magiae* (Letters on the secret works of art and nature, and on the vanity of magic) (1618). Published in Hamburg, this fascinating work contains alchemical as well as magical material. It contains a Preface which is strongly **Rosicrucian**, and the text was taken from John Dee's revision of a medieval manuscript in his library.

*Friar Bacon, his Discovery of the Miracles of Art, Nature and Magick* (1659). Published in London, this is an English translation of the *Epistolae* above.

# Bain Marie
**Latin:** *Balneum Mariae*

*See* **Baths** and **Maria Prophetissa**.

# Balsam
**Balsamus**, *Balsamum*, Balm

The Greek botanist Theophrastus describes balsam of Mecca as flowing like tears from the bark of **trees** cultivated in Syrian valleys and this is the 'Balm of Gilead', defined by *The Oxford English Dictionary* as 'golden oleo-resin once used much as antiseptic'. In general balsam denotes a resinous product, the word 'balm' being used for fragrant or medicinal resins used in ointments or medicinal concoctions. 'Friar's balsam' is still used in treating asthma.

The word became current in English, especially in poetry, through Paracelsian influence. John Donne refers to balm as healing, in his poem 'Twicknam Garden':

Hither I come to seeke the spring,
And at mine eyes, and at mine eares,
Receive such balmes as else cure every thing.

**Paracelsus** uses balsam to mean the 'interior salt', the preservative fluid which keeps the body from mortal corruption and decay. His strange work, *De vita longa* (On long life) equates balsam with 'Mummia', which was a preservative analogous to that used by the Egyptians in mummification. **Martin Ruland** in his alchemical *Lexicon* identifies baslam of the **elements** with the **quintessence**, which was derived from **mercury**: it is an agent in accomplishing the mystical marriage of alchemical principles, the *conjunctio*.

# Barchusen, Johann Conrad
**born 16 May 1666, died 1723**

Barchusen was born at the small village of Horn near Detmold in Lippe, Germany. He studied chemistry and pharmacy in Germany and in Vienna, then worked as a military physician with the Venetian army, though as yet unqualified. In 1694 he moved to Utrecht where he delivered private lectures on chemistry and built himself a laboratory on the city walls. He received an honorary degree from the university here in 1698, and became chemistry lecturer at the medical faculty. He was appointed extraordinary professor until his death in 1723.

Barchusen is one of the last chemists to exploit and explore alchemical imagery, his *Elementa chemiae* being full of alchemical illustrations (some featured in Jung's *Psychology and Alchemy*).

**Publications:**
*Pyrosophia* (Wisdom of Fire) (Leiden, 1698).
*Elementa chemiae, quibus subjuncta est confectura Lapidis Philosophiae imaginibus repraesenta* (Elements of chemistry, to which are added the making of the Stone of Philosophy pictured in images) (1718). This includes 19 plate engravings showing the stages of the alchemical opus.

# Bartholomaeus Anglicus
**English natural philosopher;** *floruit* 1230-40

Bartholomew seems to have studied with Robert Grosseteste, who taught **Roger Bacon**, and he became teacher to the Franciscans of Saxon Magdeburg. His encyclopaedia, entitled *De proprietatibus rerum* (On the properties of things), shows clear chemical knowledge, derived mostly from the medieval encyclopaedist Isidore of Seville. He is convinced that **mercury** is the element basic to all **metals**, and says it is watery, insoluble and white of substance; brimstone and lead congeal it. *De proprietatibus rerum* commences with theology, describing the names and properties of God, and the hierarchies of angels ministering divine influence. Geography, including catalogues of mountains and rivers, is prominent. The work presents most aspects of the standard medieval world view and when the **manuscript** was first printed in the reign of Elizabeth I it was a best-seller. The expanded edition of Stephen Batman, entitled *Batman uppon Bartholomew* (1583) was the source of some of Shakespeare's natural lore. Although sixteenth-century science had made giant leaps forward, Anglicus' medieval conception of a divine and magical cosmos remained remarkably unscathed.

# Basilisk

The basilisk is a creature said to have been hatched from a cock's egg by a serpent, being reptilian with the head of a fowl and the body of a **dragon**. It is typical of alchemical allegory centred on the philosophers' **egg**, which was the symbol for the Hermetic **vessel** in which the opus reached summation.

A medieval lapidary described by Lynn Thorndike gives three types of basilisk:

> The most ferocious type of basilisk is hatched from a cock's egg with serpentine form, and with Gorgon's eyes which kill a man at a glance. This is small, the size of a chicken with the feet and head of a rooster and a beak like the mouth of a toad. It has no wings, like fowl, with talons, short plumage on the neck, head and back. Such a creature, believes the author [of the medieval lapidary], was actually killed at Halle, Saxony, by a weasel. Like demons, it is best killed with a mirror, by its own reflection – preferably a steel mirror, thus it is killed with its own stare.
>
> The second type is produced artificially, being venomous according to the herbs used in creating it.
>
> The third type is generated in mines, with feet and head of a fowl, beautiful eyes like the bird herodius, and a serpent's tail; it is coal black with wings almost shining with visible small veins. This genus is said to be harmless, indeed its oil and water are valuable to alchemists. Sometimes there are gems in the head of this creature.

> Lynn Thorndike, 'Medieval Lapidaries', *Ambix*, February 1960

This shows the range of medieval animal folklore, and the kind of mining superstitions which were even believed by **Georgius Agricola**.

Theophilus, the monk writing on **colour** in the twelfth century, casts further light on mining lore in a fascinating passage quoted by John Stillman:

In manufacture of Spanish gold, 'ashes of basilisk' are used with red copper, blood and vinegar. The story goes that two cocks mate and lay eggs. Toads are used to incubate the eggs. Male chickens are hatched which, within 7 days, grow serpent tails. The basilisk is buried, reduced to ash and the blood of a red-haired man is added.

John Stillman, *The Story of Alchemy and Early Chemistry*, pp.228 – 9

This may be a clue to the growth of alchemical **myth**. Theophilus is generally sensible, down-to-earth; what he has heard is an account of a metallurgical process, told in the kind of mythic language beloved of alchemists. The blood of the red-haired man might be **cinnabar.**

# Baths, *Bain-Marie*

The alchemical warming bath still called *Bain-Marie* in France, Latin *Balneum Mariae*, takes its name from the ancient authority **Maria Prophetissa** who wrote much on chemical **apparatus**. The bath is normally kept warm by a simmering kettle or cauldron with gentle heat, being ideal for maintaining constant modest heat. It is extremely common in accounts of alchemical experiments, where bathing and cleaning are often equated with baptism, with purification following the dark, wretched state of *nigredo*, or with calcination. Washing and cleaning of calcined metal brings the *albedo*, the stage of whitening (*see* **Processes**; **Stages**).

Alchemical baths are imbued with mythic images: one harmonious picture in the *Rosarium* shows the immersion of **King and Queen**, representing **Sol and Luna**, in a hexagonal bath with a dove hovering over them as they hold outstretched twigs. There are many similar pictures of Sol and Luna naked in the bath. Usually the alchemical couple sit sedately in the bath, surrounded by mythic **beasts**. They are the same royal couple of the *conjunctio*, brother and sister, **mercury-sulphur.** A well-known picture in the *Splendor solis* (The Sun's Splendour) **manuscript** shows a bearded Christ-like figure seated in the bath with a white, radiant dove perched upon his head, symbol of the whitening *albedo*. The alchemist is using a pair of bellows to stoke the fire beneath the bath and the background shows a splendid classic arched colonnade.

There are many similar illustrations with Sol and Luna in the bath:

one picture, from **Libavius**' *Commentariorum alchymiae* (Alchemical
Commentaries) (1606) shows the King and Queen seated facing one
another beneath the Philosophers' **Tree**, under the seven planetary
bodies representing the **metals**; they lean against a balustrade, their
feet decorously in the water.

John Read quotes Artephius on the bath, which is 'the most
pleasant, faire, and cleere Fountaine, prepared onely for the King and
Queene, whom it knoweth very well and they know it; for it draws
them to itselfe, and they abide therein to wash themselves two or three
dayes, that is, two or three monthes, and it maketh them young againe
and faire . . .' (*Prelude to Chemistry*, p.143). The bath, then, is filled
with waters of rejuvenation which are an **elixir** or **medicine** of
renewal, and Artephius introduces the classic symbolism of birth,
**redemption** and resurrection:

> Let therefore the spirit of our living water be with great wit and subtlety
> fixed with the Sunne and Moone, because they are being turned into the
> nature of water, doe dye and seem like unto the dead; yet afterward being
> inspired from thence, they live, encrease, and multiply like all other
> vegetable things.

John Read explains this as follows:

> . . .before entering the Bath or Fountain of the Philosophers, the King
> and Queen divest themselves of their garments. In a like manner, gold
> and silver are divested of their impurities in the preparation of sophic
> sulphur and sophic mercury. The Bath of the Philosophers . . .is thus a
> symbol of the purification of gold and silver, for the purposes of the Great
> Work.

We might add that the metals **gold** and silver have their spiritual
archetypal dimensions as symbols of spiritual purity and perfection
and the alchemical allegory is bound to transcend chemical
operations to purify these comparatively base metals.

# Beasts and Birds

The medieval bestiary, with its picturesque folklore, is the repository
of a whole aspect of culture: **magic**, superstition and truth are the
same. The alchemical bestiary likewise is vital in its symbolism of
every aspect and **stage** of the opus. For the true adept, there is no
inanimate matter: every **process** represents a living, animate
happening. **Metals, acids** and liquids are living beings – a fierce
reaction is a fight between fierce animals, a vapour is a bird or flock

of birds rising from the solution, a metal dissolving in an acid is a **king** dying, drowning, crying from the depths. Much **myth** concerns the soteriological significance of rising from the earthly darkness of mortality and sin to the purity of divine illumination.

Alchemical tradition includes the mythic beasts the **dragon** and **basilisk** and the semi-mythic creatures the salamander, the winged serpents, red and green lions. **Giordano Bruno** draws a distinction between creatures of the dark and of the light: toads, owls and basilisks are associated with witchcraft and are ruled by Diana and the moon (*see* **Sol and Luna**); the creatures of the light are the **phoenix**, eagle, lion and ram. The latter = the sign of Aries, spring, start of the sun's course. In *On the shadows of ideas*, Bruno portrays the triumph of creatures of the light over those of the darkness – a thoroughly alchemical myth.

Above all, animals tend to represent **colours** and processes, as in **George Ripley**'s famous poem of the toad passing through the colours of the opus. Black birds tend to signify the dark chaos of *nigredo*, the initial **Prime Matter**. The grey wolf is often used for **antimony** in later (sixteenth-century) texts, as antimony is conceived

*Double-headed mercurial dragon, with clerical alchemists kneeling in prayer, and a bird representing the spiritual aspect of the world.*

*This is a strangely pagan image, with the priestly alchemists actually shown worshipping the mercurial dragon. There are Sol and Luna symbols. The scroll on the left refers to the experimental, practical aspect of the alchemical opus, that on the right to the speculative, reasoning approach to the religious study of nature.*

*From Elias Ashmole,* Theatrum chemicum Britannicum *(London, 1652).*

*By kind permission of The Bodleian Library, Oxford.*

*RR. W. 29 (9), p.213.*

as attacking metals. Animals and birds also have apocalyptic meaning: the lion of St Mark, the eagle of St John, the bull of St Luke, the angel reserved for St Matthew.

The most popular alchemical creatures are the chthonic snakes, dragons and salamandars which so often have wings. These enjoy prestige everywhere as guardians of treasure – fierce protectors as well as venomous obstacles on the path to enlightenment.

## Birds

The alchemical opus may be described almost entirely in allegories of birds and beasts, and they could fill a whole volume. Birds tend to be more prominent than beasts, since the rising of **spirits** or vapours under heat is so often symbolized by flight of birds. Black crows, ravens or eagles symbolize *nigredo*, the black beginning of the opus: in **Hermes**' *Golden Tractate* the crow cries with a loud voice from the mountain top, proclaiming its colour transformations (*see* **Colours**). The eagle is imperial, also associated with the Revelations of St John, this apocalyptic work being crucial to the prophetic alchemists (*see* **Joachim of Fiore; Prophecy**). The white doves of Diana feature much in **Newton**'s experiments, while the Peacock's Tail, the *cauda pavonis* (*see* **Peacock**) is the supreme stage of flowering and success in the opus. White swans and doves are spiritual birds. Mythic birds like the solar phoenix or the **pelican,** which inflicts injury upon itself for its young, represent themes of death and resurrection, bringing Christ's suffering into the alchemical context (*see* **Jungian Theory of Alchemy; Redemption**). As Jung so forcefully proves, the Philosophers' **Stone** of **transmutation** was so often equated with Christ the Redeemer.

One striking medieval picture shows a vision of dead birds beneath the feet of a hermaphroditic couple, with one hand holding a bat, the other a hare. The 'couple' are embraced or enfolded from behind by a ferocious-looking black eagle (*see* **Hermaphrodite**).

The symbolism of the **egg,** of incubation and hatching, is involved not only with the Hermetic **vessel,** but with other aspects of the opus (*see* **Egg**). There is a marked tendency for hybrid creatures to arise, as in the millennarian visions of Hieronymus Bosch, who may have been inspired by **alchemy**: his strange bird-humans hatching from eggs must be alchemical.

Chinese symbolism has a neater, more poetic quality than that of the West. Chinese birds and creatures are fitted into a **mandala** structured on the basis of yin and yang symbolism, or on circles of the hexagrams of the *I Ching*. The four directions are important: East – Green Dragon; West – White Tiger; South – Red Bird; North – Black

Warrior. These are ubiquitous in alchemy, as are snakes and magic tortoises. The symbolism of longevity is of most interest to Taoists, with cranes and tortoises given pride of place. The lavishly-plumed birds of Chinese art, commonly equated with the phoenix, do not die and rise from the ashes as in western tradition. Other Chinese birds are the Red Bird of the South, with plumes like a peacock (*zhu niao*), and the *feng huang*, which is paired with the dragon.

# Bernard of Trevisa
**Bernardus Trenvisanus;** *floruit c.*1380

Bernard came from Trier (Treves) on the Mosel, and is dated to the later fourteenth century. He lived at the time of the flourishing alchemical craze to which **Chaucer** bears witness in his Canones Yeomans Tale; he is also contemporary with **Flamel**. He is most interesting for his lively correspondence with Thomas of Bologna, astrologer and physician to King Charles V of France. Thomas was respected as an astrologer, but found his reputation tarnished by the failure of *aurum potabile* **medicines**, concocted of **mercury** with **gold**. In reply to a letter from Thomas, Bernard presents his own views on the **mercury-sulphur theory of metals**, arguing that mercury alone is the essential constituent of gold. He explains the concept of mercury as **hermaphrodite**, combining in itself the masculine and feminine characteristics of mercury and **sulphur**. The philosophers' mercury contains all four **elements**, the air and fire of sulphur with the earth and water normally associated with mercury.

Bernard's alchemical autobiography, *De chemico miraculo* (On the alchemical miracle), is often cited, being printed in the *Theatrum Chemicum*. It describes the birth of the Philosophers' **Stone** with the sun and moon (**Sol and Luna**) as its parents. Bernard also discusses production of the **elixir** from purest mercury, and likens the philosophers' mercury to their **egg** which symbolizes **unity** (*see* **Numerology**).

The only firm date in his life is that of the letter to Thomas of Bologna: St Denis' Day, 1385.

He shows strong animosity towards Arabs, as he expended 400 crowns on experiments from **Rhazes** and 2,000 crowns on **Geber**. By the age of 38 he had spent 6,000 crowns fruitlessly . . . .. But at the age of 62 he still travelled to the island of Rhodes to continue his experiments.

# Bodenstein, Adam von
Paracelsian physician and editor; born 1528, died 1577 in Basle

Graduating as Doctor of Arts and Medicine at Basle University, Adam studied and practised **medicine**, becoming a leading disciple of **Paracelsus**, and pouring forth editions of his master's works (which were not published during Paracelsus' lifetime). He belongs to the vitally important circle of Paracelsians working in Germany and Habsburg central Europe. This circle includes Michael Toxites, Adam Schröter, Georg Forberger, Balthasar Flöter and **Gerard Dorn**. They were mystical as well as practical alchemists, guided by the light of **nature** (*lumen naturae*) and by the light of revelation. They believed nature was God's **Creation** and therefore the physician must study 'The Book of Nature', which is itself a form of divine revelation.

Adam was enthusiastic about **Arnald of Villanova**, the leading medieval alchemist, who was also a medical man, interested in using **alchemy** to prepare medical cures. In a dedicatory epistle to his own edition of Arnald, he addressed to the Fuggers (a German commercial monopolist family) a defence of alchemy and of the new approach to Paracelsian medicine, that is, using alchemy for cures and to understand illness as partly chemical. Paracelsus himself had antagonized the powerful Fuggers by attacking the use of guiac wood as a cure for syphilis: trade in guiac wood was their main source of wealth.

Adam's *Isagoge*, or Introduction to the *Rosarium* of Arnald shows his reverence for and inspiration from medieval alchemy. His is a thorough edition and paraphrase of the medieval work.

During the 1560s and 1570s, a whole series of printed editions of Paracelsus' works was issued, edited by Adam and his circle and published in Basle, Frankfurt and Mulhausen. Jung calls Adam 'the closest disciple of Paracelsus' and his edition of the book 'On long life' (*De vita longa*) (analysed in detail by Jung in his *Alchemical Studies*) claims to be edited from the works of the master himself. This work is amongst the richest in esoteric symbolism; the edition was in Latin, translated from the original German in which Paracelsus used to teach. *De vita longa* was printed in Basle in 1562; Gerard Dorn issued his edition in Frankfurt in 1583.

**Publications:**

Isagoge in . . . Arnaldi de Villanova Rosarium chymicum, *paraphrastice et magna diligentia tradita. Epistola operis praefixa ad amplissimos et generosos dominos . . .Fuggeros in qua argumenta*

*alchymiam infirmantia et confirmantia adducuntur, quibus et eam
artem esse certissemam demonstratur* (1559).

# Boehme, Jacob
## Or Behmen; born 1575 near Gorlitz, Prussia, died 1624

This mystical shoemaker achieved renown as a prophet who was
profoundly influenced by the Paracelsian vision of the cosmos. He
was himself no more than a dabbler in chemistry, but **Paracelsus** had
created a religious, mystical philosophy of man as **microcosm**, and
of the revelatory light of **nature**, and this inspired spiritual
movements during the seventeenth century.

Boehme was born of a poor family and learnt the trade of shoemaker
before embarking on his wanderings. He returned to his native town
and was married in 1594; he had a family of four children. In 1598 he
experienced a prolonged state of mystical enlightenment, feeling
himself to be surrounded with divine light for several days. He
believed that he had seen into the heart of 'The Book of Nature', to
use the Paracelsian metaphor; he had become enlightened by the
*lumen naturae*, and he claimed that he saw the signatures or marks of
the stars in the world of **creation**, these signatures being the evidence
of divine influence in the cosmos.

In 1600 another visionary state arose as he gazed upon the sun's
dazzling reflection in a pewter dish. He continued to follow his trade,
but poured forth writings which inspired the radical Boehmist
movement. His first work was called 'Red Sky at Morning' (*Aurora*,
or *Morgenrote*), written in 1612, but published in 1682. Frances Yates
comments:

> Boehme aimed at refreshing with Paracelsian inspired alchemical
> philosophy the deadness and dryness of contemporary Lutheran piety,
> which is an aim of the Rosicrucian writers.

The titles of his works show how strongly he lived under the spell of
Paracelsian mysticism:

*On the signature of things, or on the birth and description of all being*
(1635). The doctrine of astrological signatures was a vital feature of
Paracelsian theory.

*On the three principles of Divine Being* (1660), referring to the **Tria
Principia** (three principles) of Paracelsus, the principles being
**salt**, **sulphur** and **mercury**. This trinity was easily made to

correspond to the divine Trinity as manifested in the natural world of creation.

*On the threefold life of man.*

*Mysterium Magnum, on the first book of Moses* (1682). The 'Great Mystery' for Paracelsus was the divine Creation, and Paracelsians had a new vision of an alchemical process of creation.

Thus the Paracelsian vision of the world of nature and of the astral influences therein was a basis for reviving Christian mysticism in a time of millennarian expectation. This is the age of **Michael Maier, Robert Fludd** and of the great **Rosicrucian** movement. **Alchemy** with Boehme has left the laboratory to become a system of mystical, transcendent symbolism.

# Bolos of Mendes
## *c.* 300–250 BC

The name of **Democritus** figures frequently in references to magical and alchemical books and a famous work, the *Phusika kai mustika* (On natural and initiatory things) was attributed to him. However, scholars now attribute these works to Bolos of Mendes, sometimes called 'the Democritean' – perhaps he was a disciple of the atomist Democritus of Abdera who published voluminous works.

Mendes was the seat of worship of the Egyptian goat god Mendes (equated with Greek Pan) and was famous for production of perfume. Bolos' known works are full of Egyptian **magic**, based on the principles of antipathy and sympathy, with accounts of superstitious wonders and marvels, as well as conjuring tricks. Such interests were consistent with the burgeoning Neopythagorean movement: Neoplatonist, Pythagorean and gnostic-Hermetic influences all merge in early **alchemy**. He was a versatile writer, his works covering chemistry, **medicine**, agriculture, **astrology** and Egyptian hieroglyphics. His magic is mainly Persian, derived from Zoroaster and **Ostanes**. Pliny claimed that Democritus and Ostanes were the main culprits for inciting a Hellenistic craze for all kinds of magic.

His works include *Baphika*, dealing with chemistry, recipes for dyeing and so forth, *Phusika*, concerning sympathies and antipathies in **nature**, *Cheirokmeta*, a compilation of Persian magic and Chaldaean astrology, *Georgika*, dealing with agriculture, and *Paignia*, a book of conjuring tricks.

Bolos seems to have been a main source for recipes of chemistry, dyes, medical remedies, and magical ideas of sympathy and antipathy, all vital to early alchemy.

# Bonus, Petrus of Ferrara
*floruit* 1330

Bonus composed one of the most celebrated of medieval works on **alchemy**, *Pretiosia margarita novella* (New Pearl of Great Price), a fund of ideas printed in 1546 in the edition of Janus Lacinius. The book is impressive for its admission of failure in pursuit of the **Stone**, and in its scholastic structure of argument and counter-argument. The strong case against alchemy is presented first, followed by a refutation of doubters, and this suggests the lines of general debate on the subject at this time. The argument centres on the alchemist's ability to imitate **nature** in maturing **metals** with heat in the womb of the earth. Sceptics argue that nature takes thousands of years – a tentative step towards a concept of geological time – and this was the authoritative view of **Avicenna**. The influences of the stars were also considered to be long-term, beyond the control of alchemists. Bonus argues with cogent logic that the Stone may indeed effect **transmutation**: the argument is oft-repeated that metals essentially contain quicksilver, and it is the pure element in them which may be at once transmuted by the stone (*see* **Stone**).

*See* Lynn Thorndike, 'Medieval Lapidaries', *Ambix*, February 1960, and Holmyard, *Alchemy*.

# Boyle, Robert
**English chemist; 1627–91**

Robert was the son of Richard Boyle, first Earl of Cork. He was given private tuition as a child before going to Eton, then continuing his education on the Continent, where he encountered Galileo's writings.

He returned to an England torn by the strife of the Civil War and met **Samuel Hartlib**, who encouraged his interest in **medicine** and chemistry. In 1656 he went to Oxford where he became involved with John Wilkins, John Wallis and Seth Ward, the founders of the Invisible College which was a precursor for the Royal Society. After the Restoration of 1668, he settled in London, where the Royal Society provided the forum for his scientific activities.

Boyle dedicated his life to chemistry, and his laboratory was a centre for dramatic new experimental research and chemical debate. He was a contemporary of men like **Elias Ashmole** and Sir **Isaac Newton** who still owed a tremendous debt to the Hermetic tradition, but he is known as the man who introduced modern methods and theories into chemistry, thereby contributing to the abolition of the alchemical world view. His view of matter was corpuscularian, and he contributed to original debate over the whole concept of **elements** in chemistry in the course of his *Sceptical Chymist* (1661).

**Publications:**
*New Experiments Physico-Mechanicall, touching the Spring of the Air and its Effects* (1660).
*Certain Physiological Essays* (1661). In this work Boyle expounds his corpuscularian view of matter, which was to have immense influence as the ancient view of matter as constituted of the four elements died out.
*Sceptical Chymist* (1661).
*New Experiments* (1662). This work contains his exposition of Boyle's Law, and he defends the concept of the vacuum and of atmospheric pressure. *Experiments and Considerations touching Colours* (1664). This work describes how Boyle learnt to distinguish **acids and alkalis** by their colour effects in solution.
*Hydrostatical Paradoxes* (1666).
*Origine of Formes and Qualities* (1666). Boyle here refutes the Aristotelian world view, in which matter was given its characteristics through forms and qualities. His philosophy emerges as mechanistic and corpuscular. He prefers the idea of corpuscles to ancient atomism.

# Bruno, Giordano
## born Nola in Italy, 1548, died Rome 1600

Born near Mt Vesuvius, Giordano Bruno became one of the most remarkable of the Renaissance Hermetic philosophers of **magic**, whose writings presented a new vision of the cosmos as an infinite, animate universe, pervaded by magical and astral influences. He entered the Dominican Friars at the age of fifteen, joining the monastery at Naples, but by 1576 he was in trouble with them and had to leave the order, under accusations of heresy. From then on, he wandered Europe, giving dramatic lectures and composing fascinating books on the art of memory and on cosmology and magic. After an unsuccessful stay in Geneva, he moved to Paris in 1581, where he found favour with King Henri III (the patron of Nostradamus). He gave public lectures on Egyptian Hermetic philosophy, and was soon to emerge as an advocate of a reformation of religion and philosophy, and a revival of the ancient Egyptian mystery religion. In Paris he published two books on the magical art of memory. His work *De umbris idearum* (On the shadows of ideas) appeared in 1582, dedicated to the King.

In 1583, he travelled to England where his bombastic style antagonized the university of Oxford. His famous work *Cena de la ceneri* (Ash Wednesday Supper) is a dramatic satire on the academics of his day, and has earned him fame as a Copernican philosopher. His view of the universe was magical rather than mathematical, and he supported a sun-centred universe largely because it fitted the ancient Egyptian religion of sun worship.

His work *Spaccio della bestia triofante* was dedicated to Sir Phillip Sidney. Bruno had a powerful poetic imagination, and was revered in the esoteric Sidney circle. He claimed that he had received divine revelations in his works, and became the boldest advocate of magic in the sixteenth century.

From England, he went to Germany, then, fatefully, to his native Italy. He was arrested in Venice in 1592 and long imprisonment and interrogation by the Inquisition followed. In 1600 he was burnt to death for his beliefs, one of the last of the martyrs to the dreaded Inquisition.

Although Bruno was not known as an alchemist, his Renaissance Hermetic philosophy, much influenced by **Agrippa**, was the key to all forms of practical magic in this vibrant period.

*See* F.A. Yates, *Giordano Bruno and the Hermetic Tradition*.

# Cabala
## Also 'Kabbalah' or 'Qabbalah'

From the Hebrew *cabal* (or *qabbal* = received tradition), the Cabala evolved through medieval and Renaissance times into a complex magical, mystical philosophy whose influence was incalculable. The Cabala became virtually a world view, with a governing influence on Renaissance Natural **Magic**. It first emerges as a system of biblical exegesis in Spain in the eighth century AD and spread rapidly throughout Europe. There are two main texts: the *Zohar* (Book of Splendour) and the *Sefer Yetzirah* (Book of Creation). The latter probably dates from after the third century AD, being the subject of an Arabic commentary of the tenth century by which time it was familiar. The *Zohar* was composed in Spain by Moses ben Shem-Tob (1250–1305). As with the **Hermetic texts**, these works were credited to ancient sages.

Gershom Scholem explains the system as a highly developed form of mysticism, but in magical folklore tradition it lost much of its dignity, being equated with popular magic or necromancy, using diagrams and geometrical figures. The *Book of Creation* expounds a mystical world view, the basic doctrine concerning the 10 *Sefiroth* = emanations of God. They are the names or properties of God, the number 10 being perfection in Pythagorean **numerology** (10 = 1+2+3+4). Whereas in Plato's *Timaeus* the universe is created by a demiurge, a craftsman, Cabalists believed that the Creator En Soph entrusted this sacred task to the 10 emanations, the male and female Sefiroth. The 'World of Formation' is recognizable as similar to the hierarchies of angels in Christian cosmology: the Cabalists posit 10 groups of angels, ruling planets and **elements**.

The Cabala uses three main techniques, originally applied to the Scriptures: *Notarikon* involves the abbreviation of Hebrew words; *Temurah* uses anagrams; *Gematria* is applied to the intricate numerology, so popular with Renaissance Hermetic philosophers. These techniques are cited in the Prefatory Letter to **John Dee**'s classic evocation of Cabalist **alchemy**, the *Monas Hieroglyphica* (Antwerp, 1564).

The Christian Cabala of the Renaissance exerted a vast philosophical influence. The oriental linguist and father of comparative philology Guillaume Postel was immersed in the Cabala as a system of understanding the universe as mystical **harmony**, pervaded with the spiritual emanations of the Sefiroth. He translated cabalist works, including the *Zohar*, and proposed a prophetic vision of eirenicism, or universal peace and reconciliation of faiths. Such ideas are the key to understanding John Dee and many other prophetic alchemists. The medieval Cabala animates the vision of **Ramon Lull**, and Renaissance Platonists like Pico della Mirandola and Johannes Reuchlin converted the Cabala to Christian purposes, arguing that it was a direct path to an understanding of Christ.

The Cabala introduced the idea of *Shekinah*, which really means the presence of God in the world, but which came to mean the feminine aspect or emanation of God. The doctrine of **Adam** Cadmon, the spiritual or primordial man, is also vital to the Cabala as it is to the gnostic mysticism of alchemists like **Zosimos of Panoplis** (third century AD).

**Paracelsus** and his followers, especially Leonhardt Thurneysser, were completely immersed in the Cabala; Paracelsus may have imbibed the tradition from Abbot **Trithemius** of Sponheim, who evolved the system of **angel magic** so popular with John Dee and others.

The doctrine of the cabalist **Tree** is familiar, with its diagram of centres of power or energy, often compared to the Indian yoga system of *chakras*. There is an important antithesis between the Tree of Life and the Tree of Knowledge, both potent symbols in alchemy. Man is a **microcosm** and the tree is a diagram of his inner spiritual world, as of the universe. The centres of the cabalist Tree link the microcosm with the planets, and could easily be converted for alchemical use.

The Cabala blended all too easily into the fantastic amalgam of Hermetic and Neoplatonist occult theorizing which went out of control during the Renaissance. It remained powerful during the **Rosicrucian** period: one of the most famous later works was that of Christian Knorr von Rosenroth (1636–89) who was an adept of cabalist alchemy and keenly interested in oriental languages. His *Kabbala Denudata* or 'Kabbala Unveiled' (1677) contained translations of the *Zohar* which Postel had worked on.

During the Renaissance, followers of the Neoplatonist magi liked to trace the genealogy of the cabalist and Hermetic traditions to Old Testament, Mosaic antiquity. **Thomas Vaughan**, twin brother of the

The Cave of the Illuminati, showing steps or stages of the opus, leading through a dark cavernous tunnel to the mystic light.

The inscriptions around the cave include the Tetragrammaton, indicating the cabalist religious aspirations of the author.

From Heinrich Khunrath, Amphitheatrum sapientiae aeternae (Hanover, 1619).

By kind permission of The Warburg Institute, London.

metaphysical poet Henry Vaughan, gives this eloquent idea of the Cabala. He claims that the Jewish Sanhedrin, formed to preserve the Mosaic law, was responsible for the Cabala 'for they imparted that knowledge by word of mouth to their Successors, and hence it came to pass that the science itself was styled Cabala, that is, a Reception'.

Vaughan condemns those who have 'produced a certain upstart, bastard Cabala, which consists altogether in Alphabeticall knacks, ends always in the Letter where it begins, and the Vanities of it are grown voluminous . . . As for the more ancient and Physical Traditions of the Cabala, I embrace them for so many sacred Truths.'

Like the Renaissance Christian cabalists, Vaughan esteems the Cabala as the profoundest mystical philosophy, of Mosaic origin and significance. A devout metaphysical Christian, he also esteems true **magic** as divine philosophy:

> The Cabalists agree with all the world of Magicians, that Man in spirituall Mysteries is both Agent and Patient. This is plain: for Jacob's Ladder is the greatest Mysterie in the Cabala. Here we find two extremes: Jacob is one, at the Foot of the Ladder, and God is the other, who stands above it, *immittens* (saith the Jew) *Formas, et Influxus in Jacob, sive Subjectum Hominem*, shedding some secret Influx of Spirit upon Jacob, who in this place typifies man in general. The Rounds, or Steps in the Ladder signifie the middle Natures, by which Jacob is united to God, Inferiors united to Superiors.

> *Magia Adamica* (Magic of Adam), Rudrum edition, p.180

Here we have the universal theme of religious mysticism, the concept of the ascent of the spiritual man towards union with the divine: thus the Cabala is easily harmonized with gnostic philosophy, which animated **Hellenistic alchemy**. Vaughan also alludes to another vital aspect of the Cabala – and of the alchemical world view in general – **angel magic**, which was used by a number of alchemical philosophers to contact celestial intelligences. Vaughan notes that the angels in Jacob's dream ascend first, before they descend, suggesting that they do not belong to the 'Superior Hierarchy' of angels. He suggests that Jacob's angels are of some 'secret essence'.

The role of the Cabala in the magical culture of the Renaissance is best studied through the illuminating works of Frances A. Yates. *See also* J.L. Blau, *The Christian Interpretation of the Cabala in the Renaissance*; Shumaker, *The Occult Sciences in the Renaissance*.

# Caduceus

Mercury, or **Hermes**, the Messenger of the Gods, possesses a magical staff, the winged caduceus, and **Nicolas Flamel**'s *Book of Hieroglyphs* contains this as an alchemical symbol. Around this staff are entwined the two serpents, symbolizing the **conjunctio**, the mystical marriage of the opposing principles **mercury-sulphur**. There is the legend that Mercury found two serpents fighting and, striking them, allowed them to coil around his **magic** wand, thus investing him with the divine power of the chthonic serpent. Thus the symbol represents dynamic equilibrium of opposites. The idea of mercury and sulphur poisoning one another is also vital to the death-resurrection symbolism of **alchemy** (*see* **Dragon; Mortification; Redemption**).

# Charnock, Thomas
## Elizabethan alchemical poet; *c.* 1524–81

This fascinating personality was an 'unlettered Scholar' alchemist, a contemporary if not a friend of Dr **John Dee**, who corresponded with William Blomfild. These adepts kept alive the medieval tradition of English alchemical poetry inherited from **Thomas Norton** and **George Ripley**.

Charnock's life has been documented by Sherwood Taylor, who published his fascinating hymn to the alchemical **dragon** in *Ambix*. Like **Chaucer**'s Canones Yeoman, Charnock worked as laboratory assistant, probably to one James Sauler, who handed on the secret of the Philosophers' **Stone** on his death in 1554, but in the following year, on New Year's Day, a fire destroyed his laboratory along with the secret.

He then had instruction from the erstwhile prior of Bath Abbey; **Ashmole** tells of the discovery in the ruined Abbey of 'a Glasse found in a Wall full of Red Tincture', a liquid dye strong enough to redden the dung heap upon which it was cast (but which encouraged the growth of corn). In 1557 'a gentleman that ought me great malice,/caused me to be pressed to goe to serve at Callys', that is, he was forced to serve in Queen Mary's army in defence of Calais. In his fury, he took a hatchet to his whole laboratory.

He married Agnes Norden of Bristol in 1562, and moving near Bridgewater, Somerset, established a new laboratory, much to the distress of his neighbours. He composed an alchemical book dedicated to Lord Burleigh, who was a cautious (if not generous) believer in alchemy, and a friend to **Edward Kelley**. He died in April 1581, leaving a daughter.

Charnock's versified autobiography gives us the social history of the sixteenth-century alchemist, who has learnt nothing from the mistakes of the fourteenth-century Canone and his Yeoman. He actually meets two yeomen while serving in Calais, who have **sulphur** and **mercury** to **tincture metals** along with seven **salts**, oils and corrosives.

See Frank Sherwood Taylor, *The Alchemists, Founders of Modern Chemistry*; E.J. Holmyard, *Alchemy*.

# Chaucer, Geoffrey
## Poet, diplomat, and just possibly alchemist; 1340–1400

Chaucer's portrait of the alchemical Canones Yeoman in his *Canterbury Tales* is one of the classic satires of the misguided adept: Ben Jonson's marvellous play *The Alchemist* shows that the art continued to live without learning. Chaucer was a man of immense learning, a cosmopolitan diplomat. In addition to his famous works, he translated Boethius' *Consolation of Philosophy* into English and produced a version of an Arabic work on the astrolabe for his nephew Lewis.

His Canones Yeomans Tale portrays a most unspiritual (non-Jungian!) type of **alchemy** (*see* **Jungian Theory of Alchemy**). The tale is told by a yeoman laboratory assistant who serves an alchemical Canon of the Church. Chaucer himself may have experienced the folly of 'vulgar' alchemy, for the Canon of the Royal Chapel at Windsor, with which he was associated, was an alchemist. (**Thomas Norton** tells us that many churchmen, rich and poor, were alchemists, Canon **George Ripley** of Bridlington Priory in Yorkshire being one.)

The Canones Yeoman is a martyr to the art, having spent seven years in this 'slyding science'. 'And wher my colour was both fresh and reed,/Now is it wan and of a leden hewe' – he is worn out, drowning in debt, his clothes threadbare. His materials are arsenic, sal ammoniac. brimstone (**sulphur**), verdigris, and **herbs** like agrimony, valerian and lunary. His **apparatus** consists of 'sondry vessels maad of erthe and glas', urinals, descensories, crucibles, cucurbits, etc . . .

The Yeoman's theory of alchemy seems to come from **Avicenna** (or from works attributed to him), for he has a concept of four **spirits**: quicksilver (**mercury**), orpiment (arsenic sulphide, used as yellow dye), sal ammoniac and brimstone. This bears some resemblance to the Paracelsian doctrine of three principles (***Tria Principia***): **salt**, sulphur and mercury.

A fascinating alchemical **manuscript**, with an attribution to

Chaucer himself, probably false, was acquired by **John Dee**. The text, in Middle English, gives an account of several experiments, described in vivid, mythic language.

*See* 'The Chaucer Ascription in Trinity College, Dublin Manuscript D.2.8', by Gareth W. Dunleavy, *Ambix*, February 1965, pp.2-21.

# Chinese Alchemy

**Alchemy** is found throughout India, Tibet and South-east Asia. The Chinese Taoist tradition is probably the most ancient, long predating **Hellenistic alchemy**. It has been argued that the Chinese word *Chin-je*, denoting 'gold juice' or 'elixir', may be the root of the Arabic *kimiya*. Whereas western alchemy, derived from Islamic texts, was concerned with **transmutation** of **metals**, Chinese and **Indian alchemy** are concerned mainly with **elixirs** of life and vitality. Legend carries the alchemical elixir back to the Yellow Emperor, Huang Ti (2,704-595 BC), who received instruction from three immortal maidens in **magic** as well as in the erotic arts.

## Early History

The earliest reference to the fabrication of **gold** by alchemical means comes in an imperial edict of 144 BC, which forbids such practices. In 60 BC we find that an alchemist called Liu Hsiang was given an imperial commission to create gold by transmutation. Thus both transmutation and elixirs were known at least as early as the second century BC. The first significant complete work on alchemy is by **Wei Po Yang**, its title: *Ts'an T'ung Ch'i* (Treatise on the Three Principles) (*c.*142 AD). This is a strongly magical Taoist work which is based upon the hexagrams of the *I Ching*, the Chinese oracular 'Book of Changes'. Like western works, it is strongly obscurantist in style.

Most famous was the remarkable alchemist Ko Hung, known as the father of Chinese alchemy, who was an approximate contemporary of the Greek **Zosimos of Panoplis** (*c.*300 AD). He refers to a bulk of literature on elixirs of life, derived from **cinnabar** and **mercury**, explaining that few elixirs were prepared without the inclusion of cinnabar.

Liu An, who lived from 77 to 6 BC, composed a book called *Lieh Hsien Ch'uan* (Book of Immortals), a collection of stories of Taoist sages who have attained immortality through alchemical and magical means. Taoist sages who attained to immortality were called *Hsien* and were supposed to aid the alchemist in his quest – rather as angels were thought to provide guidance to western adepts.

It is certain that Chinese and Indian alchemists exchanged ideas, and alchemy flourished in Tibet, probably mainly under the influence of Indian Tantra. Professor Needham has shown that there was Chinese influence upon the **apparatus** used in **Islamic alchemy.**

## The Chinese Concept of *Chhi* and the Birth of Metals and Minerals

Taoist alchemists used the theory of *chhi* to explain everything in **nature.** This is similar to the Greek concept of *pneuma* or the Sanskrit idea of *prana* energy: these words are used for the breath, and for the spirit or more generally to denote energy.

The Chinese used the theory of *chhi* to explain the origins of metals and minerals: stone is the kernel of *chhi*, and this mysterious energy may congeal to form cinnabar or green vitriol. Gold and jade constitute the 'seminal essence' of the *chhi*, whilst arsenic compounds and **acids** are its poisonous aspects. The *chhi* may also undergo transformations as liquid to yield mercury and alums. Professor Needham suggests that this theory may derive from Babylonian sources. It means that Chinese alchemists, like their Islamic or western counterparts, believe that metals and minerals all share an essential **unity** in substance and origin. Thus it was easy to believe in transformation and transmutation of metals and precious stones.

Islamic and western alchemy were dominated meanwhile by the **mercury-sulphur theory of the generation of metals**: if nature could foster gold in the womb of the earth by natural incubation, why should not the alchemist imitate nature in producing gold from base metals?

## The Divergence of *Wai Tan* Laboratory Alchemy from *Nei Tan* Spiritual Alchemy

In western alchemy, there is constant confusion as to the true goal of the *opus alchymicum*. There is the experimental, chemical tradition, with its practical goal of the transmutation of base metals into gold and the Jungian interpretation, emphasizing the *spiritual* goals of Christian alchemists, who equated the **Stone** of the Philosophers with the redeeming power of Christ (*see* **Jungian Theory of Alchemy**; **Redemption**). This division is also reflected in Chinese alchemy, in which two divergent traditions emerged. First, there was the advanced experimental, laboratory tradition called *Wai Tan*, which specialized in producing **medicines** and elixirs. Then, from this, arose the *Nei Tan* tradition which involves yogic spiritual and meditational practices, like Indian Tantric alchemy, for aiding vitality and longevity. This tradition uses the symbolism of chemical experiments.

The text published in translation by Richard Willhelm, with commentary by C.G. Jung, called the *Secret of the Golden Flower,* belongs to the *Nei Tan* yogic tradition.

*Nei Tan* aims to nurture three primary vitalities: *ching* (translated as 'seminal essence'), *chhi* (like the Greek *pneuma,* Sanskrit *prana,* meaning 'spiritual energy'), and *shen* (breath control, involved with thinking).

In the West, spiritual alchemy was a secret tradition, but Chinese alchemists were more explicit about their quest for lasting vitality, for 'regenerating and restoring primal vitalities' (*hsiu chen*), a formula which appears in many titles. The *Nei Tan* yogic system of alchemy depends upon a theory of the circulation of energy and vitality; there is an elaborate esoteric symbolism used to describe the circulation of spiritual energy through the vital organs, the heart, brain and kidneys. The Taoist adept seeks to actually reverse the natural process of ageing and bodily degeneration. The heart represents the heavens, the kidneys, the earth principles in the body. The Taoist theory of yin and yang, the polarity of active and passive principles in the universe, is used to explain energy and vitality flow through the body.

There are many fascinating parallels between eastern and western alchemy. In general, it is apparent that Chinese alchemists had a far clearer concept of the goal of their experimental and meditational work. Nothing like the tradition of Chinese yogic alchemy ever evolved in the West, for European alchemists remained totally confused by the texts which they inherited from Islamic and Hellenistic sources.

# Cinnabar

From earliest times this brilliant red sulphide of **mercury** was fascinating to miners and smelters of metal: it was mythologized as 'dragon's blood', undoubtedly with strong magical significance. Much alchemical symbolism, both East and West, centres on the process of heating the ore cinnabar, releasing volatile fumes of mercury to condense. Heated in a glass container, mercury condenses as a **magic** silver mirror. The birth of the silvery lunar mercury from the vermilion red cinnabar may be one source for the classic alchemical symbolism of sun and moon (*see* **Sol and Luna**), red and white **elixirs**.

Chinese Taoist alchemists founded their quest for the elixir upon the ninefold transformation of cinnabar and mercury: they aimed at complete purity. Joseph Needham tells us:

> *Tan*, which means red, was a great witch word in Chinese alchemy and mineralogy, having had the significance of cinnabar . . . as far back as can be traced. Later, due to its use by the Taoists as a drug of immortality, it came to mean any **medicine**, pill or prescription.
>
> *Shorter Science and Civilization in China*, Vol. 2

Both branches of **Chinese alchemy** contain the *Tan* root: *Nei Tan* being the esoteric search for the inner elixir, and *Wai Tan*, the laboratory craft. Ko Hung, father of Chinese alchemy, informs us that of the substantial literature he has devoured (of the third century AD), there is scarcely a recipe which does not contain mercury or cinnabar.

Cinnabar and mercury were also vital in Greco-Egyptian, **Islamic alchemy**. It is thought that the *kerotakis* (*see* **Apparatus**) was mainly used for creating this sulphide of mercury in Greek and Judaic alchemy, and that the original **colour** sequence of **stages** of the opus may come from this reaction. It was natural to think of the volatile mercury fumes as the **spirit** escaping from its ore, the *prima materia*, which was left as a deposit (*see* **Prime Matter**).

The ancient writers Pliny, Vitruvius and Theophrastus are familiar with the mining of cinnabar in Spain. The Latin word *minium* sometimes is used for cinnabar, although its real meaning is red lead: there was confusion over identification.

# Colours

The use of colour symbolism in **alchemy** is diverse and complex, and before the advent of modern chemistry, colour often provided the only way of describing a chemical reaction or a substance.

All of the **stages** or **processes** of alchemy are distinguished by colours. Greco-Egyptian alchemy used a four-colour sequence:

1)  The initial blackness of the chaos, or *prima materia* (*see* **Prime Matter**), called in Greek *melanosis* and in Latin **nigredo**.
2)  Whiteness as a result of the washing, cleansing, purification of the calcined, blackened first matter. In Greek *leukosis* = Latin *albedo*.
3)  The yellowing stage, in Greek *xanthosis*, not usually included in Latin alchemy.
4)  *Iosis*, the final stage, which is quite mysterious as the culmination of the opus. The word means 'purple', which was the imperial colour, as red is the colour of kingship.

Latin alchemists nearly always commence with the *nigredo*, the dark, black stage of melancholy, death and **mortification**. The roasting of ores in the **furnace** may have given rise to this idea of a black *prima materia*, a chaos from which separation and **Creation** take place. After the black stage, there must be a purifying, washing and whitening (*albedo*). A dramatic indicator of success in the opus is the appearance of the 'Peacock's Tail', (*cauda pavonis*) (*see* **Peacock**), the multi-coloured flowering and blossoming of the opus.

Early alchemists were fascinated by the problems of dyeing **metals** using **tinctures**, a word which came to be equivalent to the famous **elixir** or **medicine** of metals, meant to cure imperfections in metals, and western texts nearly all distinguish two elixirs: the white silver-transmuting elixir, and the red gold-transmuting elixir. The opposition of red and white presides over the philosophers' work: red is the kingly colour, associated with **gold** and **mercury**, whilst white is feminine, lunar, the queen of the opus (*see* **Sol and Luna**, as opposing principles).

To give a comprehensive survey of the use of colour symbolism would require volumes, but here are some examples of alchemical colour sequences.

A **Hermetic text** presents a black vulture crying loudly from a mountain top: 'I am the white of the black, and the red of the white and the citrine of the red and indeed I speak truthfully. And know that the head of the art is a crow, which flies without wings in the blackness of the night and the clear of day'.

A text attributed to **Paracelsus** starts with the blackness caused by heating, then when dryness and humidity begin to interact 'there will likewise arise in the Glass, various flowers of diverse colours, such as appeare like the taile of a Peacocke, and such as man never saw before'. The blackness shows 'that the Woman is pregnant'; the Peacock's Tail indicates the interaction of 'the Philosophical and Vulgar Mercuries'. Then appears 'the Matter of the Moon' which is 'white and candid as Snow', and this can tincture metals to 'Luna' (silver). This is the first mastery, production of the white elixir. Persevering with the fire, white gives way to yellow: 'Yellow and Saffron-like groweth the Colour, until it come to perfect redness.' Having reached 'the highest degree of the Red Colour; then is the substance of Gold prepared, and there is born an oriental King, sitting in his Throne, and ruling over all the Princes of the World' (taken from *Paracelsus on the Secrets of Alchymy*, trans. R. Turner).

This is typical of the **myth** imagery of the flood of popular alchemical texts.

*See* **Beasts and Birds**; **Elixir**; **Mercury**; **Sulphur** for further examples.

# Conjunctio

A key concept of **alchemy**, this idea almost symbolizes the entire inner meaning of the art. The theme of the mystic marriage, the *conjunctio*, the marriage of opposites, reaches back to the roots of prehistoric speculation about the world: in Taoism everything takes place through the interaction of yin and yang, creative and receptive principles of heaven and earth. Alchemists inherited this animistic philosophy.

Illustrations of the alchemical *conjunctio* are frank portrayals of sexual intercourse, often in water, by a crowned couple. The well-known woodcuts of the 1550 edition of the *Rosarium philosophorum* (Rose Garden of the Philosophers), for example, show variations on the theme of marital **harmony**.

We are dealing with a mystic secret, no mere chemical combination, or sexual mating of **elements**. The archetypal copulation was that of **sulphur** 'fixing' **mercury**, but the mercury and sulphur involved were the reigning principles in **nature**, not our chemical elements. The classic couple are **Sol and Luna**, sun and moon, shown often as **King and Queen** in splendid robes, or else frankly naked. Sol, the sun, is the fiery, masculine, active, fixed principle of kingship, symbol of sulphur and **gold**, whilst Luna is the volatile, feminine, liquid principle of the moon, representing silver and mercury (= quicksilver).

The variety of **myths** of this marriage is baffling, many concerned with incestuous relations of brother and sister, which sound to be of Egyptian origin. **Ripley** uses a primitive mother-son incest myth. Alchemists were more interested in variations on a single theme than they were on chemical discoveries.

The simple idea of sulphur fixing or coagulating mercury permeates most texts; but the vague concept of harmonizing and unifying, integrating opposites clearly has an esoteric mystical significance, as well as being a metaphor for chemical combination.

There is strongly literal copulation in many popular texts:

Cap III: When you have placed the Man and the Wife in the Matrimonial Bed: if you would that he may operate upon her, so that she may bring forth, it is necessary . . . that the Man have his operation upon the Woman, so that the seed of the Woman may be coagulated into the Mass, by the seed of the Man; otherwise it produceth no Fruit.

*Paracelsus on the Secrets of Alchymy*, tr. R. Turner

Mircea Eliade stresses the primitive roots of the concept of Mother Earth as the womb for gestation of the embryo **metals** and ores: their emergence is a process of birth. Mercury and sulphur are quite literally the parents of metals, their union producing the progeny of more or less pure metals. The most harmonious combination is required to produce gold.

**Edward Kelley** shows the vivid realism of this ancient imagery:

> Mercury and Sulphur, Sun and Moon, agent and patient, matter and form are the opposites. When the virgin or feminine, earth is thoroughly purified and purged from all superfluity, you must give it a husband meet for it; for when the male and female are joined together by means of the sperm, a generation must take place in the *menstruum*. The substance of Mercury is known to the Sages as the Earth and matter in which the Sulphur of nature is sown, that it may thereby putrefy, the earth being its womb.
>
> 'The Theatre of Terrestrial Astronomy' in *Alchemy*, ed. R. Grossingen

Thus the *conjunctio* is the union of male and female seed, and the combination of sulphur and mercury is regarded as sexual mating. But this crude copulation is then followed by a further *conjunctio* of body, **spirit** and soul, this Trinity being a common theme in medieval alchemy.

# Creation

The **myth** of Creation is one of the keys to **alchemy** as it is to medieval natural philosophy, for alchemists are philosophers with mystical insight into **nature**. Their justification for any form of investigation of the secrets of nature was the doctrine that man and the cosmos are God's creation. It is seen that **Adam**, in Christian, cabalist and gnostic tradition, is the image of the spiritual inner man, who as a result of the Fall, of ignorance and sin, is imprisoned within a mortal body. The adept is therefore concerned with the operations which liberate the **spirit** or the **quintessence** from gross matter, materiality.

Genesis provides the story of the seven days of Creation, and **numerology** often saw these seven days as corresponding to seven **stages** of alchemy: the image of the Spirit of God moving over the face of the waters provides an ideal image for the mystic waters of alchemy and the mercurial spirit. Alchemists generally believe a chaos, a *massa confusa*, to be their starting point, and the *prima materia* (see

God as Judge and Creator.
  Alchemy as a tradition was concerned with the nature of the world, its Creation and its
divine purpose. There is much evidence of prophetic and apocalyptic ideas amongst
alchemists, who sought the redemption of their own nature, but also of the natural world.
  By kind permission of The Bodleian Library, Oxford.
RR. W. 29 (9) p.210.

**Prime Matter**) is very often a dark mercurial water. The application of heat then starts the movement of spirit on the face of the deep (vapour). Also the stage of *separatio* is vital, commencing with the separating out of earth and water: experiment showed that solid could precipitate from liquid, thus validating Genesis!

*The Emerald Tablet*, Bible of medieval alchemy, presents a mystical view of Creation as the emergence of plurality from primal **unity**, and this actually suggests that Creation results from meditation on the divine unity. Most alchemists were inclined to **Neoplatonism**, believing in the mystical unity from which the cosmos is created.

**Paracelsus**, in his *Philosophy to the Athenians*, generates the **elements** from the *prima materia*, which he calls the *Mysterium Magnum* (Great Mystery). Creation for him is just like the first alchemical stage, moving to *separatio* from the *nigredo* or blackness of chaos (*see* **Processes**; **Stages**). God creates the world through the light shining in the darkness of chaos, and this brings the distinction and separating of all things. Thus Paracelsians evolve the concept of *lumen naturae*, the light of nature, which in Paracelsus' alchemical **medicine** is the only true guide. The light of nature supplements the light of grace or revelation, *lumen gratiae*. Creation reveals the hand of the Creator, as the Scriptures contain the word of God, and Paracelsians continually use the idea of 'The Book of Nature' as their true authority. a concept basic to **Francis Bacon** and other seventeenth-century experimental scientists.

One achievement of alchemy was to provide an alternative vision of Creation, drawing upon cabalist and **Hermetic texts** which tend to favour a concept of emanation from the divine, with the creative influence mediated through hierarchies of angels (*see* **Cabala**; **Hermetic Texts**).

**Thomas Vaughan**, steeped in Paracelsian ideas, shows how central Creation is to alchemy:

> Those students then who would be better instructed must first know there is an universal agent, Who when he was disposed to create had no other pattern or exemplar whereby to frame and mould His Creatures but Himself . . . In the second place they ought to know there is an universal patient, and this passive Nature was created by the Universal Agent. This general patient is the immediate passive character of God Himself in his Unity and trinity. In plain terms it is that substance which we commonly call the First Matter.

> Quoted in Israel Regardie, *The Philosophers' Stone*, p.165

# Croll, Oswald
## German Paracelsian physician and chemist; c. 1580–1609

Oswald Croll was born into a Lutheran family, and he studied at Marburg University from 1576. He graduated MD in 1582, afterwards studying at several universities: Heidelberg, Strasburg and Geneva. He served as tutor to the d'Esnes family in Lyons (1583–90); in Tübingen he was tutor to the household of Count Maximilian of Pappenheim.

He practised **medicine** in Prague from 1597 to 1599 and returned there from 1602 until his death in 1609. From 1598 he served Prince Christian I of Anhalt-Bernburg, Upper Palatine, as personal physician: his seminal work the *Basilica chemica* (1609) is dedicated to the Prince. He seems to have made an enemy, however, of Emperor Rudolf II, usually a spectacular patron of Hermetic arts.

Croll was extremely influential as a founder of Paracelsian-inspired alchemical medicine, but unlike many Paracelsian doctors he was also an important innovatory chemist. He was a contemporary of **Heinrich Khunrath** and **Andreas Libavius**, fellow torch-bearers of the new chemical medicine, and uses **John Dee's** *monas* symbol, which was an emblem of the **Rosicrucians**.

Professor Pagel regards Croll as 'a more mystical and religious Paracelsist' than **Severinus**, the Danish royal physician. Croll reinterpreted the Paracelsian philosophy, believing that each being has its own star, its *astrum*, if not its inner heaven (*see* **Astra**; **Astrology**). He accepts astral mysticism, but rejects rigid astrology: 'through dew, rain and seasonal changes, the upper stars and the zodiac awaken and promote life and growth, but do not influence them'. (*see* Pagel, *Van Helmont*, p.49)

Croll's long 'Admonitory Preface' to the *Basilica chemica* shows how powerful Paracelsian mystical ideas were, even in the work of an experimental chemist much in advance of **Paracelsus** himself. Some quotations from the English translation will illuminate alchemical philosophy of this vital period:

> Man is a hidden world, because visible things in him are invisible, and when they are made visible then they are diseases, not health, as truly as he is the little world and not the great one.
>
> It is not the locall Anatomy of a man and dead corpses, but the Essentiated and Elemental Anatomy of the World and man that discovereth the disease and cure.
>
> It was the Fall which brought disease and corruption into the world: the sin of Adam and Eve affects the whole of nature, and God has sowed the

'tinctures' of disease in nature as a curse to man. But man's inner microcosmic nature is pure, invisible, being tainted only by its carnal involvement.

**Publications:**

*Basilica chemica continens philosophicam propria laborumexperientia confirmatam descriptionem et usum remediorum chymicorum . . . e lumine gratiae et naturae* (Frankfurt, 1609).

The title page of this important work is obviously cabalist, suggesting as it does the threefold relation of cabalist theology, astronomical magic and medical alchemy. It shows the antithesis of the light of nature and the light of grace or revelation, derived from Paracelsus. There was an influential English edition of 1657: *Philosophy Reformed and Improved in Four Profound Tractates: The first discovering the Great and Deep Mysteries of Nature by that Learned Chymist and Physitian, O. Croll, the other three discovering the wonderful Mysteries of the Creation, by Paracelsus, being his Philosophy to the Athenians,* trans: H. Pinnell, London. It includes a complete English version of Croll's 'Admonitory Preface', explaining his Paracelsian views. (Pinnell was chaplain to the New Model Army until *c.*1648.)

*See* P.O. Hannaway, *The Chemists and the Word*; Walter Pagel, *Joan Battista van Helmont.*

# Culpeper, Nicholas
### English astrologer, physician and herbalist; 1616–54

Culpeper is best known as a herbalist, but he made a much broader contribution to pharmacy. He was apprenticed to an apothecary in St Helen's parish, Bishopsgate and in 1640 set up shop in Red Lion Street, Spitalfields. He belongs to the seventeenth-century renaissance of **astrology** and Dr Webster, in his *Great Instauration*, points out that Culpeper was an important popularizer of Paracelsian **medicine.**

One of his most important works was a valuable translation of the *Pharmacopoeia* of London, published as *A Physical Directory* (London, 1649). This had been produced on the centenary of its founding by the Royal College of Physicians, enemies of **alchemy** who nevertheless included many chemical remedies in their *Pharmacopoeia.* Culpeper drew Parliamentarian praise but Royalist anger by popularizing medicine, and his edition attacks the monopoly of the Royal College which had persecuted men like Simon

Forman, **Francis Anthony** and **Arthur Dee**. His *Pharmacopoeia* was much more than a translation; it was much augmented.

Of his other publications, his *English Physician* was a **herbal** on astrological lines, later to become *Culpeper's Herbal*, and he published a *Treatise of Aurum Potabile* (1657) and with colleagues translated Daniel Sennert's Paracelsian work as *Thirteen Books of Natural Philosophy* (London, 1659).

# D

## Dasteyn, John
Also 'Dastyn' or 'Dastin'; *floruit* 1320s

Described by E.J. Holmyard as 'the foremost alchemist of his time', Dasteyn has left us a number of testaments to his alchemical faith. He belongs to the alchemical craze of the early fourteenth century when papal decrees were needed to restrain fraud and self-deception. He wrote interesting alchemical letters to Pope John XXII, who officially condemned **alchemy**, and to Cardinal Orsini. His letter to the Pope uses the well-worn Arabic concepts of **mercury-sulphur theory of the generation of metals**: an exceptionally pure red **sulphur**, fiery in quality will produce **gold** if married with **mercury** (*see* **Conjunctio**). Gold contains the vital qualities of all **metals**, and it forms the ferment of **elixirs**. Most alchemists of this time think in terms of an elixir, or **medicine** of metals which needs a ferment or seed, just as dough, or cheese or musk for perfume need a leaven or ferment. Dasteyn puts forward the clichés of the Arabic tradition, describing the two elixirs, white and red, silver and gold, of which the red not only heals or perfects metals, but is an elixir of health and life.

*See* E.J. Holmyard, *Alchemy*.

## Dee, Arthur

Dr Arthur Dee was the eldest son of **John Dee**, and amongst his earliest memories was that of playing at quoits with transmuted silver plates in the courtyard of Trebon castle in Hungary, where his father was supported by Count Rosenberg. He belongs to the class of Paracelsian physicians (*see* **Paracelsus**), who were gaining ground in Elizabethan England. This 'new medicine' of the Paracelsians relied much on **alchemy** to prepare **medicines**.

Dee's house was at 'the signe of the Elephant and Castle by Fleet Condyt, an Apothecaryes house', and he appears in the annals of the Royal College of Physicians, for in 1606 he was in trouble for displaying a notice over his door advertising various medicaments for sale – the Royal College persecuted practitioners who lacked formal university qualifications in **medicine**, and associated Dee with **Francis Anthony**, John Napier and Simon Forman, practitioners who were basically astrological psychotherapists without paper qualifications. John Dee had been a Paracelsian alchemist, and it is not surprising to find his son at odds with the medical establishment.

In 1612 we find two doctors were appointed by the College to examine Dee and Anthony together, and in 1614 Dee was summoned and accused of refusing to answer previous summonses. His testimonial from the University of Basle, dated 4 May 1609, proved he was indeed qualified, but the College summoned him again in 1615, by which time he was able to boast that he was the Queen's personal physician. He was later elected as physician to the Hospital of Charterhouse.

Arthur Dee was a remarkable man, and a testimonial to him survives from James I, dated 11 June 1621, informing the Russian Tsar of his loyal service as royal physician. John Dee had previously been offered an appointment in Russia, and Arthur Dee accepted an offer to stay in Moscow where he remained for 14 years in the Tsar's employment. However, his wife suffered a fatal illness in the ferocious Muscovite winters and she died in 1634, precipitating his return to England. By 1635 he was already Physician Extraordinary to King Charles I, from which position he retired to Norwich where he was a friend of Sir Thomas Browne. He died in October 1651.

J.H. Appleby describes a **manuscript** in the British Museum Library entitled *Arca arcanorum* (Citadel of Secrets), which is a revised version of Dee's *Fasciculus chemicus* of 1652, carefully edited, translated from the Latin and published by **Elias Ashmole** (Sloane Manuscript, 1876). It includes a Preface addressed to the **Rosicrucians** – and it is noteworthy that an edition of **Roger Bacon**'s writings on **magic** was published in 1616 in Hamburg, including notes by John Dee, with a strong Rosicrucian Preface. Arthur Dee thus appears as part of the English support for the Rosicrucians, standing with men like **Thomas Vaughan** and **Robert Fludd**. Appleby describes a drawing in Dee's manuscript: opposite the Frontispiece is a drawing of **Adam and Eve** 'with an angel brandishing a pickaxe ready to strike Eve, and a man with a club poised to hammer Adam'. The motto above the drawing indicates that Adam and Eve are to be interpreted as symbolizing the **Prime Matter**.

*See* J.H. Appleby, 'Arthur Dee and Johannes Banfi Hunyades', *Ambix*, July 1977.

# Dee, John
## Tudor mathematician, cosmographer and cabalist alchemist; 1527–1608

Dr John Dee was the outstanding scientific personality of the Tudor age, with a European-wide reputation for expertise as a mathematician and cosmographer, but his deep fascination for **astrology**, **alchemy** and **angel magic** caused accusations of witchcraft and sorcery in a superstitious age. He amassed a vast library of some 3,000 books on all subjects, especially scientific, philosophical and magical. A whole section was devoted to Paracelsian works and Dee was a forerunner of the Paracelsian movement (see **Paracelsus**). He was a devoted alchemist, and one wing of his house at Mortlake on Thames was used as laboratory.

Dee graduated from St John's College, Cambridge (BA 1546; MA 1547), then studied cartography and cosmography with Gerard Mercator and Gemma Frisius who had founded a map-making school at Louvain in the Netherlands. He delivered lectures on Euclid in Paris, expounding a Pythagorean philosophy, probably already cabalist (see **Cabala**). During the 1550s he taught cosmography in England, whilst expanding his studies of alchemy and astrology. The fruit of these studies was the first of his original works to be published, the *Propaideumata aphoristica* of 1558, a series of aphorisms on his theory of the universe, including alchemy. He held that the stars and planets diffused both unseen and visible rays of influence, thus providing a physical theory of astrology based on a concept of radiation which sounds surprisingly modern.

Like Simon Forman and others, Dee held an astrological practice, retrieving lost objects and so forth. In a letter of 1574 to Lord Burleigh about finding lost treasure and mines he explains a magical theory of sympathy and antipathy.

His main alchemical work was the **Monas hieroglyphica** (Hieroglyphic monad), published in Antwerp in 1564 by Willem Silvius, beautifully printed with diagrams illustrating its 24 Theorems. This work seems to have been a key influence upon the **Rosicrucian** movement.

Of his other works, his *Mathematicall Praeface to Euclid* (1570) provided an imaginative survey of the uses of mathematics in every imaginable discipline, including **medicine**, where he shows a 'Cross of Graduation' for assessing the strengths of remedies. At this time the Paracelsians were introducing alchemical methods into medicine.

During the 1550s and again in the 1570s John Dee was involved with Tudor exploration, both in the regions of the far North-east, towards

Russia, and in the search for a North-west passage to Cathay. If alchemy could not provide fabled wealth to Elizabethan England, Dee and his friends dreamt of an easy passage to the spice islands at the very least.

During the 1580s Dee became most deeply involved with séances of angel magic: his friend the alchemist **Edward Kelley** acted as 'scryer' or medium, transmitting long messages from the angelic intelligences thought to inhabit the cosmos. The first recorded *actio* or séance is dated 22 December 1581 at Mortlake, when Kelley summoned the angel Anael. On 10 March 1581, Kelley had called on Dee and held a séance with Dee's stone, to which *aliqui angeli boni* were said to be 'answerable'. The archangel Uriel had appeared with a new crystal or stone and gave instructions for the layout of the 'holy table' and the 'seal of god' (Sloane manuscript 3188, f.30).

Records of the angelic conversations were published by Meric Casaubon in his book *A True and Faithful Relation of what passed for many Yeers between Dr John Dee and some Spirits* (London, 1659), and it was these transcripts which effectively ruined Dee's reputation for posterity. However, these texts appear to me to be replete with mainly alchemical and apocalyptic imagery, and they have scarcely been studied or examined.

Séances not included in the Casaubon edition have meanwhile been published by C.H. Josten in *Elias Ashmole*. These **manuscripts,** preserved by Elias Ashmole in transcript, reveal the powerful prophetic atmosphere of the angel magic of Dee and Kelley. It is vital to realize that contact with divine beings was an integral part of alchemy from earliest, Hellenistic times. The angelic manuscripts contain very detailed instructions for contacting divine beings, for example in the manuscript entitled *48 claves angelicae* (The 48 Angelic Keys), and the *Liber scientiae terrestris auxilii et victoriae* (The Book of the Science of Terrestrial Help and Victory).

There were several dramatic crises in the course of the séances: on 10 April 1586, the angels instructed Dee and Kelley to burn their books, which they did (or so the transcript maintains). The books were then miraculously restored by the angels on 30 April 1586. These were:

*De heptarchia mystica collecteanorum, liber I.*
*A Book of 'invocations and Calls wherein the Holy Names are raised out of those Tables'.*

The other manuscripts of séances were:

1)  *48 claves angelicae* (The 48 Angelic Keys).

2)  *Liber scientiae terrestris auxilii et victoriae* (The Book of the Science of Terrestrial Help and Victory).

In 1583 the Polish Prince Albrecht Laski visited England and he soon became involved in the angelic séances. On 21 September 1583, in an atmosphere of top secrecy, Dee and his family, with Kelley and his wife, left England with Laski. On 3 February 1583, they were at Cracow in Poland where they sought out the Emperor Rudolf II, a notorious patron of magicians and alchemists. They also met King Stephen of Poland, but were soon in trouble with the papal representative. However, they were rescued by Count Rosemberg, who allowed them to stay at his castle of Trebon during 1586. There Dee and Kelley indulged their alchemical **dreams**. (*See* John Dee's *Diary*.)

In 1588-9, Dee returned to England leaving Kelley to his fate (*see* **Kelley**) – both by now were legendary as having possessed a powder of **transmutation** for turning **metals** to silver and **gold**, but their angelic séances had ended after their young woman **spirit** guide Madimi had appeared naked, advising wife-swapping.

In the British Museum there is a 'shew stone' or 'holy stone', said to have been given to Dee by an angel. It is a marvellous crystal ball, perfectly translucent, made of finest quartz. There are also extant waxen tablets with magical hieroglyphs engraved thereon, and a black obsidian mirror, apparently of Aztec origin.

*See* C.H. Josten, *Elias Ashmole*; N.H. Clulee, *John Dee's Natural Philosophy*.

# Democritus of Abdera
## Greek atomist philosopher; *c.* 460–370 BC

The father of atomism, with Leukippos, Democritus is said to have travelled to Egypt, Persia and even India, where he may have imbibed Hindu scientific wisdom. He formulated atomistic concepts of matter only confirmed after the work of **Boyle** and **Newton**: the concept of a void, the law of conservation of matter, the idea of necessity as natural law, the existence of 'uncuttable' smallest particles of matter (Greek *a-toma* = uncuttable), and the view that atoms have weight and form objects by combination. He believed in 'soul atoms' as did **Aristotle**, comparing them to dust particles in sunlight, ever moving even in still air. Atomists believed that atoms move and collide in empty space. Atoms seem to have been considered variable in shape, and the mind or soul was said to consist of smooth, spherical storms of fire.

The atomism of Democritus and Leukippos exerted a tremendous influence, being vividly presented in the poem of Lucretius *De natura rerum* (On the nature of things), and enigmatically summarized by Aristotle. Although works of Democrius himself were lost, thinkers like Sir Walter Ralegh's assistant Thomas Harriot, **Giordano Bruno** (1548–1600) and **Robert Boyle** drew their inspiration directly from classical sources. Early alchemical texts attributed to Democritus of Abdera appear to be the work of **Bolos of Mendes**, often called 'pseudo-Democritus' (*floruit c.*200 BC.)

# Digby, Sir Kenelm
## 1603–65

Digby belongs to the class of chemical alchemists who created scientific chemistry, being a contemporary of **Elias Ashmole** and **Robert Boyle**. Although very much a gentleman dilettante, he was also a scientist. John Aubrey refers to his 'undaunted courage', his wide travels and his knowledge of '10 or 12 languages', and he was 'well versed in all kinds of learning'. He was the son of Sir Everard Digby, executed for complicity in the Gunpowder Plot. After studying at Gloucester Hall, Oxford, with Thomas Allen, astrologer and mathematician of note, he travelled to Paris, Florence and Madrid, returning with Prince Charles in 1623. He then embarked on a successful piracy expedition in the Mediterranean, winning royal praise on his return.

His wife's death in 1633 made an eccentric chemist of Digby, and he was involved with Gresham College, the prototype for a scientific university in London. His Royalist sympathies landed him in severe trouble during 1640s, but he was favoured after the Restoration.

Digby was profoundly impressed by the Paracelsian 'Powder of Sympathy', the weapon salve which nearly destroyed the life of **Joan Battista van Helmont**. (The salve was to anoint the weapon rather than the wound.) He was a friend of the alchemist Johannes Banfi Hunneades, a Hungarian who became professor at Gresham College in the 1630s. He was also a friend of Sir Thomas Browne, admiring his *Religio Medici*.

Digby's alchemical chemistry gives much insight into the strange hybrid 'chymistry' which paved the way for **Newton**'s alchemical craze. After his death, his assistant George Hartman published *A Choice Collection of Chymical Secrets*, which included preparation of **medicines**, *menstruums*, and **alkahests**, 'with the true secret of volatilizing fixt salt of tarter'.

*See* B.J. Dobbs, *The Foundations of Newton's Alchemy*; E.J. Holmyard, *Alchemy*.

# Distillation

This is perhaps the most important of alchemical **processes** and much **apparatus** was designed for the purpose. Hellenistic alchemical texts display *ambix* (*see* **Alembic**), *kerotakis* and *tribikos*, all famous as distillation apparatus. The heating of **cinnabar** to produce **mercury** in vapour form was known from earliest times both in China (*see* **Chinese Alchemy**) and the West, and it inspired much alchemical **myth**. It is possible that the alchemists' endless obsession with white and red **elixirs** resulted from the vermilion colour of magical cinnabar, and the white, silvery colour of mercury (*see* **Colours**; *Conjunctio*).

An important breakthrough in the history of **alchemy** and chemistry was the discovery of the **distillation** of alcohol, already known at the medical school of Salerno in the eleventh century, and of great importance to **Arnald of Villanova** and John of Rupescissa in the early fourteenth century. It was called *aqua vitae* (water of life), *aqua vini* (water of wine), *aqua ardens* (burning water), and there were mysterious explanations of this pure liquid as an elixir or universal **quintessence.**

Alchemical symbolism shows that distillation was a mystic process by which the more gross material **elements**, earth and water, became rarified and purer, nearer to the divine spiritual quintessence.

Renaissance distillation was brought to a fine art by best-selling textbooks like the work of Jerome Brunschweig (first edition, Strasburg, 1500) translated into English as *The Vertuose Boke of Distyllacyon* by Lawrence Andrews. This was the first English textbook of chemistry and **medicine**, anticipating the Paracelsian movement. Another landmark in medical pharmacy was *The Treasure of Euonymus* by Conradt Gesner (translated into English in 1559).

# Dorn, Gerard
**Flemish Paracelsian; born in Belgium, *floruit* Basle and Frankfurt 1560–80s**

The dates of Gerard Dorn's life are unknown, but he started publishing books from 1565. Marie-Louise von Franz, a convinced Jungian, has provided a study of Dorn's highly original alchemical writings. She comments:

We also know that he was a physician, a general practitioner . . . He also advanced pharmacology to a certain extent because, unlike most general practitioners at that time, he did not only use herbal medicines.

Marie-Louise von Franz, *Alchemical Active Imagination*

Dorn was a fierce protagonist for **Paracelsus**. He made important contributions to science and to chemical **medicine**, but he was also an adept, with a mystical outlook.

He studied with **Adam von Bodenstein**, to whom his first book is dedicated, and knew Michael Toxites. These two men retrieved Paracelsus' **manuscript** works and printed them for the first time, while Dorn translated many into Latin for the Basle publisher Peter Perna. He was in Basle during the late 1570s, and in Frankfurt in the early 1580s. He used **John Dee**'s *monas* symbol in the title of his *Chymisticum artificium* (Chemical Skill).

Dorn produced an important dictionary (*Congeries*) of Paracelsian terms, and an account of **Trithemius**' views on the spagyric art (Ursellis' *Theatrum Chemicum* (Theatre of Chemistry) (1602) contains a number of his works).

To give an idea of his influence, the following titles were found in the library of **John Winthrop** (seventeenth century):

*Chymisticum artificium naturae, theoricum et practicum . . . liber plane philosophicus* (Chemical skill in nature, theoretical and practical) (1568).

*Artificii chymistici physici, metaphysici, secunda pars and tertia . . . accessit etiam tertiaede parti, de praeparationibus metallicis in utroque lapidis philosophorum opere maiore minoreque* (Physical and metaphysical skill in chemistry, to which is added on the preparation of metals in both the major and minor works of the Philosophers' Stone) (1569).

*Monarchia triadis, in unitate, soli deo sacro* (Monarchy of the triad, in unity) (1577).

Same volume: *Paracelsus, aurora thesaurusque philosophorum* (Dawn and treasure of the philosophers) (Basle, Guarini).

*Congeries paracelsicae chemiae de transmutationibus metallorum, ex omnibus quae de his ab ipso scripta reperire licuit hactenus. Accessit genealogia Mineralium atque metallorum omnium.* (Collection of Paracelsian chemistry on transmutation of metals, a collection from all the writings of Paracelsus to be discovered so far) (Works of Paracelsus translated by Dorn) (Andreas Wechel, Frankfurt, 1581).

*Trevisanus* (by **Bernard of Trevisa**): *De chymico miraculo, quod lapidem philosophiae appellant* (Conrad Waldkirch, Basle, 1600).

This work is taken from various authors, princes of the art: **Democritus, Geber, Lull, Arnald of Villanova,** collected and illustrated by Dorn.

# Dragon

Of all alchemical symbols, the fire-breathing dragon is probably the most famous, being a close cousin of the **uroboros**, the self-devouring serpent which was the earliest emblem of **alchemy**. The Greek word *drako* means 'serpent', and there are many early **myths** of slaying the serpent, the symbol of chthonic, underworld powers, while snakes or serpents were always sacred in ancient Greece, being associated with health.

Our image of the dragon comes from Christian art, and its shape has most in common with the Chinese dragon (*see also* **Chinese**

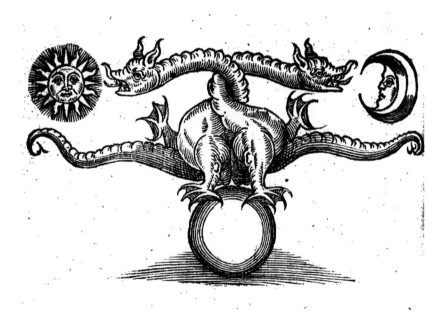

*Two intertwined dragons, their heads towards sun and moon symbols.*

*Sol and Luna denote not only sun and moon, but the cosmic principles of sulphur and mercury. The dragon is always the classic symbol for the cosmic mercury of the philosophers, which is full of ambivalence, a hermaphroditic symbol.*

*From Elias Ashmole,* Theatrum chemicum Britannicum *(London, 1652). This work is a celebrated collection of English alchemical poetry with some of the finest extant alchemical woodcuts.*

*By kind permission of The Bodleian Library, Oxford.*

*RR. W. 29 (9) p.212.*

Alchemy). Slaying the dragon in order to free the damsel in distress or to reach the 'treasure hard to attain' is a universal archetypal myth (see Jung's exhaustive study in 'Symbols of Transformation', Vol. 5, Collected Works). In medieval legend, the dragon is often called the worm.

The alchemical dragon is guardian of the treasure of the opus. It undergoes countless transformations, for the monster represents the elusive mercurius. Thus there is a winged, fiery dragon representing the volatile **mercury**, and a wingless dragon symbolizing the fixed state. The **hermaphrodite** or Rebis is often shown standing upon the winged, fire-breathing dragon.

### Textual Examples

One of the most vivid accounts of the alchemical dragon is given by the Elizabethan **Thomas Charnock**:

> The dragon speaketh:
> Souldiers in armour bright
> Should not have kylled me in fyelde of fighte,
> Mr Charnock neither for all his philosophie
> Iff by pryson and famyne he had not famysshed me.
> Gye of Warwick nor Berys of Southampton
> Nere slew such a venemous dragon.
> Hercules fought with Hidra the Serpent
> And yet he coulde not have his intent.

'Salomon the wyse' used a tomb of brass as prison, but the dragon mercury was to be 'shutt upp in a doungeon of glasse' (i.e. in the vas hermeticum, or **vessel** of **transmutation**). Like the uroboric serpent, he feeds upon himself:

> For very hunger I eate myne owne bodye
> And soe by corruption I become black and redde
> But that precious stone that is in my hedd
> Wyll be worth a mle [mille = 1,000] to him that hath skyll
> And for that stone's sake he wysely dyd me kyll.

This refers to the work with the philosophers' mercury, which gives birth to the Philosophers' **Stone**: the head being, apparently, the head of the **alembic** or still. The killing of dragon is the fixing of mercury: 'killing' is a common metaphor for fixing or solidifying, known also in Indian texts.

Charnock's unsophisticated verses give more direct insight into the adept oral tradition of myth and symbol. His dragon represents the course of the opus, from the *nigredo* stage of death and putrefaction, through to the red (*rubedo*) stage to the mastery (*magisterium*) of the Stone itself.

The process of mortifying the mercury (*see* **Mortification**), or slaying the dragon, is vital, and it is suggested that only the most famous adepts have really succeeded:

> My great grawnfather was killyd by Ramunde Lulli, knyght of Spayne.
> My grawnfather by Sir George Ripley, Chanone of England Sartayne.

Every aspect of the opus is included in the myth or allegory. The slaying of the dragon is vital for attaining the **elixir** which is the means of transmutation, as well as the elixir of life. The dragon generously forgives his killer, admitting that in life he was 'but strong poyson' (an allusion to the poisonous quality of mercury).

It is easy to discern the projection of unconscious archetypes: the process of spiritual suffering, of death and resurrection, required to achieve mastery (*see* **Redemption**):

> Dying in mine owne blood
> For now I doe excell all other worldeley good
> And a new name is given me of those that be wise
> For now I am named Elixer of great price
> Which if you will make prouffe, put to me my Sister Mercury
> And I will conjoyne her into Sylver in the twinkling of an eye.

Having passed through the stages of dying, of putrefaction and of poison, the elixir is born to be united with the feminine mercury (*see* **Conjunctio**, the mystic marriage of opposites in alchemy).

*See* F. Sherwood Taylor, *Alchemy*, for these quotations from Thomas Charnock.

# Dreams and Visions

Although it obviously has a chemical-experimental aspect, the esoteric kernel of the alchemical tradition involves dreams and visions. The Jungian interpretation (*see* **Jungian Theory of Alchemy**) rejects the chemical explanation entirely, and in his book *Psychology and Alchemy* (1944) Jung used alchemical symbolism to illustrate a series of dreams representing the individuation process of psychic maturation. He emphasizes the **mandala** symbolism of dreams, a symbolism we also find in **alchemy**, where balance and **harmony**, concepts of mystical **unity**, of quaternity and

**numerology**, always appear. Many alchemical icons are clearly meditation mandala symbols. Jung argues that the human unconscious has a universal collective depth, flowing beneath the more obvious personal unconscious.

Dreams were interpreted by Freud in sexual terms, using personal memory associations, and much alchemical symbol and **myth** seems to be repressed sexual fantasies. Jung, however, emphasizes the archetypal quality of dreams, especially visionary ones which transcend the personal ego. Visions can reveal some of the archetypal, primordial depth of the psyche. He describes the alchemical tradition as flowing like dreams beneath the conventional surface of dogma and doctrine. This is why alchemical imagery is so often heretical, with themes of incest and sexual intercourse prominent (and quite openly portrayed in **manuscript** illuminations).

Dreams and allegory play a vital part in medieval culture, with Middle English poems like 'The Pearl' and 'The Vision of Piers Plowman' as well as Chaucerian works using dreams for imaginative expansion. As alchemical visions are full of dreams and allegory, so medieval dream theory is vital to deciphering alchemy. Medieval dream theory arose from works like Cicero's *Dream of Scipio*, with Macrobius' commentary, and more popular works like *The Dream Book of Daniel*, which used the biblical dreams of Joseph and Daniel. The *Aurora consurgens* (attributed to St Thomas Aquinas) is also full of allegories and citations from visionary biblical texts, along with *The Wisdom of Solomon*, which exerted fantastic influence.

Dreams were given categories, the lowest being those of humoral or bodily origin (e.g. from eating cheese or onions or from drunkenness or indigestion). More important were prophetic or religious dreams, universally revered.

Alchemists were deeply involved with these ideas of vision and prophecy. Canon **George Ripley** uses a vision of a chameleon toad to symbolize the sequence of **colours** in the opus, and his poetry is full of disturbing incest fantasy. The ancient work of **Zosimos of Panoplis** (third century AD) describes what is supposed to be a terrifying dream vision, a fantastic nightmare.

The paintings of Hieronymus Bosch have been interpreted in alchemical terms, as the garden and the **fountain**, symbols shared with alchemy, feature very prominently. The apocalyptic visions of Bosch correspond to the apocalyptic or prophetic ideas of alchemists who drew upon biblical visions (*see* **Prophecy**). **Joachim of Fiore**, for example, used a dream of a ten-stringed psaltery as the basis for his prophetic numerology, much used by alchemists.

# Duchesne, Joseph
Latin *Quercetanus*; born in Gascony in 1544 (or 1521),
died in 1609 in Paris

Graduating from Basle as MD in 1573, Duchesne took up his position
as physician to the French King Henry IV in Paris in 1593. He soon
became a leading apologist of Paracelsian **medicine**, although he is
not credited with any (iatro-)chemical originality. The translation of
his work by John Hester into English was an important factor in
inspiring English Paracelsians (*see* **Paracelsus**).

Duchesne made enemies rapidly through his arrogant assertion of
Paracelsian 'heresy', and soon found himself condemned by the
medical profession of the Sorbonne. His book *On the material of the
old medicine of the ancient philosophers* (1603) provoked attacks, but
also the defence of Theodore Turquet de Mayerne, who was a more
advanced pharmacist and fellow royal physician. His *Apologia* for
Duchesne argues that chemically-prepared medicines do not violate
the laws of Galenic Hippocratic academic medicine.

Duchesne taught that illness was caused by seeds (*semina*), like
those of plants. He espoused the Paracelsian doctrine of the three
principles (*Tria Principia*), **salt**, **sulphur** and **mercury**, underlying
the world and being present in all bodies. He used the astrological
doctrine of signatures, and believed in a *sal generalis* capable of
creating philosophical **gold**. He regarded the salts of sulphur and
mercury as volatile, with saltpetre as solid. He also used **antimony**,
highly fashionable with medical chemists of the time.

**Publications:**
*Sclopetarius*, a work on gunshot wounds, with the *Antidotarium
spagyricum* (Spagyric Antidotes), an alchemical or *spagyricum*
work on pharmacy (Lyons, 1576; Frankfurt, 1602). John Hester
translated *Sclopetarius* into English and published it in 1596, and
it was also translated into French: *Traitte de la Cure Generale en
Particulière des Arcebuscades avec l'Antidotaire Spagyrique pour
preparer et composer les medicaments* (Jean Lertout, Lyons, 1576).
*Pharmacopoeia dogmaticorum restituta* (Pharmacopia restored) (Paris,
1607). This work contains various forms of healing waters, wines,
decoctions and syrups.

An interesting work by Jo Lertotius was published in Lyons in 1575,
being a 'brief reply of Duchesne to the exposition of Jacobus
Aubertus Vindonis, on the origins and causes of metals', a book

ostensibly attacking the Paracelsians and their remedies. The book includes Duchesne's work *On the exquisite spagyric preparation of mineral, animal and vegetable medicaments,* describing itself as 'a useful and perceptive tract'.

# Earth

*See* **Elements**.

# Egg

Like most alchemical iconography, the egg is subject to variety of interpretation. The emblem comes eighth in Maier's series of emblems in the *Atalanta fugiens* (1608); the motto being, 'Take the egg and pierce it with a fiery sword.' Although this is a seventeenth-century work, the symbol is amongst the most ancient in **alchemy**. Maier's egg stands on a square table as a soldier raises his sword to strike it, the background shows the black and white tiling of a courtyard, and there is a fire and a tunnel in the courtyard wall. The engraving is partly an exercise in mathematical perspective.

This symbol represents the dividing of the cosmic or philosophical egg, the early stage of separation out of the four **elements**. The alchemist must commence the opus by dividing the cosmic **unity** and in this he is imitating the Creator (*see* **Creation**) who constructs the universe by separating out the elements from the cosmogonic unity of the **Prime Matter** (*prima materia*).

Maier explains the symbol as meaning the attack of the fiery sword of Vulcan with the aid of Mars (iron) upon the egg, whose yellow yoke is surrounded by white. Yellow is the natural symbol for **gold**, also sophic **sulphur**, whilst white represents the *albedo* (whitening) (*see* **Colours**). The chick hatching from the egg is an obvious symbol for growth, for the incubation and hatching of the Philosophers' **Stone**, which requires the action both of gentle heat and of the more forceful cracking heat of the **furnace**.

There is an epigram from the medieval text, 'Work of Women and Play for Boys' (Latin: *Opus mulierum et ludus puerorum*) which translates:

*The alchemist as knight, with sword poised to strike the philosophical egg. The unity of the egg must first be divided into its elements. Note the geometrical harmony of the background.*
*Emblem from Michael Maier,* Atalanta fugiens *(Oppenheimer, 1617).*
*By kind permission of The Warburg Institute, London.*

There is a bird in the world, more sublime than all,
Let it be your only care to find its egg.
The albumen softly surrounds the golden yolk;
Attack it cautiously with a fiery sword, (as is the custom)
Let Mars assist Vulcan; the bird arising from it
Will be conqueror of iron and fire.

It is clear from many texts that the egg means the *vas hermeticum*, the hermetically-sealed vase or **vessel** in which the Stone (*Lapis*) incubates like an embryo in the womb: note that **metals** in primitive animistic thought are believed to incubate in the womb of Mother Earth. The alchemist always seeks a cosmic dimension for every stage of his laboratory operations, thus the mysterious events in his Hermetic vessel are a recreation of the divine Creation of the cosmos. In the *Turba philosophorum* (The Crowd of Philosophers), one of the most popular works translated from Arabic for medieval alchemists, there is a long comparison of the *opus alchymicum* with the egg. Pandolphus is the fifth speaker in the *Turba*, and he discusses earth and air in the Creation. The four elements are all contained in the egg:

Its hard shell is earth, the albumen is the water, the thin membrane inside of the eggshell separates earth and water, because . . . it is air which separates water and earth; the red of the egg [ = the yolk] is fire, and the membrane around the yolk is air, which separates fire and water.

The speakers in the 'Crowd of Philosophers' are the early Greek pre-Socratic philosophers, and the cosmic egg was vital to the cosmology of the Orphic sect. Their mysteries may have been an influence on **Hellenistic alchemy**.

It should be noted too that the cosmic egg was well known to the Chinese, being an archetypal symbol. A Chinese text shows that the yolk of the egg symbolizes the earth, surrounded by water on its surface with sky and heavens above (cited in Volume 2 of Joseph Needham's *Shorter Science and Civilization in China*).

The 'Work of Women' shows that the standard idea of the egg is the Hermetic vessel, and it is here that 'our Stone' is to be laid, 'so that it is perfected by fire and art'. Maier quotes the ancient text of **Morienus** as well as **Albertus Magnus**, in a work *On the generation of the Stone*:

One place is the principle of generation, and this brings about the development of that which is put into it by the properties of heaven which, through the radiations of the stars, penetrate that which is made to develope.

The opus is based on the concept of using natural, celestial influences (*see* **Astrology**) to accomplish in the artificial Hermetic vessel that which **nature** accomplishes in the earth. Plato in the (spurious) *Book of the Four Quarters* compares the motion of the firmament, which causes the cycle of transformations of the elemental bodies, with the work of the philosophers. In the cosmos at large, subtle or light things ascend, whilst heavy or gross things descend, and the alchemist thinks in terms of **distillation** as the means of freeing the more subtle **quintessence** from the gross materiality where it is imprisoned. The egg is often likened to the prison of the **dragon**, the 'doungel of glasse', as **Thomas Charnock** calls it. The philosophers' incubation vessel for the Stone must be hermetically sealed and well secured, 'for in it the whole firmament follows its circular course'. The Hermetic vessel, where the essential process of **transmutation** is carried out, is to filter through the celestial influences, and must sustain circulation, a concept also familiar to **Chinese alchemy**. The sources are unanimous that the egg means the Hermetic vessel, and there can be no doubt that this equation is universal. (There is much illuminating material in the facsimile edition of Maier's *Atalanta fugiens* edited by L. Wuthrich.)

As the egg is a key symbol for understanding the entire opus, it may help to refer also to **John Dee**'s *Monas hieroglyphica* of 1564. Dee, an expert astronomer as well as cabalist, knew that the orbit of **Mercury** as a planet is eccentric (not perfectly circular) – as we now know, the orbit is elliptical, nearer to being egg-shaped – and this was known half a century before Kepler discovered elliptical orbits. Dee considers it a profound mystery that the planet Mercury described an orbit which is egg-shaped, for mercury in the opus represents the unity, the ambivalence and the synthesis of opposites in the opus, as well as being the Prime Matter of metals. The concept of dividing the unity of the cosmic egg unity, symbolized by the egg, is shown in Dee's poem, included by Elias Ashmole in *Theatrum Chemicum Britannicum* (1652), and quoted by C.H. Josten 'John Dee's *Monas Hieroglyphica*', *Ambix* 1964, p.92:

> Cut that in three which Nature hath made One
> Then strengthen hyt, even by itself alone,
> Werewith then cutte the poudred Sonne in twayne,
> By length of tyme, and heale the wounde againe.

Such riddles are not to be solved by non-adepts such as myself. But in general, it is easy to see that the egg is an archetypal symbol of unity, of growth, incubation, of nature's miraculous hatching of chicks from seemingly inanimate matter, which needs only warmth to accomplish and bring to perfection. Alchemists constantly setting up the antithesis of **microcosm** and macrocosm: the Stone is so often called a 'triune Microcosm', and cosmic symbols of creation are constantly used to represent the humble (and fruitless) experiments in the adept's laboratory. The secret of success lay in man's imitating the marvellous workings of nature, recreating the miraculous processes of birth and generation, linked with the processes of putrefaction, death and suffering.

# Elements

Early Greek pre-Socratic philosophers sought to derive all matter from a primal element, which formed a **Prime Matter** of the universe.

Thales derived all matter from water (*see* **Aqua**), Herakleitos from fire, and Xenophanes from earth. Empedocles presented the theory of four elements, earth, air fire and water, ruled over by the twin principles love and strife, and **Aristotle**'s account of the elements, with their paired qualities, formed the basis for all natural philosophy until the time of **Robert Boyle**.

In this theory the four elements – earth, air, fire and water – arise from the pairing of qualities: hot, cold, wet, dry. Transformation of one element into another is perfectly possible by change of quality, and this concept was vital to the alchemical concept of transformation and **transmutation**. An element in the Aristotelian sense is defined as a body which cannot be broken down into other elements, but it does form a component of the material world. The **Creation** involved the separation of the elements, division of heaven and earth, and the emergence of land from the sea. The cosmos is arranged with the four elements surrounding the earth within the sphere of the moon. Beyond the sphere of the moon is the realm not of mortal, transformable elements, but of the **quintessence**, which has such immense alchemical significance. This fifth essence has a durability, a permanence.

The *Liber Platonis quartorum* (Plato's 'Book of Quaternities') cited by Jung in *Psychology and Alchemy*, gives a typical table of elements with correspondences and this typifies the medieval way of using the universe as a place system or as a 'theatre of memory' (*see* F.A. Yates, *The Theatre of Memory*).

**Paracelsus** retained the theory of four elements, but made the universe dependent upon three principles (*see* **Tria Prima**) of **salt**, **sulphur** and **mercury**, which animate the phenomenal world. **John Dee** introduces the quaternity of four elements into his ***Monas hieroglyphica*** (1564), suggesting that the quaternary rests upon the ternary: i.e. the four elements rest upon the trinity (*see* **Numerology**)

**Thomas Vaughan**, in his graphic seventeenth-century prose, gives an authentic alchemical account of the inner meaning of the doctrine of elements:

Earth . . . being the Subsidence, or Remains of that Primitive Masse, which God formed out of Darknesse, must needs be a faeculent impure Body: for the Extractions which the Divine Spirit made, were pure, oleous, aethereall substances: but the crude, phlegmatick, indigested humours settled like Lees towards the Centre.

Water: This is the first Element we read of in Scripture, the most Ancient Principles, and the Mother of all things amongst Visibles. Without the mediation of this, the Earth can receive no blessing at all, for moysture is the proper cause of mixture and Fusion . . . . The Common Element water is not altogether contemptible, for there are hidden treasures in it.

Vaughan says there are only two real elements, earth and water, although the Peripatetics claim four elements.

Air: This is no Element, but a certain miraculous Hermaphrodite, the Caement of two worlds, and a Medley of Extremes . . . . In this are innumerable magicall Forms of Men and Beasts, Fish and Fowle, Trees, Herbs, and all creeping things.

He calls the air a 'sea of invisible things', and a 'Magicians backdoor'. He then passes to the fourth element, fire, which is 'the last substance, the Highest in the *Scala Naturae* [the Ladder of Nature]':

This Fire passeth through all things in the world, and it is Natures Charriot, in this she rides; when she moves this moves, and when she stands this stands, like the wheeles in Ezekiel whose motion dependeth on that of the spirit. This is the mask and skreen of the Almighty, wheresoever he is, this Train of Fire attends Him. Thus he appears to Moses in the Bush . . ..

# Elixir
## 'Our medicine'; *medicina*

Mammon: He that has once the flower of the sun,
The perfect ruby, which he calls elixir,
Not only can do that, but, by its virtue
Can confer honour, love, respect, long life,
Give safety, valour, yea, and victory
To whom he will. In eight and twenty days
I'll make an old man, of fourscore, a child.

Ben Jonson, *The Alchemist*, II. i.

Ben Jonson's play *The Alchemist* conveys the age-old idea of the elixir, the panacea, which restores youth, renewing a man 'like an eagle,/To the fifth age'. He will beget sons and daughters who are young giants (which was how children of the philosophers were before the flood), and further, and taking but one mustard-grain of it will 'fright the plague/Out o'the kingdom in three months'.

The elixir of life, of youth and vitality was an essential, established part of medieval **alchemy. Roger Bacon** and **Arnald of Villanova** wrote popular tracts on the subject. The elixir is usually bound up with the concepts of the **Stone** of the Philosophers and the **tincture** – in fact these are often used as synonyms. The reason for this is that the Philosophers' Stone was described as a 'medicine of metals': both the Stone and elixir have the function of healing the defects or corruption in **metals**, raising them to the perfection of **gold**. This theory of the healing **medicine** or elixir of metals is found in the popular writings of **John Dasteyn**, who wrote at the height of the medieval craze. After outlining his theory of **transmutation** of metals, he adds that the elixir is also a panacea, a medicine to cure all disease and sickness in man.

Paracelsians seem to have purveyed hundreds of different elixirs, above all the famous *aurum potabile*, or potable gold, which was publicly defended against medical attack by **Francis Anthony** in the early seventeenth century.

One text, the *Glory of the World*, comments that **Adam** would never have lived for 300 years without the *Mysterium Magnum* (Great Mystery) of the elixir. There were also legends that the fourteenth-century alchemist **Nicholas Flamel** and his wife Perenelle lived for hundreds of years as a result of their experiments.

In general, however, the elixir tradition is less obvious in western alchemy than it is in eastern, **Chinese** and **Indian alchemy**. The position with **Hellenistic alchemy** is quite obscure, and in medieval Christendom the idea of prolonging life beyond natural limits was inconsistent with divine law.

Chinese alchemy, on the other hand, raised the arts of concocting elixirs to unheard-of popularity, and most adepts believed implicitly in the power of alchemy to confer immortality. Indeed, adepts were helped by supernatural 'genies' (equivalent to western angels). These beings had achieved varying degrees of spiritual immortality.

**Wei Po Yang** (*floruit* 142 AD) is one of the fathers of Chinese alchemy, and there is the famous story of himself, his white dog and his trusting disciple Yu going to the mountains to try their elixir. At first they appeared to expire, but later attained immortality. Such stories were earnestly believed by Ko Hung, the other father of Chinese elixir alchemy, and we now know that there were basically two Chinese traditions, one involving chemical or medicinal elixirs, the other a form of yoga, with breathing exercises and dietary regimen to prolong life (*see* **Chinese Alchemy**). Ko Hung tells us that of the hundreds of books he had read, only a handful failed to recommend both **mercury** and its ore **cinnabar** as food for elixirs:

The volumes I have studied as I examined writings on the nurturing of life and collected recipes for acquiring everlasting vision must number in the thousands; yet there was not one amongst them that did not insist that revated [recombined] cinnabar and Potable Gold were the things of highest importance. These bring the adept to the summit of the divine process.

# The Emerald Tablet
## Tabula Smaragdina

The name of this text reverberates through the history of **alchemy**, and yet it is a most untransmutatory document, whose philosophy is completely obscure in its Latin translation. The text has been published in a number of versions and translations, and has now been traced back to the Islamic Jabirian corpus (*see* **Jabir ibn Hayyan**).

The legend of its discovery belongs to the attempts to ennoble the alchemical tradition by attributing its texts to biblical antiquity; it was said that Sara, wife of Abraham, discovered it in the very tomb of **Hermes Trismegistus**.

E.J. Holmyard, who discovered the text amongst the Jabirian corpus, concludes that 'the oldest known form of the *Table*, namely the Arabic, was probably translated from Syriac but it may ultimately have been based on a Greek original'.

The text claims that its assertions are completely true and certain. Its first proposition: 'That which is above is like that which is below', reminds us of Herakleitos: 'The way up and the way down are one and the same.' It was used to justify **astrology** as a vital part of alchemy. The text goes on to say that all things exist or come into being through contemplation, or meditation through 'adaptation'. Many alchemical emblems portray the father of the **Stone** as the sun, the mother as moon (*see* **Sol and Luna**), and the text also tells us that it was carried in the womb of the wind and nursed by the earth.

The Stone of the Philosophers is not named, and the text speaks of a **unity**, but this clearly means a mystic Stone with miraculous attributes. The unity harmonizes superior and inferior (celestial and terrestrial) things:

Thus thou wilt possess the glory of the brightness of all things, and all obscurity will fly far away from thee.

The significance of the text was its proof that the alchemical opus is a cosmic process, and the doctrine of **microcosm-macrocosm** seems implicit in it. It expounds the very secrets of **Creation** of the world.

See E.J. Holmyard, *Alchemy*.

# F

## Fermentation

Metaphors of vegetation are common in **alchemy** and the maturation of **metals** is seen as a process of growth or incubation within the womb of the earth. Fermentation is often a key process in the opus and **Morienus** describes the two opposing principles **Sol and Luna** (sun and moon) as ferments, that is, as the seeds (*semina*) of metals. Perhaps the image originates in the early processes of dyeing, which used vegetable ferments to produce dyes or **tinctures**. The ferment helps in preparing the **elixir** or 'medicine of metals', which then tinctures or **colours** the metals. A ferment of **gold** or **sulphur** is vital to produce the red elixir, while silver or **mercury** is vital for the white elixir. Sometimes the red elixir is equated with the **quintessence** of gold: it is the elixir of life and the spiritual ferment which serves both to transmute metals and to preserve man's bodily health:

> The Philosophers' Stone was often pictured as a 'ferment' which could insinuate itself between the particles of imperfect metals, thereby attracting to itself all the particles of its own nature: thus the red stone, or golden ferment, would yield gold, and the white stone, or silver ferment, would yield silver.
>
> John Read, *Prelude to Chemistry*, p.140

## Fire

*See* **Elements**.

## Flamel, Nicholas
### born 1330, died 22 March 1417

Perhaps the most famous of the medieval alchemists, Flamel and his wife Pernelle's immense wealth encouraged the fourteenth-century craze for transmutatory **alchemy**. His interest began when, while working as a wealthy Paris notary, he came across a gilded book with strange letters inscribed on leaves of bark. The work declared itself to be written by **Abraham Eleazar**, Astrologer and Philosopher, Prince amongst Jews of the Dispersion. On every seventh leaf was painted one of three strange icons:

1) a **caduceus** with intertwined serpents;
2) a serpent crucified on a cross;
3) a snake-infested desert with beautiful **fountains**;

While the fourth leaf displayed a familiar image of winged **Mercury** with the figure of Saturn with hour-glass and scythe (*see* **Metals and Planets**), and there was also a mountain with a rose blown by the north wind, its stalk blue, its flowers white and red (*see* **Colours**). Flamel and his wife embarked upon a life-long quest for its meaning, and at last found a Jew who recognized the work as that of the Rabbi Abraham, a work of the **Cabala** considered lost.

On 17 January 1382, using the book as well as other guidance, the couple believed they had achieved **transmutation**, by the boring experimental cliché of projection of the red **stone** upon half a pound of mercury. First they contemplated the admirable works of **nature**, then became suddenly rich.

Under Flamel's will 14 hospitals were founded, three chapels built and seven churches endowed. His marble tombstone was later appropriated for chopping **herbs**. It displayed carvings of St Peter and St Paul on either side of a figure of Christ holding a globe and cross – only sun and moon symbols on each side betrayed that the owner had been an alchemist, an adept of **Sol and Luna**.

*See* E.J. Holmyard, *Alchemy*; Titus Burckhardt, *Alchemy*.

# Fludd, Robert
**Physician, alchemist and Hermetic philosopher; 1574–1637**

Robert Fludd's father, Sir Thomas Fludd, had served as Treasurer to the army in Flanders before retiring to Milgate House, Bearsted in Kent. Fludd studied at St John's College, Oxford, proceeding BA in 1596, MA in 1597. He may have studied his main interests with Thomas Allen, mathematician of Pembroke Hall, for his passion for **astrology**, music and mathematical schemes was born at Oxford, but it burgeoned during his later continental travels, when he imbibed mystical Paracelsian ideas. In France he was tutor to the Duke de Guise, and he met William Harvey in Italy. Professor Pagel argues that Harvey's world view was influenced by the doctrine of the **microcosm**, and Harvey and Fludd remained the closest friends. Returning to England in 1604 Fludd studied **medicine** at Christchurch, Oxford, then as MD sought admission to the Royal College of Physicians in London. The College was persecuting men like Simon Forman and **Arthur Dee** for unauthorized medical practice, and with his strong Paracelsian leanings Fludd failed repeatedly to gain admittance. On 20 September 1609, however, he did gain admission as Fellow and thereafter he rose to eminence as Censor of the College in 1618, 1627, 1633 and 1634.

He was a wealthy practitioner of medicine, and a stout **Rosicrucian** supporter, publishing an apologia for the brotherhood in 1616 which fended off attacks by the Protestant chemist **Andreas Libavius**. Also in 1616 he met **Michael Maier** in England.

Fludd's writing was prolific, and infused with cabalist thinking. He regarded himself as a 'Mosaicall' interpreter of the **Creation**. His famous volume on the *Physics and Technics* of both 'cosmi' expounds an ambitious vision of Macrocosm-Microcosm. There are many beautiful engravings in this lavish book: one shows the Creator as Tertragrammaton, radiating creative emanation through spheres of angels. **Nature** as a naked woman is chained to God above, but holds an earthly monkey on a chain below. The cosmos is that familiar in **Aristotle**, with the four **elements** and the worlds of animal, vegetable and mineral. Fludd attacked Aristotle, however, favouring Plato, and he uses Paracelsian ideas of *Tria Principia*, the three principles of **salt**, **sulphur** and **mercury** in his works. He belongs to the mainstream of mystical, anti-Aristotelian speculation which followed **Paracelsus**.

Mystical alchemists like **Croll** and **Boehme** were concerned with alchemical interpretation of the Mosaic view of Creation, and they believed that the **Cabala** and Hermetic **magic** were vital tools in understanding nature and in curing disease. Fludd was like **van Helmont** and Sir **Kennelm Digby** in fiercely defending the weapon salve, the 'Powder of Sympathy' which others attacked as witchcraft: the salve used sympathetic magic, for it was used to anoint the weapon which inflicted the wound.

C.H. Josten has made available a marvellous alchemical work by Fludd on the germination of wheat: *see* C.H. Josten, 'Truth's Golden Harrow', *Ambix*, 1949.

*See also* Allen G. Debus, *The English Paracelsians*.

# Fountain, Mercurial
*Fons mercurialis*

The fountain is another frequent alchemical image whose exact meaning seems to vary. In many pictures it is found in a beautiful garden, being associated with flourishing and growth in the opus.

A beautiful engraving in the *Rosarium* (1550) shows the mercurial fountain with three spouts, from which issue *lac virginis* (virgin's milk), *acetum fontis* (vinegar or corrosive acid), and *aqua vitae* (**quintessence**, alcohol). The stem of the fountain bears words *triplex nomine* = threefold in name, and around the basin or cauldron the inscription refers to the **unity** of animal, vegetable and mineral. There are four stars at the corners, representing the quaternity of **elements**, with an upper central star being the quintessence, symbol of spiritual unity. Above there is a trinity, around the two-headed coiled mercurial serpent which licks the upper stars.

Thus the fountain represents a **vessel** in which **mercury** is transformed into its various alchemical guises: it is also a symbol of the underlying unity of the trickster god. Jung explains that this is like the philosophical **bath**, being a font of health and rejuvenation, but the fountain's mercurial character means that it is ambivalent, being poisonous as well as healing.

On the fifth page of **Nicholas Flamel**'s **manuscript** by **Abraham Eleazar** was a rose bush in flower in the midst of a beautiful garden. At the foot of this was a very white spring or fountain gushing and flowing away in cascades into the distance, but the multitude of seekers were blindly digging everywhere, unable to find the spring or source of the white or silvery water, the *fons mercurialis* itself . . .

Amongst the hieroglyphs of this book there is also a picture of a beautiful desert with snakes twining here and there. Snakes are the classic symbol for mercury. Such imagery is obsure, but the idea of the alchemical garden of roses (*Rosarium*) is common, and mercury is the very fount or source of the opus.

# French, John
**Paracelsian English physician of the seventeenth century**

Born at Broughton near Banbury in Oxfordshire, John French was a protegé of the local lord, and he entered the Parliamentarian army of General Fairfax as a physician. His studies were at New Inn Hall in Oxford (BA 1637, MA 1640), and after the Civil War he was physician at the Savoy Hospital.

*This picture, from* Ashmole's Theatrum chemicum Britannicum, *shows a busy laboratory, with furnaces heating a variety of vessels, including distillation apparatus. By kind permission of The Bodleian Library, Oxford.*
RR. W. 29 (9) p.102.

French's publications were a vital contribution to the Paracelsian movement for alchemical **medicine** (*see* **Paracelsus**). He was involved with **Hartlib**'s circle and issued a translation of **H.C. Agrippa**'s *Book of Occult Philosophy*, dedicated to Hartlib's friend Robert Child: *Three Books of Occult Philosophy* (London, 1657).

**Publications:**
*A New Light of Alchymie, written by Michael Sendivogius . . . Also Nine Books of the Nature of Things, written by Paracelsus . . . Also a Chymicall Dictionary explaining . . . the writings of Paracelsus, and other obscure authors* (1650).

*The Art of Distillation, or a Treatise of the choicest Spagyricall Preparations performed by way of Distillation, being partly taken out of the most select Chymicall Authors of severall Languages, and partly out taken of the most select Chymicall Authors of severall Languages, and partly out of the Authors manuall Experience* (1651).

*The Art of Distillation . . . with the Description of the Chiefest Furnaces and vessels used by Ancient and Modern Chymists* (1653).

*See* Charles Webster, *The Great Instauration*.

# Furnaces

Furnaces belong to the age-old practice of metallurgy, and the smelting of **metals** and ores was carried on with the greatest skill in prehistoric times. The Bronze Age in fact gains its name from the subtle skill of those who manufactured alloys of copper and tin. Modern archaeologists have found it difficult to reproduce such alloys and the ancient furnaces which created very high temperatures, but Mircea Eliade argues that early **alchemy** derived directly from the ancient arts and mythology of the furnace. It seems that some alchemists were equipped with powerful furnaces, and we know much about medieval and Renaissance mining and metal-working from **Georg Agricola**.

Sir **Isaac Newton** provides this fascinating list of furnaces (taken from Newton's Manuscript 'Don', b.5, f.3, in the Bodleian Library, Oxford, and quoted by R. Westfall in *Never at Rest*, p.284):

1) Wind furnace: this is 'for calcination, fusion, cementation'; it 'blows it selfe by attracting ye aire through a narrow passage'.
2) Distilling furnace: 'for things yt require a strong fire for distillation'. This differs little from the wind furnace, 'only ye

glasse rests on a crosse barr of iron under which bar is a hole to put in the fire, which in ye wind furnace is put in at ye top'.

3) Reverberatory furnace: 'where ye flame only circulating under an arched roof acts upon ye body'.

4) Sand furnace: 'when ye vessel is set in sand or sifted ashes heated by a fire underneath'.

5) Newton also includes the *Balneum Mariae* (*see* **Baths**): 'when ye body is set to distill or digest in hot water'.

6) The *Balneum Roris* or *Vaporosum*: 'ye glasse hanging in ye steame of boiling water'.

7) **Athanor**, also *Piger henricus*, or *Furnace acediae*.

# G

## Geber

'Geber' is only a name, the Latin for Jabir. The **manuscripts** attributed to Geber during the Middle Ages were immensely influential in encouraging medieval practical **alchemy** (*alchimia practica*, as opposed to *alchimia speculativa*, philosophical or speculative alchemy), and medieval alchemists believed these texts were by the famous Islamic alchemical philosopher **Jabir ibn Hayyan**. Scholars now agree that this is not the case, hence Geber and Jabir are given separate entries here. In fact the texts are medieval and of quite uncertain authorship.

Of the texts, the *Summa perfectionis* (Summit of Perfection) was most famous, and *Investigatio perfectionis* (Investigation of Perfection), *Inventio veritatis* (Discovery of Truth), a book on **furnaces** and a testament were also believed to be Geber's. E.J. Holmyard does not consider them part of the Islamic Jabirian corpus, as 'we look in vain in them for any references to the characteristically Jabirian ideas of "balance" and alphabetic Numerology'. He cites practicality and concise expression as their main features.

The Geber manuscripts belong to the class of texts which present an exoteric tradition of practical experimental alchemy, which wrestles with the problem of the possibility of actual, physical **transmutation** of **metals**. There is an exposition of the classic doctrine of the generation of metals from **mercury** and **sulphur** (*see* **Mercury-Sulphur Theory of the Generation of Metals**). Exoteric alchemy propounds a theory of perfecting metals by use of the healing **elixir** or **stone**. There are white and red elixirs: white for silver and red for **gold**. The stone is identified with the elixir, which depends upon the universal principles of mercury and sulphur.

## Gnosticism

Gnosticism, the most debated of terms in comparative religious studies, is vital to understanding early **alchemy**, as Jung has extensively argued. The father of **Hellenistic alchemy, Zosimos of Panoplis**, belonged to the Poimandres gnostic sect, and although he was not a Christian, later alchemists like Stephanus of Alexandria were gnostic Christians. Although Christian bishops attacked gnostics as heretics, Gnosticism provided a path of access for Christian doctrines, especially the concepts of purification and **redemption** of the dark material world. The word *gnosis* means knowledge in the sense of realization of the divine.

Christian writers attacked the diversity of gnostic sects as a many-headed Hydra, but there are broad doctrinal outlines. Where Hindus and Buddhists call the world of birth, death and rebirth *samsara*, an ever-running stream of mortality, gnostics see the material world of arising and passing away as fundamentally evil. The divine spark of light in man is the result of the mythic Fall (*see* **Adam and Eve**). This dualistic vision of the cosmos is easily seen in the myth of Pistis Sophia (female goddess of wisdom), whose creative work places a curtain between the material world and the heavenly light. The curtain casts a shadow, which is the source of matter and of boundless chaos.

It is easy to detect in alchemy traces of the gnostic concepts of primal chaos, the *massa confusa*, for alchemical texts rarely obey Genesis. Zosimos of Panoplis expounds the gnostic doctrine of the inner spiritual man, the man of light, a doctrine central to the teaching of **Paracelsus** (*see also* **Microcosm-Macrocosm**). Man's body is a prison for the spark of immortality of **spirit** and light which is divine, representing the true inner man. Gnostic conceptions of man provide the basis for the microcosm-macrocosm analogy, which runs the length and breadth of the alchemical tradition, and the concept of redeeming or freeing the inner man of light is the key to the idea of redemption, which is the spiritual core of the alchemical message.

Gnostics also used that archetypal symbol of alchemy, the **uroboros**, (the **dragon** or serpent devouring its own tail). The creature has a black upper half in some pictures, representing the dark forces of matter which feed upon the light, lower half of the serpent. This provides a symbol for the eternal **unity** of all things, the cycle of birth and death from which the true adept seeks release and liberation.

The spirit of the **Hermetic texts** is also in close agreement with gnostic visions of the cosmos, of **Creation**, and of man as microcosm, who must find some way to rise from this dark realm of material chaos and indeed evil.

# Gold

**Geber** offers us this definition of gold:

> . . . a Metallick Body, Citrine, ponderous, mute, fulgid, equally digested in the Bowels of the Earth, and very long washed with Mineral Water; under the Hammer extensible, fusible and sustaining the trial of the Cupel . . . . According to this Definition, you may conclude, that nothing is true gold, unless it hath all the Causes and Differences of the Definition of Gold.

In the exoteric western tradition, the goal of the opus is to produce a **tincture, elixir** or **stone** which will accomplish **transmutation** of base **metals** into gold. The idea arose of using the precious metal itself as a ferment to aid transmutation, and gold was regarded as a **medicine** which by magical sympathy would prolong life and improve health.

Chinese alchemists also sought transmutation of base metals into gold, but their aim was generally to make use of gold as a medicinal elixir of youth and vitality (*see* **Chinese Alchemy**). Geber suggests such a tradition:

> Gold is of all metals the most precious, and it is the Tincture of Redness; because it tingeth and transforms every Body. It is calcined and dissolved without profit, and is a Medicine rejoycing, and conserving the Body in Youth.

The physical properties of gold naturally encouraged attribution of such magical properties as prolonging life and youth. *Aurum potabile*, or 'potable gold' was popular amongst Paracelsian alchemists (*see* **Francis Anthony**). Gold is also the most difficult metal to dissolve, being easily separated from impurities or from other metals by use of **acids** or solvents.

Jung, in *Psychology and Alchemy*, launches a strong attack on any notion of **alchemy** as a quest for physical gold, and he makes much of the distinction between physical and the philosophical gold: alchemists, he believes, are always using riddles to conceal their true work, the opus of transformation, from the vulgar gold-seekers who are probably represented by Chaucer's Canone and by Ben Jonson's alchemists. The true adept seeks no 'ordinary gold (*aurum vulgi*) – it is the philosophical gold or even the marvellous stone, the *lapis invisibilitatis* (the Stone of Invisibility), or the *lapis aethereus* (the Ethereal Stone), or finally the 'unimaginable hermaphroditic Rebis' which he seeks. The true adept, in Jung's view, in the end eschews all chemical recipes.

Many texts undoubtedly do nourish a very literal view of transmutation, but it is easy to show that in a vast number of texts symbolism and myth are the life-blood of alchemical literature, with the allegories of birth, death, resurrection and **redemption** as universal themes.

The **myth** of gold is the myth of **Sol and Luna**, of the sun and moon, for the sun is the symbol of the radiant splendour of gold, the moon of the dimmer, reflective quality of silver.

Georg Heym delivers this lucid account of the myth of 'King Gold':

> The alchemical myth of King Gold – the sun – who must be killed and buried so that he can awaken to a new life and attain his fulfilment by transcending the seven 'rulers' (planets), is the alchemical interpretation of the ancient symbolical universe of astrology. The latter, however, is the cosmic picture of an inner system of opposites. The sun is the divine spark, that seemingly dies when the sun enters the house of Saturn, but is reborn and ascends the seven phases of consciousness to become the 'red lion', the Great Elixir that can transform the world.
>
> Quoted from Georg Heym's review of T. Burckhardt, *Alchemy*, in *Ambix*,
> October 1960

# Grail, The Holy

The connection of the Grail legends with **alchemy** is not at first apparent. Medieval romances show a divergence of opinions on what the Grail really is. In general it is supposed to be the chalice which received the blood of Christ as he was taken down from the Cross, and it thus has mystical and magical significance beyond compare. It was said to have been brought by Joseph of Arimathea to Glastonbury, and hence a whole cycle of Arthurian legends surrounds the mystic **vessel**. However, in the poems of Wolfram von Eschenbach, it becomes clear that the Grail is a **stone**, perhaps like the Philosophers' Stone:

> They [the Arthurian knights] take their life from a Stone
> Which is most pure
> Perhaps you do not recognize it:
> It is called the *Lapsit exillis*.

This is often compared to the *Lapis exilis*, referred to in **Arnald of Villanova**'s *Rosarium*: the Philosophers' Stone is that 'which the builders rejected, and which has become the corner stone' – hence the concept of the alchemical stone as 'exiled'.

The Grail, like the stone or mystic **elixir** of alchemy, is a mystery which passeth all understanding, having associations with the garden of perfection and purity (*see* **Adam and Eve** for the significance of the Paradise Garden in alchemy). It is the transforming vessel of the soul. *Lapsit exillis* may in fact mean *lapis elixir.*

It is also worth noting that a whole cycle of alchemical legends concerns the sickness and death of the alchemical **King** (*see also* **Sol and Luna**). The Grail legend centres upon the sickness of the ailing Fisher King who must be redeemed by a knight who asks the right question (*see* **Redemption**). The themes of medieval alchemy find their echoes in the **myth**, legend, allegory and religious doctrine of the age, and it is a mistake to seek to isolate alchemy from its cultural context.

*See* Emma Jung, *The Grail Legend*, 1971 edition, p.148-9.

# Harmony and Symmetry in Hermetic Philosophy

> We must understand that the Order and Symmetry of the universe is so settled by the laws of Creation, that the lowest things should be immediately subservient to the Middle, the Middle to those above; and these to the Supreme Rulers becke.

This is **Elias Ashmole**'s vision of the cosmic harmony and symmetry, which he presents in the forceful, highly original Preface composed for his *Theatrum chemicum Britannicum*, which contains his compilation of alchemical poetry. (For his views on the philosophical *Lapis*, see Philosophers' **Stone**.) This is the classic philosophy of **Agrippa** and the natural Magicians (*see* **Magic**), who divide the cosmos into terrestrial, celestial and supercelestial. It is fascinating to find such a cogent statement of faith in the ancient Hermetic philosophy from a seventeenth-century scholar who became a founding member of the Royal Society. An exact contemporary of the alchemical **Newton**, Ashmole believed implicitly in astral mysticism and practised divinatory **astrology**. His vision is presented more clearly than is usually found in classic texts.

Ashmole subscribes to the perennial alchemical cosmology of *The Emerald Tablet*, holding that 'what is above is the same as that which is belowe':

> These Superiours and Inferiours have an Analogicall likenesse, and by a secret Bond have likewise a fast coherence between themselves through insensible Mediums, freely combining in Obedience to the same supreme Ruler.

He quotes *The Emerald Tablet*, ascribing it to **Hermes**: '*Quod est superius, est sicut id quod est inferius*' ('That which is above is just like that which is below'):

> And upon this ground Wise men conceive it no way Irrationall that it should be possible for us to ascend by the same degrees through each

world, to the Originall world itself, the Maker of all things and first Cause. But how to conjoine the Inferiours with the vertue of the Superiours (which is marrying Elmes and Vines) or how to call out of the hidden places into open light, the dispersed and seminated Vertue (i.e. *Virtutes in centro centrilatentes* [virtues lying hidden in the centre of the centre]) is, the work of Magi, or Hermetick Philosophers onely.

Thus Ashmole is suggesting that the wise man, the true philosopher, is something other than the 'vulgar chymist', the village 'puffer'. The true alchemist must 'invite and allure the propitious Spirit to descend from Heaven and to unite with that which is Internall'. This **unity** creates a *vinculum*, a bond or chain which has the power to 'hold and fix the Celestiall Influences, from recoyling back into their united Centres'.

Ashmole believed implicitly in the paraphernalia of **magic**, the magic sigills or seals, the horary and natal astrology, the spiritualist or **angel magic** associated with **John Dee**. Like so many of his contemporaries in an age of scientific revolution, he was a profound exponent of the philosophy of the *prisci theologi*, and he traces the art of **medicine**, as a Hermetic art, back to Solomon and Moses.

# Hartlib, Samuel

One of the key figures in the scientific revolution which led to the founding of the Royal Society, Hartlib came from Elbing to study at Cambridge from 1625 to 1626. This was the time when **Francis Bacon** was producing his plan for a 'Great Instauration' of science in England. A refugee from the devastation of the Thirty Years War, Hartlib seems to have entered Emmanuel College, Cambridge, whence he embarked upon a program of educational reform which involved him with a whole circle of scientists. The Hartlib circle included men like **Boyle** and **Digby**, who worked on the borderline of **alchemy** and chemistry. He planned an 'Office of Public Address' to deal with correspondence and information, and this is now regarded as a precursor for the Royal Society. He was a catalyst for the influence of German mysticism, as **Boehme** and the **Rosicrucians** became known in England, and was responsible for inviting Jan Comenius to England.

Hartlib was deeply interested in every aspect of science, but especially in chemistry. His most popular work was in husbandry. He kept a diary, called *Ephemerides*, from 1634 to his death in 1660, and this is a rich source for studying the alchemical character of much

seventeenth-century chemistry. Betty Jo Dobbs draws attention to a collection of Hartlib's letters which concern experiments, **aurum potabile** ('potable gold'), and the mystic **alkahest** or universal solvent, and give an account of Digby's laboratory in Gresham College.
The following publication gives insight into Hartlibian alchemy:

*Chymical, Medicinal and Chyrurgical Addresses: Made to Samuel Hartlib, Esquire, viz:*
*1) Whether the Vrim and Thummin were given in the mount, or perfected by Art.*
*2) Sir George Ripley's Epistle to King Edward unfolded.*
*3) Gabriel Plat's Caveat for Alchymists.*
*4) A conference concerning the Philosophers Stone.*
*5) An Invitation for a free and generous Communication for Secrets and Receits in Physick.*
*6) Whether or no each Several Disease hath a Particular Remedy? and other tracts* (London, 1655).

*See* Betty Jo Dobbs, *Foundations*; Charles Webster, *The Great Instauration*; *also* **Philalethes**; **Thomas Vaughan**.

# Hellenistic Alchemy

The Hellenistic tradition of **alchemy** is probably the least accessible of all. Alchemy arose, apparently, in Hellenistic Egypt, perhaps around the time of Alexander the Great, and this opens the question of whether eastern influences inspired it. The Babylonians may have had a tradition of metallurgical initiation, if not alchemy, and a eighth-century BC Assyrian tablet has instructions for purification rites for building and using a **furnace**. An obscure reference to embryos may indicate a theory of organic, embryonic growth in the development of minerals and **metals**, while a Chinese story of the first century BC suggests that alchemy was used to produce **gold**, which was then used for drinking **vessels**, and to prolong life (*see* **Elixirs**).
Hellenistic alchemy represents a confusion between the mystical, religious aspect of the quests and the exoteric aim of **transmutation** of base metals. Whereas the Chinese and Indian alchemical traditions both stress the aim of health and longevity through using elixirs, Hellenistic alchemy shows a fascination with tingeing and dyeing metals. The Emperor Diocletian issued a decree (*c.*290 AD) condemning *chemeia* as a gold-forging art, and commanding the

destruction of books concerning it.

Early alchemical texts in Greek are attributed to Democritos, Isis, Iamblichus, Moses, **Ostanes, Maria Prophetissa**, Kleopatra, Agathodaimon, **Hermes** and Komarios. As with magical and alchemical works of the Middle Ages, there is a striving to invent for alchemy a genealogy of biblical antiquity.

The work called *Phusika kai mustika* (On natural and initiatory things) in Greek was attributed to Demosthenes, who is referred to by later writers as 'the philosopher', but modern critics attribute the book to **Bolos of Mendes**, who was author of a work on dyeing (*baphika*). *Phusika* refers to the things of **nature**, and *mustika* means not so much 'mystical things', as 'initiatory things'. This fascinating book describes how the master magus dies before communicating the secrets of 'bringing the natures into harmony', and his disciples seek to contact him through necromancy. During a feast in the temple, one of the columns of the temple bursts open to reveal not a secret text of alchemy, but a simple motto: 'Nature rejoices in nature, nature conquers nature, nature masters nature.' This reinforces the point that alchemy is already a philosophy of nature. It is also initiatory, and strongly magical.

Surviving books of recipes reveal the exoteric aspect of alchemy as an experimental tradition to do with paints, dyes and **tinctures** of metals and with disguising the true nature of metals and creating fake gems (*see* **Manuscripts**).

**Zosimos of Panoplis** is the earliest alchemist whose writings betray a consistent account both of mystical and transmutatory aspects of the opus. Living in Alexandria in the late third century AD, he compiled an encyclopaedia of alchemy entitled *Cheirokmeta*, in which he discusses the root of the word *chemeia*, which he uses to denote alchemy. Surviving fragments of the work indicate the link with esoteric Egyptian priestly tradition of mystical metallurgy. Maria Prophetissa is quoted with humility by Zosimos for her expertise in designing equipment, notably the *tribikos* (*see* **Alembic**; **Apparatus**; **Baths**). He also quotes Agathodaimon and **Democritus**.

There is undoubtedly the closest symbiosis between early alchemy and mystical *gnosis* and it is certain that Zosimos belonged to the Poimandres sect of **Gnosticism**. Stephanus of Alexandria and later alchemists of Hellenistic times are now regarded as being gnostics rather than showing any interest in chemistry.

Jung quotes a fascinating passage from a *Dialogue of Kleopatra and the Philosophers*, which speaks of an elixir or **medicine** of life which descends to revive the corpses in hell. There is also a concept of mystical ascent and descent in this text. Zosimos' visions show that there is a descent of 15 steps into darkness, and an ascent of 15 steps to the light, and an altar is the scene of his bizarre vision of the torture and rending of an unfortunate priest.

There can be no doubt that the concept of **colour stages** in the opus is basic to Greek alchemy, this theory being elaborated first by **Islamic alchemy**, then by medieval Christian alchemy. There is also the theory that the colour of the metal is in fact a **spirit** of the metal, independent of its inert material constitution.

A.J. Hopkins makes the colour sequence the key to Greek alchemy, and he cites Zosimos' tribute to Maria Prophetissa as originator of the colours (*see* **Processes; Stages**). He argues that the 'kerotakis method' involves the following sequence:

1) *Melanosis* (= blackening = *nigredo*): this stage involves production of a black metal alloy, the *tetrasomia*.
2) *Leukosis* (= *albedo* = whitening): next, by ablution and purification (*see* **Baths**), this black alloy is whitened, like silver.
3) *Xanthosis* (= yellowing): the cleansed white metal is then tinged or coloured to yellow or gold.
4) *Iosis* (= purple, turning purple): this stage is difficult to define. It seems to correspond to the *rubedo* in Latin alchemy. *Ios* has a reproductive power, like the **Stone** or elixir, which is like a ferment, achieving the projection and multiplying of gold-making elixir.

*See* F. Sherwood Taylor, 'The Origins of Greek Alchemy', *Ambix*, May 1937; J. Lindsay, *The Origins of Alchemy in Greco-Roman Egypt*; A.J. Hopkins, 'A Study of the Kerotakis Process as given by Zosimos and Later Alchemical Writers', *Isis*, November 1938.

# Helmont, Joan Battista van
## 1579–1644

Born in Brussels on 12 January 1579, van Helmont belongs to that vital class of figures who still were devoted to the tradition of **alchemy** and natural **magic**, yet who forged a scientific revolution at the turn of the sixteenth to the seventeenth century. Apart from **Paracelsus**, van Helmont is probably the most important scientific figure in this book (not forgetting **Newton**).

Completely disillusioned by academic study with its Aristotelian obsession, during his studies at Louvain University he turned to herbal and medical studies, but still found no satisfaction. He gained his medical degree in 1599, but was only convinced of the inefficacy of contemporary methods. He then toured Europe, including London, and worked in Amsterdam during a plague epidemic (1605).

Somewhat in the manner of **Francis Bacon**, van Helmont used his private means to retire into a scientific retreat. He felt he had a religious call to the Hermetic arts of the chemist, to 'pyrotechnia'. Tragedy struck his private researches, however, for he became embroiled in a dispute over a tract published in Paris without his permission, and he was persecuted and kept under house arrest by the Jesuits, being nearly condemned for heresy. The initial cause of his troubles was a Paracelsian work *The Magnetic Cure of Wounds* (1621), concerning the theory of the magical cure of wounds by anointing the offending weapon.

Van Helmont was a powerfully independent thinker who rejected ancient notions of the four **elements**, and made innovative discoveries in chemistry, using the medieval and Paracelsian tradition of spagyric alchemy, or 'pyrotechny', the art of the **furnace**. To do justice to the rich fund of observation and speculation to be found in his work goes beyond the scope of this book: Walter Pagel provides a masterly study in his *Joan Battista van Helmont*.

From **Paracelsus**, van Helmont evolved his own idea of an 'Archeus', or 'Master-Workman', responsible for giving life and form to the human body. This he defines as a kind of vital air, rather like the ancient Stoic doctrine of the **spirit**-*pneuma* in the body. This theory links with his concern with gases, which he discovered, and with a new theory of the elements. He regarded water as the vital element in life and growth: his experiment with growing a **tree** suggested to him that the vital ingredient in vegetative growth was precisely water, and this seemed eminently consistent with the book of Genesis (*see* **Creation**). (Note how these thinkers always found their scientific speculation upon Genesis: such diverse men as **Fludd**, Newton, **Thomas Vaughan** or **John Dee** all make clear that their real concern is with the secrets of Creation, with singing a hymn of praise to the Creator.)

**Boyle** and van Helmont may be considered the founders of modern chemistry, both strongly influenced by the powerful Paracelsian and **Rosicrucian** movements of their time.

Van Helmont's published work wrought a revolution in attitudes to **medicine**, but was only issued after his death, edited by his son. His collected medical writings were published as the *Ortus medicinae*, or the 'Dawn of Medicine' (Amsterdam, 1648 and 1659). The important English translation was by John Chandler, entitled *Oriatrike* (London, 1662).

# Helvetius

**Real name: Johann Friedrich Schweitzer (= Swiss, *Helvetius*); Born Kothen, Anhalt, in 1625, died The Hague, 1709**

This man belongs to the class of legends of actual **transmutation**, coming at the close of the alchemical tradition. He became physician to the Prince of Orange and was distinguished as a medical man. In 1667 he published a circumstantial account of transmutation. He recounts that on 27 December 1666 he was visited by a rustic stranger at his residence in The Hague. He seemed to be from the north of Scotland and expressed his concern that Helvetius had published an attack upon **Kennelm Digby**'s famous 'Powder of Sympathy'. The Scot was a brass-founder by trade, and asked the Swiss physician if he believed in the panacea (or **elixir**) to cure all sickness, and whether he would recognize the Philosophers' **Stone** if he met it. Helvetius admitted to having read **Paracelsus** and **van Helmont** on the subject, whereupon the alchemist produced three 'ponderous lumps of stone' from a neat ivory box. Eventually Helvetius obtained enough of the stone to perform a transmutatory experiment, and he convinced himself that the 'medicine' had actually transformed lead into **gold**: 'The melted lead after projection, showed on the fire the rarest and most beautiful colours imaginable, settling in green, and when poured forth into an ingot, it had the lively fresh colour of blood.' This is an interesting example of alchemical **colours** appearing. When cooled, there appeared aurified lead, which a goldsmith certified as pure gold.

See A.E. Waite, *Lives of the Alchemystical Philosophers*.

# Herbs and Herbals

**Alchemy** is normally associated with **metals** and minerals, but there were three types of **Stone** of the Philosophers – animal, vegetable and mineral – and there can be no doubt that herbal lore was part of alchemy. All three stones are described by **Elias Ashmole** and he explains the 'Vegetable Stone' as helping to cultivate **trees** and herbs. He speaks of how the Glastonbury Thorn, 'so greatly famed for shooting forth leaves and Flowers at Christmas' might be the product of the search for the 'Vegetable Stone'. He adds, 'If the lower part be expos'd abroad in a dark Night, Birds will repair to (and circulate about) it, as a Fly round a Candle, and submit themselves to the Captivity of the Hand' (cited in John Read's *Prelude to Chemistry*, p.125).

Ashmole also preserves a beautiful poem about a herb of great importance to alchemists:

Her ys an Erbe men calls Lunayrie,
I-blesset mowte hys maker bee.
Asterion he ys I-callet alle so,
And other namys many and mo;
He is an Erbe of grete myght,
Of Sol the Sunn he taketh hys lyght . . .

The symbolism of **Sol and Luna** extends throughout **nature**, for the heavens imprint their influence in the animal, vegetable and mineral worlds. The marvellous herb Lunary is a panacea, an **elixir**:

The Rote is black, the Stalke is red;
The wyche schall ther never be dede . . .
Hys Flower shynith, fayre and cler,
In alle the Worlde thaye have non pere . . .
With many a vertu both fayre and cler,
As ther ben dayes in alle the yere,
Fro fallyng Ewel and alle Sekeneys,
From Sorowe he brengyth man to Bles.

The 'fallyng Ewel' is the falling sickness, or epilepsy. Gerard's Elizabethan herbal credits the *Liunaria* or Moone wort with powers to heal wounds, and he refers to the superstitions of witches and alchemists. John Read also cites a fascinating mention in *Bloomefields Blossoms*: 'The Moone that is called the lesser Lunary, Wife unto Phoebus, shining by night, To others gives her Garments through her herb Lunary.'

Concepts of the organic growth of metals and minerals are vital to alchemy (*see also* **Tree**). S. Mahdihassan argues that the whole idea of the alchemical **hermaphrodite** arises from the **creation** of a 'herbo-metallic complex'. Metals were often calcined with herbs and great magical significance was attached to the idea of fusing or uniting metallic and herbal 'souls'.

The **medicine** of medieval and Renaissance times was dependent upon herbal remedies, derived via the tradition of Dioscorides. Medieval herbals are full of magical lore, with pictures of the *Mandragora* and other mythic plants.

# Hermaphrodite
Also called Androgyny, composed of Greek words for man and woman, and *Rebis* from Latin meaning 'double thing'

This is one of the most famous images in **alchemy**, its meaning inscrutable. It belongs to the mythology of *conjunctio*, the mystical marriage of alchemical **sulphur** and **mercury**. The name comes from the supposed birth of Hermaphrodite to **Hermes** and Aphrodite. Psychologically, the symbol is extremely powerful, representing the undifferentiated unconscious which bears the potential for masculine as well as feminine development.

Most primitive mythology sees the world as animated by opposing sexual principles. **Chinese alchemy** and natural philosophy use the yin and yang principles, and Indian philosophers use the god and goddess Shiva and Shakti to symbolism cosmic sexual duality. Medieval alchemists probably had no idea of the primitive roots of this sexual chemistry, but this cycle of symbols is the key to understanding alchemy.

The gnostic philosophers as well as the **Hermetic texts** are the source for the **myth** of the hermaphrodite: in the Hermetic *Poimandres* text, the **Creation** is brought about by a hermaphroditic mind (Greek *Nous*). **Adam** was hermaphroditic, in that Eve was created from his body, and alchemists like the gnostic **Zosimos** used the myth of the *anthropos*, the primal man of light. There seems little doubt that the state of gnostic enlightenment or liberation from the prison of materiality involves discovery of a state of sexual union (*see* **Gnosticism**).

The central symbol of alchemy is the **uroboros**, the **dragon** or cosmic serpent, which is said to symbolize the **unity** of all things, and it is equated with mercury as cosmic emblem of the tradition. The mercurial serpent represents a whole series of opposites, and is able to impregnate itself. Mercurius is always portrayed in alchemical illustrations associated with serpents, and with a dual nature, for he is a winged, volatile figure, but may also be fixed: the hermaphrodite is a mercurial figure, shown with wings (*see* **Beasts and Birds**). One impressive manuscript illustration shows the hermaphroditic couple held by the talons of a huge black eagle, representing the mercurial **Prime Matter**. At their feet is a heap of dead eagles. The myth behind this is that of the birth of the hermaphroditic union from the stage of death and decay or putrefaction of the Prime Matter. The birth of the hermaphrodite generally follows the *conjunctio*, the sexual union of **Sol and Luna**, and represents the culmination of the work, the birth of the mystic Philosopers' **Stone**, the *Lapis Philosophorum*.

The way in which this complex sequence of myth themes was used by alchemists in explaining the sequence of the opus is most clearly evident in the famous series of illustrations published in the printed edition of the *Rosarium* (The Rose Garden of the Philosophers). The woodcuts show the figures of Sol and Luna, sun and moon, as crowned **King and Queen**, through successive stages of the *conjunctio*. The couple are shown in the alchemical **bath** as practically merged together. The final illustration shows the triumphant figure of the hermaphrodite, who is clearly meant to represent the redeeming Philosophers' Stone which purges all corruption and impurity. The text gives this verse on 'her' birth:

> Here is born the noble and rich empress,
> Whom masters of the art name as their daughter.
> She multiplies herself, giving birth to numberless children
> They are quite pure and without taint.

Jung explains the psychological meaning of this set in his *Psychology of the Transference*: 'The final production of the *lapis* in the form of the crowned hermaphrodite is called the *aenigma regis*.' This emblem is one of the best examples of symbols which are profoundly psychic: Jung says this is the image of the self, which transcends ego-consciousness. It is an image of chemical union and power of mastery of the art as well as an emanation from the psyche.

Jung also points out that the 'empress' comes tenth in the series of *Rosarium* images, and ten is the perfect Pythagorean number (*see* **Numerology**). Thus we see the integrated structure of alchemical number mysticism and psychic symbolism, evoking the deeper mysteries and confusions of the collective unconscious on its progress towards realization of the inner unity in man's conflict-ridden nature.

See C.G. Jung, *The Psychology of the Transference*; also his *Mysterium Conjunctionis*, Vol.14.

# Hermes Trismegistus

Hermes is the Greek messenger of the gods, in Latin Mercurius. Hermes the Thrice Great god was regarded as a historical founder of **alchemy** and Hellenistic magical astral mysticism. Many vital texts are credited to him: alchemists believed their **Emerald Tablet** (*Tabula smaragdina*) had been found in his tomb, and the *Golden Tractate* was universally attributed to him.

The Islamic alchemists had many texts ascribed to Hermes, but the bulky Hellenistic Hermetic corpus did not reach the West until the Renaissance. Medieval Latin versions of the *Asclepius* circulated widely, but only during the late fifteenth century did the full extent of

magical writings appear in Latin, translated by Marsilio Ficino on the urgent commission of Cosimo Medici. Ficino is the founder of Renaissance **Neoplatonism** and Platonist theology.
*See also* **Hermetic Texts**.

# Hermetic Texts

**Alchemy** is characterized as the Hermetic tradition, its mythic patron being Thrice Great Hermes (*Hermes Trismegistus*). Hermes is the Greek name for **Mercury**, the messenger of the gods, and the **metal** and **spirit** mercury is vital to alchemy. Hermes Trismegistus was believed to have composed a vast volume of writings in the time of Moses, and these texts are extant in Greek, apparently containing a synthesis of Hellenistic magical philosophy from various sources, including Greek and Egyptian doctrines. He was often identified as Thoth Hermes, Thoth being the ancient Egyptian scribe of the gods. Thoth was associated with the moon, with the realm of the dead, and with time. During Hellenistic times a corpus of works in Greek was attributed to Hermes, including magical as well as alchemical and philosophical works. Alchemy arose in relation to **magic** as well as to the religious Hermetic philosophy, concerned with the salvation of man from the mortal and corrupt world of the **elements**.

During the Renaissance the Hermetic texts were vastly influential: in 1471 Marsilio Ficino published a Latin translation, for his patron Cosimo dei Medici. These texts were the ones concerned with Egyptian theology and philosophy, and Ficino compares them favourably with Christian doctrines. Texts ascribed to Hermes concerning magic, **astrology** and alchemy were known to the Arabs, and Islamic sources brought them to medieval Europe: *The Emerald Tablet* was ascribed to Hermes, and was supposed to have been discovered in his tomb. The theological texts are written in the form of revelations, some of them decidedly gnostic in character (*see* **Gnosticism**).

Notable amongst these is the *Poimandres*, a mystical text concerning the divine, transcendent mind (Greek *nous*). Here Poimander as divine Mind speaks to Hermes, who sees a vision of infinite light. Then a serpentine darkness appears within the light, and a luminous word, a divine *logos*, appears from the light as the Son of God. As the vision unfolds, the whole process of **Creation** is revealed to Hermes, including the creation of man, who partakes of the divine nature. Enshrined in these texts is the doctrine of enlightenment or liberation, to be achieved only by passing through the celestial spheres, which are the prison confining man's immortal spirit.

Another famous text, vital to Renaissance *magia naturalis*, was the *Asclepius*, which contains the description of man as *magnum miraculum*, as a being passing into the godlike nature. The text also explains the classic Hermetic doctrine of the creation of everything from the divine **Unity**, the One: divine influence flows from the stars and planets into the elemental world. There is a hierarchy of being and spiritual intelligences (*see* **Astrology**, and **Angel Magic**), and man is seen as dual in nature, with body and spirit: alchemists were obsessed with this duality, as passing throughout **nature**.

The *Asclepius* refers also to the human capacity to 'make gods', i.e. to construct statues imbued with spirit and life, an ancient Egyptian art. Such ideas inspired the magical philosophy of the Renaissance, which was closely involved with alchemy and science. The Hermetic philosopher and magus believed that through penetrating the secrets of nature, he could achieve great things in the world, transforming and using natural forces.

The cosmology and astrology of the Hermetic texts is highly intricate, but during the seventeenth century, Isaac Casaubon shocked Hermeticists by revealing that this system was not ancient, of Mosaic antiquity. Rather it is the Hellenistic doctrine of the cosmos, inhabited by astral beings and gods.

Frances Yates traces the Hermetic tradition of the Renaissance as including many of the personalities in this *Dictionary*: Ficino and della Mirandola founded the tradition, forging strong links with Platonism and with the **Cabala**, and **H.C. Agrippa** produced a synthesis of Renaissance natural magic which profoundly influenced **John Dee**, as well as the **Rosicrucian** alchemists **Robert Fludd** and **Thomas Vaughan**. **Giordano Bruno**, a leading apostle and preacher of religious Hermeticism, was not an alchemist, but had a powerful impact on the mystical outlook of his age: he was burnt as a heretic in 1600 as a result of his Copernican views and for his advocacy of a return to the religion of the ancient Egyptians, as he interpreted that religion from his Hermetic studies.

The Renaissance tradition largely died out with the close of the seventeenth century, when alchemy, astrology and natural magic were largely eclipsed by the philosophical movement of the Enlightenment. Only in our own century has study of this difficult subject been revived, much enriched by the discovery of Hermetic texts in the Nag Hammadi library of gnostic works.

*See* F.A. Yates, *Giordano Bruno and the Hermetic Tradition*.

# I

# Indian Alchemy

There is no study of Indian alchemy comparable with Joseph Needham's vast work on Chinese chemistry and alchemical yoga, but there are many alchemical texts from India, and the quest for alchemical **elixirs** still goes on there. Mircea Eliade in his book *The Forge and the Crucible* sketches yogic connections, and Dr S. Mahdihassan, an Indian scholar, in articles in *Ambix* and *Janus* argues for a link between elixir **alchemy** and the ancient Vedic worship of *soma*, the *amrita* of the gods. He suggests oriental sources as the origin of western alchemy, and much symbolism in western tradition has very ancient roots: the philosophical cosmic **egg** is familiar in the *Rig-Veda*, for example, and the Hindu Vedic philosophy emphasizes cosmic **harmony**, which is all-pervasive in the **Cabala** and in Renaissance **Neoplatonism**.

Indian alchemy is best known in its Tantric form, contemporary with the burgeoning of **Islamic alchemy**. It is called *Rasayana: rasa* = juice, or **mercury**; note that Chinese *chin-je* = **gold**-making juice, or gold elixir. Mercury seems to have been vital in the search for Tantric liberation. Tantric texts include dialogues between Shiva and Shakti, who are sometimes made parallel to the yin-yang polarity of the Chinese, or to the **mercury-sulphur** opposites of western alchemy. Shiva is god of **Creation** and destruction, interpreted as intellect, **spirit**, knower, Atman; Shakti is the whole mind-body continuum, Maya, mistress of illusion and change. Shakti is the play of the world, the life-death cycle; Shiva remains constant. The Indians called mercury 'the semen of Shiva', and semen acquires strong magical and mystical significance in yoga, both in its Indian and Chinese forms. Shiva is Lord of Transformation, and an offering of a phallus shaped from mercury was made to the god. Hindu Tantric myth is constantly concerned with **nature** as creator and destroyer, and Shakti appears both as kindly Mother Nature, and as destructive Kali, goddess of death. Note that the earliest Hellenistic alchemists were philosophers of nature, their motto being 'Nature rejoices in nature, nature conquers nature, nature dominates nature.' In the West there is this same ambivalence in the quest involving death and suffering that leads to resurrection and **redemption** or liberation. Western alchemy is much concerned with the 'seeds of the metals', and with the germination and fermentation of the elixir of **metals**, and throughout the tradition there is much vegetative metaphor.

Alchemical texts have been attributed to 'Nagarjuna', identified with the great Buddhist Madhyamaka philosopher of that name who was often credited with astonishing longevity and with having performed alchemical feats to help struggling Buddhist communities. The best-known of these texts is the *Rasaratnakara*, a compilation which refers to 'killing Mercury' and to the mercury-phallus offering to Shiva. These texts are now thought to be the work of a later Nagarjuna, but alchemy seems to have spread throughout the East at the time of the conversion of South-east Asia to Buddhism: it seems that Tibetan alchemy is more Indian than Chinese. Recent research shows that alchemy spread over vast areas, through Persia and Islam, from India through Tibet, then into Burma, Korea and Japan.

It was once argued that Indian alchemy arose through Islamic influence, but Indian elixir traditions extend back over millennia. Professor Needham draws attention to substantial Tamil literature on alchemy and magic, which he considers independent of Sanskrit influence, though subject to influence from Chinese trade. Dr Mahdihassan argues that the concept of a metallic elixir or **Stone** of the Philosophers arises through the introduction of a herbal ferment into metallic processes. Thus an elixir acquires vegetable as well as mineral soul, a living, growing magical spirit as well as inert, lifeless body or matter. The union of vegetable ferment and metal or mineral solution is used by Dr Mahdihassan to explain the **hermaphrodite** figure. Western alchemists are always obsessed with the death of the body, and the reuniting of body and soul or spirit.

Mircea Eliade establishes the yoga-alchemy connection, reinforcing Professor Needham's work on the Chinese yogic *Nei Tan* tradition of preparing elixirs of life by alchemical means. He argues that the alchemical goal of **transmutation** is amongst the *siddhas*, or magical accomplishments which come with advanced yogic or Tantric practices. Hatha yoga and Tantra operate with the concept of the **astral body**, and this alchemy is as much transmutation of man, the **microcosm**, as it is chemical **magic**. Eliade finds the death-resurrection motif in Tantra and Indian alchemy – 'killing Mercury'. There is also the dualism of body and soul (*purusha* = spirit; *prakrti* = substance, body, nature), corresponding to the dualism of Shiva-Shakti, who represent an archetype of the *conjunctio* motif, the mystic marriage so vital to western adepts. Shakti is Maya, ruling the bodily *chakras*, the yogic centres of psychic energy and dynamism (*see also* **Spirit**).

Indian alchemy is still alive and kicking, cognate with the yoga traditions which have survived in unbroken tradition. In China and India, as in most of Asia, alchemy is the quest for longevity, for elixirs of vitality, with gold being the symbol or the magical ingredient of long life, operating in **medicines** by sympathetic magic. Actual transmutation of metals figures in the Tantras, but is of less importance than elixirs. This is in contrast with the West, where the elixir tradition tends to be suppressed, although the transmutation is carried out by an elixir, a ferment or a 'medicine of metals', and this is often, in passing, credited with miraculous healing powers. Longevity was less interesting to the West (but *see* **Roger Bacon**), and the eastern spiritual practices of breath control, profound trances and meditation *samadhi* never caught on, for spiritual alchemy clung to the Christian doctrine of **redemption** through the *Lapis-Christus* parallel (*see* **Stone**). However, the all-pervading doctrine of the microcosm, the spiritual man, is analogous to the eastern yogic concept of the diamond body, or astral man. **Paracelsus** certainly believed in an astral body.

A review by H.J. Sheppard, in *Ambix*, of Arturo Schwarz's *Introduzione dell'alchimia Indiana* (Introduction to Indian Alchemy) (Latera and Figli, 1984) neatly summarizes Hindu alchemy:

> Like China and Europe, Indian alchemy shows dual aspects: a spiritual side involving knowledge of the self, and a practical one in which metals are subjected to operations corresponding to those on a psychic level. For the Hindu the world is created and governed by two cosmic principles – Siva and Shakti, the former being masculine and representing passivity and immobility, the latter feminine and therefore directly responsible for creation and life at every level.

Dr Sheppard emphasizes the liberation or redemption motif: Buddhist philosophy offers a path to liberation from the ever-turning cycle of *samsara*, the ever-running stream of life, and Hinduism also seeks freedom from cyclical time. The Tantric path involves union or *conjunctio* of the twin cosmic principles Shiva and Shakti. Sexual union (*marthuna*) is vital in Tantra, as it is in western 'Christian' texts with their vivid diagrams of coition. Mystical diagrams and **mandalas** are highly complex in Tantric yoga, usually less so in the West. Through the possession of mercury the yogi-alchemist purifies himself supernaturally and achieves a celestial body which serves to support him in attaining the state of deliverance.

*See* Mircea Eliade, *The Forge and the Crucible*, Chapter 12 on Indian alchemy; Professor Joseph Needham, *Science and Civilization in China*, Vol. 5, Part 5, for a comparison of Chinese and Indian traditions; Dr Mahdihassan's articles in *Janus* and *Ambix*, especially 'Dualistic Symbolism in a Medieval Work on Pharmacy', *Janus*, 1964.

# Iosis in Hellenistic Alchemy

A. J. Hopkins argues that **Hellenistic alchemy** is based on the 'Kerotakis method', involving the four **colours**, or **stages** of the opus:

1) *Melanosis*: the production of the black metals alloy, the Tetrasomy.
2) *Leukosis* (whitening): transforming the black to white or a silvery colour.
3) *Xanthosis* (yellowing): the silver changing to yellow or 'gold'.
4) *Iosis* (gold turning to violet). The Ios has reproductive power.

In Egypt the names of the **metals** were interchangeable with the colours: thus yellow means **gold**; white, silver; copper, red. The surface of copper touched by **mercury** gives a superficial silver **tincture**. In Greek alchemy, Hopkins argues that the colour of the metal is its **spirit**, being independent of its inactive body. The individuality and reactive force of the metal arises from the spirit.

In the *iosis*, this spiritual colour becomes so concentrated that it is nearly free from the retarding influence of the body. Here occurs, for the first time in the history of alchemy, the vision of a spirit or sperm of such reproductive power that it could transmute lower metals into higher!

Berthelot: 'In other words, if you possess a material in which the colour quality resides in the manner of a [concentrated dye-extract] you have the Philosophers' Stone (= *ios*).' The *ios* therefore is the tincture of gold, which produces pure gold.

*See* A.J. Hopkins, 'A Study of the Kerotakis Process as given by Zosimos and Later Alchemical Writers', in *Isis*, 1938.

# Islamic Alchemy

The introduction of Islamic philosophy and science into the world of Christendom during the twelfth and thirteenth centuries transformed medieval culture, and **alchemy** formed a vital part of the Islamic influence. Medieval alchemy was entirely derived from the translation of Arabic sources, the first known work being the *Book of the Composition of Alchemy* by the Christian hermit **Morienus** (trans. 1144), who was supposed to have studied with the Arab Prince Khaled ibn Yazid (d.708 AD).

Islamic political and religious dominion extended over a vast area, and Islam was open to influences from Persia, Syria and India, as well as from the world of Hellenistic Greek learning. Alchemical works were translated into Arabic from Syriac and Greek sources. The Caliph Haroun al Raschid, for example, commissioned a vast program of translating Greek works, including those on alchemy, while the caliphs of the Ummayyad and Abbasid dynasty were patrons of alchemy. Works like the *Turba Philosophorum* and *The Emerald Tablet*, which became classics of medieval Hermetic alchemy, reached the West from Arabic translations.

Hermetic, magical and astrological works exerted a tremendous influence upon Islam. The Shi'ite sect was particularly interested in Hermetic and Neoplatonist ideas, and the followers of **Jabir ibn Hayyan** seem to have been Shi'ites (*see* **Hermetic Texts; Neoplatonism**). Islam knew of a category of 'hidden' or occult sciences (*khafiyyahl*). S.L.H. Nasr explains how these sciences or arts were forbidden on the exoteric level, being associated with esoteric gnosis and mysticism: they were vehicles for divine revelation and vision.

Arabic alchemy embraced wholeheartedly both the scientific areas of metallurgy and chemistry, and Hermetic wisdom and **magic**. Al Razi (**Rhazes**) (c.825–925) was an exemplary chemist, and the author of a work *On salts and alums*. Jabir ibn Hayyan was also a formidable chemist, with a substantial laboratory, but he was more open to Neoplatonist **numerology** and mysticism, popular with the Shi'ites.

The word 'alchemy' itself derives from Arabic *al kimiya, kimiya* being the name for the Hermetic art but also for the transmuting substance. The word 'elixir' (*al iksir*) is also vital to western and Arabic alchemy.

**Transmutation** was undoubtedly a goal of many Islamic alchemists, and there was an open debate over the possibility of transmuting **metals**. The Arabs developed the theory that metals were produced from **mercury-sulphur generation**, and most philosophers accepted this theory of the birth of metals in the womb of the earth. The controversial point was whether human arts could imitate, indeed excell, **nature** in transmuting metals: **Avicenna** argued that art could not imitate nature in a brief time-span.

# J

## Jabir ibn Hayyan
Latin *Geber*, qv; born *c*. 721–2 AD, died *c*. 815

Jabir is the father of European as well as **Islamic alchemy**, and his theories reflect the ambiguity of the tradition, being strongly influenced by the Islamic mysticism of the Shi'ites, yet oriented towards laboratory practice and experiment. He was born at Tus in Persia, where he is also said to have died. He was the son of an apothecary who was executed for agitation against the Umayyad dynasty, which was succeeded by the Abbasid caliphs. Jabir studied the Koran and mathematics, and is said to have been a close friend of the famous sixth Shi'ite Imam, Ja'far al-Sadiq, although there is some debate about this legend, but religious philosophy is certainly the corner-stone of the Jabirian tradition which flourished after his death.

Jabir rose to prominence as alchemist at the court of the Abbasid Caliph of Baghdad, revered for his use of medical **elixirs**. He had access to the Caliph's library, as well as collecting his own books, and he wrote widely, on astronomy, philosophy and mathematics as well as on **alchemy**. His works on alchemy have the ingredients which are the basis of European tradition, but the writings of the Latin **Geber** are certainly not those of Jabir. Jabir's concept of the four **elements** and qualities was taken over from the Greeks, but the **mercury-sulphur theory of the generation of metals** was Islamic, superseding the Aristotelian theory of moist and dry exhalations. E.J. Holmyard discovered that **The Emerald Tablet**, the bible of medieval alchemy in Europe, was known to him.

Vital to Jabirian adepts is the **numerology** of the Pythagoreans: a central role is played by the so-called **magic** square, with the number series $1 : 3 : 5 : 8 = 17$ in total, 17 assuming universal significance. The magic square with 9 components yields a total of 28, another key number. The Jabirian school uses Pythagorean numbers with Arabic letters in a way reminiscent of the **Cabala**. According to S.H. Nasr, Jabir distinguishes between various elixirs and the Philosophers'

**Stone**, and **transmutation** is to be understood in terms of numerology of composition, weight and proportions of **metals**. Jabir uses the balance to determine weight and quantity, and the art of grading, or determining the degree of heat, cold or moisture. (*See* **Arnald of Villanova**, and **John Dee**).

The authenticity of Jabirian works is not easy to determine, for his disciples created a substantial corpus of alchemical writings.

See E.J. Holmyard, *Alchemy*; S.H. Nasr, *Islamic Cosmological Doctrines*.

# Joachim of Fiore
## born c. 1135 in Celico, Calabria; died 1202

Although not an alchemist, Joachim's millennarian **prophecy** is a vital part of the alchemical tradition. A comment by Martin Luther indicates that esoteric **alchemy** was regarded as prophetic, concerned with the Last Judgement, and this is confirmed by **Petrus Bonus of Ferrara**. In a world which felt the menace of Islam, whilst enjoying the fruits of its scientific learning, Joachim sought prophetic meaning in the Scriptures, above all in Revelations, and an image of history as a process towards a goal, as divine purpose fulfilled. He seems to have made a pilgrimage to the Holy Land, gaining the patronage of Pope Lucius III whom he met at Veroli in 1184; the Pope commissioned his book on the Old and New Testaments (*Liber concordiae novi et veteris testamenti*). By 1184 he had already risen to become abbot of the Cistercian monastery of Curazzo, Calabria, but as he puzzled over the real meaning of the Scriptures, he sought solitude for meditation in Casmari monastery, and went thence to a hermit's retreat. As disciples flocked to him, he was granted papal permission to form his own order at San Giovanni in Fiore.

Joachim's longing for revelation led to moods of despair, but in his *Exposition on the Apocalypse* he describes a vision on Easter Eve of a psaltery with ten strings. This inspired his work on biblical prophetic **numerology**, the *Psalterium of Ten Strings*. Ten was the perfect Pythagorean number.

Joachim interprets history as a threefold **tree**, branching into the different aspects of the Trinity. The tree symbol also occurs in alchemy and in **Lull**'s philosophical systems. He uses the Revelations text where Christ says 'I am the Alpha and the Omega' (*see* **Alpha and Omega**), and sees history as Trinitarian: the Old Testament is the age of the father, of the Law, the New Testament is that of the Son, the spiritual age of the Holy Ghost is still to come.

# Jungian Theory of Alchemy

Jung viewed alchemy as a system of **dream and vision** symbolism, helpful in explaining the archetypal roots of the modern mind. He commenced his work studying with Freud, and sexual symbolism is vital to the alchemical quest in the yogic alchemy of India and China, as well as to western ideas of **Sol and Luna** (*see* **Chinese Alchemy**; **Indian Alchemy**).

During a serious breakdown just before the First World War, Jung encountered for himself the power of the collective unconscious, and his visionary experiences led to his search for clues in alchemy. His study of alchemy started in 1920 and his book *Psychologie und Alchimie* (Psychology and Alchemy) appeared in Zurich in 1944. The work is a magnificent exploration of the whole world of dream symbolism as related to alchemical imagery and **myth**.

Jung interpreted medieval Christian alchemy as a kind of dream undercurrent, flowing beneath the surface of conventional Christianity. The alchemical tradition made possible heretical speculations in secret, and could thereby release various imaginative energies of the mind. In *Psychology and Alchemy*, Jung presents a theory of human 'individuation', that is, the maturing of the personality from its psychic roots. He was very impressed by the universal presence of **mandala** symbolism in differing cultures, representing the quest for **harmony** and balance of the human self. There are many alchemical illustrations which resemble mandalas, being diagrams for meditation, reflection and self-exploration.

Jung also emphasizes the religious and gnostic roots of the tradition: he was actually obsessed with **Gnosticism**. He is the first alchemical scholar to provide really strong evidence that western alchemy is concerned essentially with the doctrine of the **redemption** of man and **nature** and thus involves a whole theory of **Creation**.

Not only did Jung illuminate western alchemical tradition, he also provided an introduction to Richard Willhelm's edition of the Taoist Chinese work *The Secret of the Golden Flower*, realizing that it was a form of alchemical yoga. He also studied the *I Ching* (*see* Willhelm's edition) whose theory of natural philosophy, based on the system of hexagrams and their images, is vital to the sophisticated system of Taoist alchemy.

Jung provides classic studies of **Zosimos of Panoplis** and his astonishing visions, of **Paracelsus** and of the alchemical **tree**. He was a superb scholar, but his first book suffers from a lack of historical background to the tradition. Walter Pagel and Dr Charles Webster have recently provided a wealth of evidence of the vital importance of alchemical thought in **medicine** and philosophy during the sixteenth and seventeenth centuries, but Jung lacked any study of **Newton**'s alchemy. In *Mysterium Conjunctionis* (1963), however, Jung provides a wealth of quotation and citation of the most abstruse sources, and the work awaits wider study and appreciation (*see also Conjunctio*; **The Mercury-Sulphur Theory of the Generation of Metals; Sol and Luna**).

Jung was in his own right a kind of prophet and alchemist of the unconscious, and his works should perhaps be seen as a part of the flow of the tradition, liberating alchemy from some of the accumulated dross.

# K

## Kelley, Edward
### born Worcester, 1555, died Bohemia, 1595

Edward Kelley achieved fame, or notoriety, for his work as spiritualist scryer for Dr **John Dee** during the 1580s. He has been accused of duping the credulous Dr Dee, but most alchemists believed in **angel magic**, and formidable scientists like **van Helmont** believed in the Paracelsian weapon salve (*see also* **Digby**; **Fludd**) which worked through sympathetic **magic**.

Kelley was a dubious character. His original name being Talbot, his ears were cropped for forging ancient title deeds – no good recommendation for his **alchemy** and spiritualism. He was also accused of necromancy, and of exhuming a corpse at Walton-le-Dale Park for magic. He may have studied at Oxford without gaining a degree. He met Dr Dee at his house in Mortlake and impressed him with his séances.

Kelley's 'angelic communications' are in fact truly remarkable, being far from casual charlatanry. The angels communicated in an original language, Enochian, and the records suggest some process of unconscious regurgitating of alchemical and apocalyptic texts, attributed to angels. This was learned magic, in the Hermetic tradition, much influenced by Abbot **Trithemius**, the famous fifteenth-century humanist scholar. It is now not so easy to dismiss this Hermetic magic as nonsense, at least within the contemporary world view.

Most of the séances Dee and Kelley held took place during their continental travels. The Dee family left England with Kelley and his wife in 1583. They tried to gain support from Emperor Rudolf II, and gained strong patronage of Count Rosenberg, staying in his castle at Trebon in Bohemia. The séances ended, however, when a woman **spirit**, Madimi, advocated wife-sharing.

In January 1588, Dee claims to have delivered to Kelley the **elixir** (possessing the virtues of the Philosophers' **Stone**). This elixir was supposed to have been discovered originally in the ruins of

Glastonbury Abbey by Kelley himself. The find included books, glasses and **apparatus** (*see* similar story about **Charnock**). Dee and Kelley were rumoured to have achieved actual **transmutation** using their powder or elixir and **Arthur Dee**, John's eldest son, remembered playing quoits with transmuted pewter plates at Trebon Castle.

When Dee returned to England in 1589, Kelley remained in Bohemia, then returned to Prague. In 1591 he was created a 'Golden Knight' by Rudolf II and his **gold**-making pretensions were taken seriously. The great Lord Burleigh was credulous enough to send agents to urge Kelley to return to England; two letters from Burleigh dated May 1591 show generous respect for Kelley's 'Royal Profession' (i.e. alchemy), and beg his return. It is certain that Burleigh believed in the secret of transmutation, for there is extant a letter to Sir Edward Dyer (a friend of Dee's), dated May 1591, in which he asks for some of Kelley's mystic powder to be sent in a 'secret box' to convince Queen Elizabeth I of the reality of transmutation.

But Kelley's secrets and pretensions destroyed him. He was imprisoned for two years and tortured, then killed whilst trying to escape from the custody of the Emperor.

Kelley's alchemical treatise was printed in Hamburg and Amsterdam in 1676, as *Tractatus duo de lapide philosophorum* (Two tracts on the Philosophers' Stone). The work is interesting and succinct, with the conventional imagery of the opus.

# Khunrath, Heinrich
## born Leipzig 1560, died 1605

Khunrath is one of the most influential alchemists of the period of Paracelsian spiritual and medical alchemical influence – the time of **Boehme** and **Oswald Croll**, and of **Libavius**. His *Amphitheatre of Eternal Wisdom* blends perfectly into the spirit of **Rosicrucian** philosophy, strongly cabalist in tone. He obtained his MD at Basle in 1588 and became a satellite of the court of Emperor Rudolf II, where alchemists congregated. **John Dee** notes a meeting with him in 1598. His *Confessio* gives his religious faith in **alchemy**: he believed in divine revelation through the 'Book of Nature' (a Paracelsian metaphor), and draws the analogy of Christ with the Philosophers' **Stone**, because of its redemptive quality.

Khunrath's *Amphitheatrum* (The Amphitheatre of Eternal Wisdom) consists of a series of 365 meditations to cover each day of the year and he gives alchemical interpretations of biblical texts, using especially Proverbs and the apocryphal Wisdom of Solomon. The engravings in the work include the alchemical citadel, with the author surrounded by his enemies; there is a bespectacled owl between two candles, further illuminated by two blazing torches, crossed in front of the wise bird. The German verse asks: 'Of what use are torches when people do not even want to see?'

Perhaps the most famous plate from this work shows the devout alchemist kneeling in prayer in the midst of his magnificent oratory, littered with alchemical paraphernalia and musical instruments – the latter to convey the divine **harmony** of the cosmos. He calls himself a 'lover of both kinds of medicine', presumably spiritual as well as bodily: the Stone is often called 'medicine of metals'.

Khunrath reiterates many quotes of the medieval tradition: the Stone is the **phoenix** which kills and revivifies itself; it is body, soul and **spirit**; and he quotes Senior Zadith, the Arabic alchemist, that it is like a **tree**, whose roots, branches and blossom are contained within the seed. *Viriditas*, 'greenness', and the concept of germination are given mystical interpretation: the greenness is manifestation of *Ruach Elohim* (Hebrew for 'the Spirit of God'). He equates the alchemical Chaos, from which proceeds the mystical **Creation**, with both the **egg** and the **microcosm** – a magnificent example of the essential synonymity of large areas of alchemical symbolism, which is an attempt of the unconscious to circulate around its meaning.

*See* John Read, *Prelude to Chemistry*; Adam McLean, *Hermetic Journal*, Autumn 1981.

# King and Queen

The King and Queen figure prominently in alchemical illustrations, and are closely related to **Sol and Luna**, for they represent the sun and moon. Symbolism of sun, moon and planets is to be found everywhere in **alchemy** (*see* **Metals and Planets**). The sun represents the pure radiance and magical power of **gold**, the King, whereas the moon stands for silver, or the Queen. Solar virtue, radiance and splendour are universally the qualities of kingship, whilst the moon is so often associated with the feminine principle and with queenship.

This pair also stand for **sulphur** (the King, or masculine principle) and **mercury** (the Queen, or feminine principle). The famous series of illustrations to the *Rosarium* show the mystic marriage of King and Queen (*see* **Conjunctio**), and it is clear that their relationship symbolizes the harmonious marriage of opposing principles needed to generate the **metals** (*see* **Mercury-Sulphur Theory of the Generation of Metals**).

The mythic ramifications of this symbolism of King and Queen are complex. Gold is the king of metals, and the sun is the king of planets. During the Renaissance there was a powerful revival of the ancient Hermetic religion of Egypt, in which the sun, as the magical source of life and energy, plays the ruling part; indeed, it is likely that Copernicus was influenced by Renaissance Hermeticism in putting the case for a heliocentric universe (*see* **Giordano Bruno; Hermetic Texts**).

The idea of the death and resurrection of the King features in many texts and pictures (*see* ***Nigredo***), and this may be rooted in the ancient Egyptian religion of the sun. Pharaoh Akhenaten made the sun the centre of Egyptian religion, and his philosophy was based upon the idea of the transformation of the sun during its nightly journey towards a new dawn or resurrection. The whole idea of sun and moon as a royal pair may be rooted in the Egyptian mythology of Isis and Osiris, who were used to represent masculine and feminine principles in the universe. In classical myth the King and Queen are Apollo and Artemis.

# L

## Libavius, Andreas
### born Halle, c. 1560, died 1616

The son of a poor linen weaver, Johann Libau, Andreas rose to be one of the foremost writers in the history of **alchemy** and chemistry, an energetic polemicist on behalf of his subject. He attended the Gymnasium of Halle, and in 1578 went to the University of Wittenberg, where in 1581 he gained his PhD, along with the title of Poet Laureate. He then gained the position of schoolmaster at Ilmenau. He spent the rest of his life in education: in 1586 he became Stadt Rector in Coburg and then from 1588 he studied **medicine** at Basle, where he graduated MD. From 1588 he was also Professor of History and Poetry at Jena University. In 1591 he moved to Rotheburg as Municipal Physician, and in the following year he became Inspector of Schools. In 1607 he retired to Coburg, as a result of quarrels with the Rector of the Gymnasium. He produced a vast output of published writings.

**Publications:**
*Neoparacelsica* (1594): in this he attacked the use of the *aurum potabile* as universal panacea (*see* **Elixirs**).
*Rerum chymicarum epistolica forma* (1595): a collection of letters to philosophers and physicians in Germany, warning of the evils of over-enthusiasm for the new Paracelsian chemistry. Libavius was an apologist for alchemy, but attacked the alchemical idea of perfecting **nature**, since God's **Creation** is already perfect. He attacked above all the magical, Hermetic philosophy associated with Paracelsians. However, he was a friend of **Duchesne** and of Turquet de Mayerne, both leading apostles of Paracelsian iatrochemistry.
*Alchemia* (1597), his most famous work, which went through various editions and translations. Here he declares his belief in transmutation, notably of iron into copper.
*Singularium* (1599-1601), a collection of lectures on natural

philosophy. Libavius attacked Catholics, above all the Jesuits, whilst espousing a rather conservative, Aristotelian standpoint.

*Defensio . . . alchymicae transmutatoriae* (1604), an attack on the French physician Nicolas Guibert for denying the truth of **transmutation** of **metals** into **gold**. Libavius supported the fact that the Philosophers' **Stone** was actually known to the alchemists.

*Alchymia triumphans* (1607), being 926 pages. In this work Libavius enters the highly confused battles of his day involving Paracelsians, Hermetists and Galenists.

He also published many other works, including attacks upon the **Rosicrucians**. His works in general are an attempt to assert common sense and science, while at the same time defending the idea of alchemical transmutation. Although he seemed sometimes to be attacking the Paracelsians, his works were tremendously valuable in furthering the case of Paracelsian alchemical medicine.

# Lull, Ramon
**born Majorca, c. 1235, died North Africa, 1316**

As with so many ancient and medieval names, the name of the great 'doctor illuminatus' Ramon Lull was used to confer authority on alchemical texts. Lull was one of the most influential philosophers of his time, and famous 'Lullian method' inspired a new philosophical movement. Although the alchemical texts attributed to Lull or Lully are spurious, there can be no doubting that alchemists used Lull's method in explaining their art.

Our understanding of Lull's ideas has been immensely enriched by the writings of Frances Yates, especially her book *The Theatre of Memory*, and she refers to a vast 'Lullian literature written by his followers'.

A contemporary of Aquinas and **Albertus Magnus**, Lull lived at a time when the craze for **alchemy** derived from Islamic sources was at its height, being especially popular in monasteries and amongst even very high authorities in the Church. He was born around 1235 in Majorca, and, lacking formal scholastic education, is said to have distinguished himself as a poet and troubadour. He soon rose to favour at the court of King James I of Aragon and tutored the royal family.

Lull underwent a conversion to the role of missionary amongst the infidels after experiencing a vision on Mount Randa in Majorca, dated to 1272. He studied Arabic in Majorca, intending to use this in his work as a missionary. In the vision, which he regarded as an illumination, he beheld the **Creation** as a hierarchy, emanating from God.

His vision directly inspired the creation of the legendary Lullian art, which is founded upon the names and qualities, or 'Dignities', of God, as Lord of Creation. Yates explains the art as partly an art of memory, for Lull created a vast cosmic place system based on the scholastic cosmology of his day; within this cosmic diagram any item to be stored in memory can find a place. The Trinity forms the basis of the whole system (see **Numerology**).

The philosophy underlying the system is that the 'Dignities' of God are the actual causes of phenomena: 'All Lull's arts are based on these *Dignitates Dei* which are divine names or attributes, thought of as primordial causes.' This approach derives from the Augustinian tradition, and Frances Yates cites J. Scotus Erigena as the main influence upon Lull. She further explains vital links between Lullian method and the **Cabala** (the *Zohar* appeared in Spain during his lifetime): 'The Sephiroth of the Cabala are really Divine Names as creative principles. The sacred Hebrew alphabet is, mystically speaking, supposed to contain all the Names of God.'

Lull's system involves using concentric discs, revolving freely, one within another, to create different combinations of letters, the letters being used to represented the divine dignities. Alchemical students of this art natural leapt to the conclusion that their Hermetic quest might be aided greatly by such devices, and a scheme of Lullian alchemy arose.

The key to understanding Lull's philosophy is the missionary aspect of it. The art is intended as a universally applicable, logically clear system of knowledge and philosophy. Lull detested Averroism, and hoped to use his art to disprove all error or heresy. The story goes that he was a Christian martyr, and that he was stoned to death while on a journey in North Africa as a missionary. It is important to see the true alchemical tradition as a prophetic tradition, and a number of alchemists were involved with Joachimite **prophecy** and millennarianism (see **Joachim of Fiore**). Men like **John Dee** dreamed of a universal peace resulting from converting unbelievers.

Alchemical legend has it that one Raymond Lully was introduced to King Edward III in England, and was employed by the monarch to create **gold** within the confines of the Tower of London. Lull is said to have insisted that his alchemical work could only be used to finance a crusade in the Holy Land. The King refused to stick to his side of the bargain and Lull was imprisoned, but he later escaped. He is supposed to have taught an abbot of Westminster Abbey the secrets of adeptship.

Another legend connects Lull with the production of some gold nobles, struck by Edward IV, with alchemical help. The first issue of rose nobles is 1465, at a time when **Thomas Norton** and **George Ripley** were giving alchemy a new impetus.

The summation of Lull's writings was the *Ars Magna* (The Great Art), dating from 1305-8, which he composed during his seventies.

# Magic
## Magia naturalis

**Alchemy** has from earliest times been closely associated with magic. Early magical papyri display the image of the serpent devouring its own tail, the central symbol of alchemy (*see* **Uroboros**). Alchemy is called the Hermetic tradition, and many texts ascribed to **Hermes Trisemegistus** were magical, and also to do with alchemy and **astrology**. Most forms of magic relate to the astrological theories that occult influences radiate from stars and planets, bathing the elemental world in occult sympathy and antipathy. The successful magus is able to deal with and manipulate these supernatural forces.

The concept of sympathy and antipathy as key principles in magic dates from Hellenistic times, where we find in the *Physika kai mustika* (*c.*300 BC) a group of alchemists seeking the secrets of the art by summoning the **spirit** of their master **Ostanes**: this practice of necromancy leads to the discovery of a temple inscription. This story shows that **Hellenistic alchemy** was related to Persian and Egyptian magic.

During the Middle Ages, alchemy is found in close association with magical and astrological or **herbal** works. Thus *The Secret of Secrets*, a work which attracted **Roger Bacon**, is full of magical ideas.

It was, however, during the Renaissance that magic achieved its fullest dignity and status. During the 1470s Marsilio Ficino was commissioned by Cosimo dei Medici to translate the newly acquired texts of the *Corpus Hermeticum*, packed with Hellenistic magic, into immaculate humanist Latin. This even took priority over the translation of Plato. Ficino was a keen practitioner of astrological magic, and he handed on the mantle of learned magus to Pico della Mirandola, one of the most brilliant of the Renaissance humanists.

The Hellenistic image of the magus was forcefully revived during the Renaissance, and distinguished scholars sought to insist that the **Cabala**, **angel magic**, and natural or sympathetic magic were entirely consistent with the Christian faith; indeed, that the study of the wonders of **nature** was a direct path towards understanding the truth of divine **Creation** and the reality of the Redeemer (*see* **Redemption; Stone**). Marsilio Ficino justified 'natural magic' as being entirely consistent with the Christian philosophy of **Neoplatonism**, while Pico della Mirandola further enhanced the reputation of Christian *magia naturalis* by his powerful defence of Christian Cabala. **H.C. Agrippa** provided a coherent textbook of Renaissance natural magic, justified within a Christian context, and another important protagonist of Renaissance *magia naturalis* was Giambattista della Porta. Although **Giordano Bruno** was burnt at the stake for his flamboyant espousal of the cause of Renaissance Hermeticism and natural magic, the movement gained a tremendous prestige from the **Rosicrucian** manifestos, which continued the assertion that magic, alchemy and the Cabala were entirely consistent with Christian natural philosophy.

Leading alchemists tended to be involved with magic at some level or other, despite official repression and persecution, and alchemists were often accused of involvement with necromancy and other forms of nefarious magic. Dr **John Dee**, writing and teaching in Tudor England, sought to free magic from the taint of demonism: he composed a manuscript defending Roger Bacon from the charge of accomplishing wonders by the aid of demons. Men like Dee defended magic as a Christian use of natural forces, especially astral influences, and with the help of **Edward Kelley**, Dee himself sought communion with the angelic intelligences in the cosmos.

Thus magic was not just a matter of theories of the universe, it was also a matter of energetic, experimental practice: Agrippan magic involved a whole theory of the **harmony** of the universe, and of the powers of sympathy and antipathy to influence events.

Throughout Hellenistic, Islamic, medieval and Renaissance times, the world view was, to our eyes, magical and supernatural. Above all, early scientists and natural philosophers could not contemplate an inanimate, abstract, material universe. The cosmos was always believed to be populated by angels and demons. Alchemists were at pains to escape the witch-crazes by the demarcation of natural magic, alchemy and the Cabala from the realm of necromancy and demonism. But there can be no doubt that at a popular level alchemy was often linked with ideas of summoning spirits, casting spells, astral charms and rituals.

Prospero in Shakespeare's *Tempest* is now thought to have been modelled on John Dee as learned magus, a man of positive dignity and power. Works like Marlowe's *Doctor Faustus* or Ben Jonson's marvellous play of *The Alchemist*, however, portray the less reputable side of popular magic. In *Religion and the Decline of Magic*, Keith Thomas provides a richly documented account of popular magical practice during the sixteenth and seventeenth centuries, showing the extensive links between spiritual magic, alchemy and astrology.

The writings of Frances Yates have provided a wealth of material on learned magic during the Renaissance (*see especially* her *Giordano Bruno and the Hermetic Tradition*, and *The Occult Philosophy in the Renaissance*).

# Magnesia

Also ther was a disciple of Plato,
That on a tyme seyde to his maister to,
As his book *Senior* wol bere witnesse,
And this was his demande in soothfastnesse:
'Tel me the name of the privy stoon?'
And Plato answerde unto him anoon,
'Take the stoon that Titanos men name.'
'Which is that?' quod he. 'Magnesia is the same,'
Seyde Plato. 'Ye, sir, and is it thus?
This is *ignotium per ignotius*.
What is Magnesia, good sir, I yow preye?'
'It is a water that is maad, I seye,
Of elementes foure,' quoth Plato.
'Tel me the rote, good sir,' quod he tho,
'Of that water, if that it be your wille?'
'Nay, nay,' quod Plato, 'certein, that I nille.'

Chaucer, Canones Yeomans Tale

This is worth quoting as helping us towards an understanding of the central mystery of the quest, the **Stone** of the Philosophers which has so many synonyms. Plato refuses to define magnesia, which is mentioned as a mystic substance as early as Stephanos of Alexandria, and which is central to **Khunrath**'s Paracelsian **alchemy** in the seventeenth century.

The following passage from the *Testamentum* of Cremer (*see* **Ramon Lull**) suggests how alchemists sought a chemical meaning to this riddle:

Magnesia is the smelted ore of iron. When the mixture is still black it is called the Black Raven. As it turns water white, it is named Virgin's Milk, or the Bone of the Whale. In its red stage, it is the Red Lion. When it is blue, it is called the Blue Lion. When it is all colours, the sages name it the rainbow. But the Number of such names is legion . . . .

This gives invaluable insight into the terminology of alchemy, which uses endless synonyms, **myths** and symbols to circulate around the central mystery, which is not to be spoken.

(The above passages are both quoted in Robert M. Schuler, 'The Renaissance Chaucer as Alchemist', *Viator*, 1984, 15, pp.305–33.)

Magnesia is a term full of arcane significance in the quest for the Stone or **elixir**. It was an esoteric name popular with Greek alchemists: for them magnesia or *magnes* (which is Greek for the magnet) is a transforming substance, hermaphroditic in character. Rosinus ad Sarratantem: 'Take therefore this animate stone, the stone which has a soul in it, the mercurial, which is sensitive and sensible to the presence and influence of the magnesia and the magnet.' (This treatise of Rosinus is contained in the *Artis Auriferae* collection, published 1593.)

Khunrath, in the seventeenth century, puts the mystical Christian interpretation: for him magnesia is the primal chaos, and he defines it as 'a Catholic or Universal, that is a Cosmic Ens or Entity, Three-in-One, naturally compounded of Body, Spirit and Soul, the one and only true *Subjectum Catholicum* and true Universal Material *Lapidis Philosophorum*'.

# Maier, Michael
## born Holstein, 1568, died Magdeburg, 1622

Maier belongs to the **Rosicrucian** era of **alchemy**, when the Paracelsian movement was at its height (*see* **Paracelsus**). His remarkable books of emblems, notably *Atalanta fugiens*, provide a summary of the medieval alchemical tradition. Frances Yates, in *The Rosicrucian Enlightenment*, considers Maier as a key figure in the Rosicrucian movement, closely related to **Robert Fludd**, who was his friend. His *Atalanta* was published by de Bry of Oppenheim, who in the same year issued part of Fludd's epic work on *The History of the Microcosm and the Macrocosm* (*see also* **Microcosm-Macrocosm**). Alchemical emblem books were then in fashion, others being issued by Luca Jennis (*see* **Mylius**; **Stolz**).

Maier was born in Holstein, studied **medicine** and then practised first at Rostock and then at Prague as physician to Emperor Rudolph II, patron of alchemists and magicians. He visited England and met the personal physician of King James I, Sir William Paddy.

His first book was *Arcana arcanissima* (Most Secret Secrets), 1614, and in 1618 appeared his *Viatorium*, (On the seven mountains of the planets), on the search for the **Prime Matter**. His *Symbola aurea*

(Symbols of gold) appeared in 1617, followed by the most famous *Atalanta fugiens* (Fleeing Atalanta) of 1618. His fine emblem books are replete with allusions to classical **myth**. He died during the occupation of Magdeburg, at the start of the Thirty Years War. His works show how popular expensive alchemical emblem books were in this Rosicrucian period, and he presented his readers with a brilliant synthesis of the complex medieval tradition, enriched by his Paracelsian and Rosicrucian fervour.

# Mandala

The iconography of **alchemy** shows that images and symbols are the life-blood of the tradition, and there is little realistic illustration of chemistry or **apparatus**. Medieval **manuscript** illuminations frequently show a mandala structure, in which balance and **harmony** are more important than realism.

The word 'mandala' is a Sanskrit term, adopted by Jung in his attempt to portray alchemy as a meditative, spiritual tradition (*see* **Jungian Theory of Alchemy**). In his *Psychology and Alchemy,* a whole section is dedicated to the mandala. Jung provides a series of mandala **dreams**, which he interprets using comparative symbolic material from alchemy. He explains his use of the word: 'The term Mandala was chosen because this word denotes the ritual or magic circles used in Lamaism and also in Tantric yoga as a yantra or aid to contemplation.' The Tibetan Buddhism mandalas, called *kyilkor*, which means literally 'circle', are in fact highly complex productions, being the product of sophisticated formal artistic tradition, rather than spontaneous products of the unconscious, as are many alchemical visions.

Talking to a Tibetan lama in India, Jung drew the conclusion that the only true mandala 'is always an inner image, which is gradually built up through (active) imagination, at such times when psychic equilibrium is disturbed or when a thought cannot be found and must be sought for, because not contained in holy doctrine'. The balance or equilibrium of the picture is clearly designed to protect and defend the mind from the assaults of inner 'demons' and disturbances, and it helps to concentrate the meditative, therapeutic process of the mind.

Meditation and active imagination are at the heart of alchemy, and Adam McLean has recently published a book, *Alchemical Mandalas,* with some highly baroque mandala illustrations from later alchemical texts.

Most alchemical illustrations have some form of mandala structure. There are the series of pictures from the famous edition of the *Rosarium*, for example, which are displayed and analysed in Jung's *Psychology of the Transference*. The Fountain of Mercury, or Fountain of the Philosophers which opens this series is a brilliant example (*see also* **Fountain**). It is contained within a square, at the corners of which are four stars, with a fifth star representing the **quintessence** (= fifth essence, apart from the four **elements**), which is between adjacent sun and moon symbols. The fountain itself is a symbol of **unity**, providing three spouts for the three products of the philosophical **mercury**. The image of the **King and Queen** repeats itself in the *Rosarium* series; they are shown each holding a branch with twin flowers. A dove provides the fifth flower. Thus the figure provides the image for a union of opposites.

In a wider sense, the entire medieval world view presents the cosmos as a mandala (*see* **Creation**; **Harmony**), with a symmetrical, harmonious structure. Meditating upon the wonders of creation, the alchemist transcends his narrower self and ventures into a state or level of spiritual awareness where the vulgar wealth of gross precious **metals** is of no value beside the mystic vision of eternity.

# Manuscripts

Many alchemical texts were collected and printed during the sixteenth and seventeenth centuries, but **alchemy** is essentially a manuscript tradition. When it first arrived in Europe, during the Middle Ages, there was a very wide circulation of diverse alchemical works: chemical lists of experiments, works on **colours**, mystical inspirational texts like *The Emerald Tablet*, and endless manuscripts attributed to Moses, Solomon, Adam, Plato and **Aristotle**, not to mention the great scholastics like Aquinas and **Albertus Magnus**.

Of the most important manuscripts, the Manuscript *Marcianus 299*, from Venice, which was copied in the tenth or eleventh century, apparently from a Byzantine collection of the eighth century, is one of the most influential, also the Manuscript *Parisinus Graecus* (2325), which is thirteenth century in date.

Important evidence for the chemical, exoteric aspect of the tradition comes from two papyrus collections, those called the Leiden papyrus and the Stockholm papyrus, which provide lists of recipes for dyeing or creating precious stones.

Fine collections of manuscript illustrations include the **Ripley**

*Scrowle*, the *Splendor solis* and many others.
*See* Berthelot, *Collection des anciens alchimistes grecs.*

# Maria Prophetissa
## Maria the Jewess; uncertain dates, perhaps first century BC

**Hellenistic alchemy** is an enigma of great depth, and a key figure in the founding of a tradition of Greek texts was Maria the Prophetess, who seems to have been Jewish. Women alchemists may have been common in this tradition: several texts involve dialogues of Kleopatra, who is quite unknown. Maria was a revered figure, as **Zosimos** makes clear: she was responsible for innovations in **apparatus** in the adept's laboratory. She is credited with inventing the *tribikos* and seems to have used the *kerotakis*. She was famous for her mystical cry or exclamation: 'One becomes two, two becomes three, and out of the third comes the one as the fourth.' This is typical of alchemical **numerology**, and it may be that the same mystical notions were available to **Thomas Thymme** or **John Dee**, who attach supreme importance to **unity** amidst diversity, the mystical union of opposites. Maria may have originated the whole idea of a **colour** sequence in ancient **alchemy**: there being four colours to represent **stages** in Hellenistic times.

Maria was called 'Prophetess', and in legend was the sister of Moses, perhaps in a symbolic sense. She seems to have embraced both aspects of the tradition: the mystical, prophetic, gnostic approach, as well as the strictly practical laboratory, experimental aspect – the two aspects in medieval alchemy termed *alchimia practica* and *alchimia theoretica*. Tradition quotes her maxim about marrying two gums, the white and the red gum. This suggests that the concept of the *conjunctio*, the mystic marriage, was already known in the earliest stages of the tradition.

There is a revealing passage written by an Islamic alchemist, Ibn Umail, who suggests that Maria mythologized the waters of experiment in a familiar way:

> Maria also said: 'The water which I mentioned is an Angel and descends from the sky and the earth accepts it on account of [the earth's] moistness. The water of the sky is held by the water of the earth, and the water of the earth acts as its servant and its sand [serves] for the purpose of honouring it. Both the waters are gathered together, and the water holds the water. The vital principle holds the vital principle, and the vital principle is whitened by the vital principle.
>
> Quoted from Jack Lindsay, *The Origins of Alchemy in Greco-Roman Egypt*

Ibn Umail explains that this is coition of the soul with the **spirit**, i.e.
mystical marriage. The two must form a unity. The rise and descent
of water, as vapour then condensation, inspires the mystical notion of
the descent and ascent of a divine messenger, an angel.

# Materials used by Alchemists

The **Jungian theory of alchemy** seeks to cast aside the impossible
problem of matching alchemical **myth** and symbol to chemical
processes. Instead, analysis and contemplation focuses upon the
myths, images and icons as psychological material, embodying
projection from the unconscious mind.

The Elizabethan writer Reginald Scot includes **alchemy** in his
brilliant survey of **magic**, *The Discoverie of Witchcraft* (1586). His list
of materials used by alchemists is interesting:

> . . . orpiment, sublimed Mercury, iron squames, Mercurie crude,
> groundlie large, bole armoniacke, verdegree, borace, boles, gall,
> arsenick, sal armoniake, brimstone, salt, paper, burnt bones, unslaked
> lime, clay, saltpeter, vitriall, saltartre, alcalie, sal preparat, clay made with
> horses dung, mans haire, oile of tartare, allum, glass, woort, yest, argoll,
> resogar [ = realgar], gleir of an eie, powders, ashes, doong, pisse, etc . . . .

One dreads to think of the more amateur practitioners who plied their
trade as alchemists, deserving to be categorized as naïve magi, even
as witches. Besides such materials, Scot says, 'They have waters
corosive, and lincall, waters of albification, and waters rubifying, &c.
Also oiles, ablutions, and metals fusible. Also their lamps, their
urinalles, discensories, sublimatories, alembocks, viols, croslets,
curcurbits, stillatories, and their fornace of calcination . . . .'

*See also* **Chaucer** for his list of materials.

# Medicine

From earliest times the **elixir** of the alchemists was described as a
'medicine' to cure the defects in corrupt **metals**. This medicine is
synonymous, then, with the Philosophers' **Stone** as well. *See* Ben
Jonson's play, *The Alchemist*, II. i. 37-42:

> Mammon: But when you see th'effects of the great Medicine,
> Of which one part projected on a hundred
> Of Mercury or Venus, or the Moon,
> Shall turn it, to as many of the Sun . . .

There was always the closest connection between medicine and **alchemy**: **Avicenna**, the Islamic philosopher, was a physician, as was **Rhazes**. In the Middle Ages, **Arnald of Villanova** was the direct predecessor of **Paracelsus** in using alchemy to prepare medicines. During the Renaissance Paracelsus created a new movement in medical practice, insisting on the value of alchemy in preparing mineral or metallic remedies using the arts of **distillation** and the **furnace**. *Aurum potabile*, or potable **gold**, was a famous remedy.

Following this lead, many of the foremost physicians of the sixteenth and seventeenth centuries combined alchemy closely with medicine, although in England, from Elizabethan times, the Royal College of Physicians was inclined to persecute Paracelsian alchemists, for example **Francis Anthony** (who became embroiled in controversy for his use of *aurum potabile*) and even for a while Dr **Arthur Dee**.

The association of medicine and alchemy has continued vigorously into the twentieth century. C.G. Jung used alchemical **myth** and imagery to enrich his interpretation of **dreams**, and to throw light upon man's quest for the eternal, for the light of **redemption** to be found within man's soul. For Jung as a psychiatrist, alchemy was a profoundly practical guide to man's psychic dilemma (*see* **Jungian Theory of Alchemy**).

# Mercury
## Mercurius; Quicksilver = *Argentum vivum*

With mercury, we enter with trepidation the sacred *temenos*, the shrine of alchemical mysteries.

Of all alchemical symbols, it is this god **metal**, this liquid **spirit** which is most difficult to define or confine within any concept. By his very nature, the spirit *Mercurius* is highly elusive, volatile, often called the *cervus fugitivus*, the fugitive stag. **Alchemy** is the art of transformation and metamorphosis and it is Mercury, the spiritual messenger of the gods (*see* **Hermes**), the holder of the winged **caduceus**, who is most subject to metamorphosis, for he is in actual fact the essential symbol of every aspect of the opus, from its initial **dragon** *Prima materia* (*see* **Prime Matter**) to its culmination and fruition in the **elixir**, or the **Stone**, or *magisterium*.

### The Metal Mercury, or Quicksilver

As a metal, quicksilver is one of the most fascinating, being the only metal which is liquid at room temperature, so ideal for thermometers because of its immediate responsiveness to temperature changes. This ambivalence led to alchemists creating endless myths out of mercury as divine principle in the world, as being **hermaphrodite**, showing qualities of being both volatile and fixed. The fact that the other metals also liquefy (albeit under intense heat) suggested that they were in essence mercury, and many seventeenth-century chemists, like **Boyle** and **Newton**, believed that they could 'extract' a liquid mercury from *any and every* metal, and that the philosophical mercury was the only pre-requisite for **transmutation** (*see* **John Dasteyn**, who explains this theory of metals).

Common mercury is very volatile, changing with mildest heat from liquid into a vapour and the early **distillation apparatus** of the Hellenistic alchemists seems to have been used mainly to purify mercury, the extract it from its vermilion ore **cinnabar.** There can be no doubt that the liberation of volatile mercury from its solid, sulphide ore, cinnabar, inspired magical speculation and mystical fantasy. The vapour of mercury was always called the 'spirit mercury'. (Vapours always = spirits.)

## Mercury as the Water of Creation

The **Creation myth** of Genesis was constantly employed in alchemy, and mercury was regarded as the primordial water of Creation, the primal **aqua**, often called *aqua permanens*: as vapour, it is the 'spirit which moves upon the face of the waters'. It is easy to see that here we have come a long way from the simple mirror liquid denoted in modern chemistry as Hg. **Zosimos** knows mercury as a 'divine water', a divine mystery of the opus.

In *The Book of Eight Chapters*, attributed to **Albertus Magnus**, we are told that mercury has the cold and moist qualities of water, and that it was from this water that God created all minerals. There is much interweaving of biblical passages, expounding the theology of **redemption**, which was the key to esoteric, mystical alchemy. Mercury is also credited with a penetrating property, and is seen as a purifying baptismal font (*see* **Bath**; **Fountain**).

## Mercury as Solvent

What soon becomes apparent is that mercury is used to denote solvents which are nothing to do with quicksilver. As primordial water, mercury is regarded not only as the water of death in which metals decompose but also as the water of resurrection from which transmuted metals arise – everywhere there is ambivalence, because mercury is the symbol of transcendence and **unity**, of that mystic psychic wholeness which all religions seek.

The sea of mercury drowns the **King**, who cries for help from the dark depths; there is a famous illustration of this in the *Splendor solis*.

## Mercury as Prime Matter, as the Beginning and the End

In mythic terms, Mercury is a saviour, the mystic guide or psychopomp who leads souls from darkness of ignorance to the light of realization. He thus represents the entire progress of the opus from beginning to end, and he is described as the **alpha and omega**.

## The God Mercury

Mercurius is the Roman name for **Hermes**, the messenger of the gods, who links the infernal world of Hades with the upper Olympian world. He is thus the ideal alchemical god, the mystagogue who guides the adept down into the depths of the psyche, the suffering of the *nigredo*, thence rising to the ultimate perfection of the *magisterium*, the attainment of the elixir or the Stone. He is shown with winged helmet, winged sandals and caduceus or **magic** wand, which he used to conduct spirits to the underworld.

*See also* **Hermetic Texts**.

## The Mythology of Mercury

Jung, in his essay on 'The Spirit Mercurius' and in his writings on alchemy in general, has shown the universal applicability of the name Mercurius to every form of alchemical symbol and myth. Hermes or Mercury has a dual nature 'being a chthonic god of revelation and also the spirit of quicksilver', thus the hermaphrodite is repeatedly called Mercury, and the dragon or **uroboros** is also said to represent Mercurius. Medieval writers were puzzled and fascinated by this way of describing the chameleon quality of the unconscious, myth-making mind. Mercury is a helpful servant, called *servus* or *cervus fugitivus* (fugitive servant – but also fugitive stag). 'He is dragon, lion, eagle, raven, to mention only the most important of them' (Jung, Vol.12, p.66). As beginning and end of the opus (alpha and omega), Mercury is both Prime Matter and the fabled *Lapis* or Stone of the Philosophers. His dual nature makes him something of a devil – Mercury was god of thieves and dishonesty – but he is vital as helper of the alchemist.

**Thomas Vaughan**, in his brilliant work entitled *Magia Adamica* (Adamic Magic) states:

The Mercurie of the Wisemen is a waterie Element, Cold and moyst; this is their Permanent water, the spirit of the Bodie, the unctuous vapour, the Blessed water, the virtuous water, the water of the Wisemen, the

Philosophers' Vinacre, the Mineral water, the Dew of heavenly grace, the
Virgin's Milk, the Bodily Mercurie, and with other numberless names is
it named in the Bookes of the Philosophers, which names truly, though
they are divers, notwithstanding always signifie one and the same thing,
namely the Mercurie of the Wisemen. Out of this Mercurie alone all the
Virtue of the art is extracted, and according to its Nature, the Tincture,
both Red and White.

Rudrum edition, p.218

## The Mercury of the Philosophers

In his *Magia Adamica*, Thomas Vaughan cites the work of 'an extant
very learned Author' (op. cit., p.210), who is probably a member of
the **Rosicrucians**:

> As the world (saith he) was generated out of that water, upon which the
> Spirit of God did move, all things proceeding thence, both Caelestiall
> and Terrestriall; so this chaos is generated out of a certain water that is
> not common, not out of Dew, nor Ayre condensed in the caverns of the
> Earth, or artificially in the Receiver; not out of water drawn out of the Sea,
> Fountains, Pitts, or Rivers, but out of a certain tortured water, that hath
> suffered some alteration, obvious it is to All, but known to very few. This
> water hath all in it, that is necessarie to the perfection of the work,
> without any Extrinsecall Addition.

Mercury, then, is the water of Creation upon the face of which the
spirit of God moves, as the Genesis creation myth tells us. The
alchemists constantly hark back to the creation, to **Adam and Eve**,
as the foundation of their philosophy. The alchemical opus is, in fact,
a **microcosm** of the divine Creation. The torturing of the water seems
to be an allusion to the process of repeated distillation, required to
purify common mercury; common or vulgar mercury being
constantly contrasted with the sublime philosopher's mercury which
constitutes in fact the Prime Matter of the Stone, the beginning and
end of the opus.

One of the best accounts of the multifarious function of the mercury
concept in alchemy is the oft-quoted passage from the *De mineralibus*
of Albertus Magnus:

> The Mercurie of the Wisemen is a waterie Element, Cold and moyst; this
> is their Permanent Water, the spirit of the Bodie, the unctuous vapour, the
> Blessed Water, the virtuous water, the water of the Wisemen, the
> philosophers Vinacre, the Minerall Water, the Dew of Heavenly Grace,
> the Virgin's Milk, the Bodily Mercurie, and with other numberless names
> is it named in the Bookes of the Philosophers, which names truly, though

they are divers, notwithstanding always signifie one and the same thing, namely the Mercury of the Wisemen. Out of this Mercury alone all the virtue of the Art is extracted, and according to its Nature the Tincture, both Red and White.

This shows how mercury moves from being the word for our liquid metal element quicksilver to become the foundation concept of all alchemical work. There are countless synonyms for mercury, which is the *aqua permanens*, the permanent water which has to stand heat in the process of circular distillation; the condensing mercury is often called dew. It is the basis for creating the red and white elixir or **tincture**.

Mercury is also often called the seed or sperm, and the following quote from Rhodian, instructor of Kanid, King of Persia, shows how mercury and the Stone or elixir are synonymous concepts: 'The Sperm is white and liquid, afterwards red. This Sperm is the flying stone, and it is aereal and volatil, cold and moyst, hot and drie.'

*Liber trium verborum*, 'The Book of Three Words', is also quoted by Vaughan. *The Book of Three Words* is in fact a book of three principles; it is 'the Book of Precious Stone, which is a Body aereall and volatil, cold and moyst, watrie and adustive, and in it is Heat and Drought, Coldnesse and Moysture, one virtue inwardly, the other outwardly'.

From the same work, the paradoxical character of the Stone as being mercury itself is hinted at:

Amongst all great philosophers it is Magisteriall, that our stone is no stone, but amongst the Ignorant it is ridiculous and incredible. For who will believe that water can be made a stone, and a stone water, nothing beirg more difficult than these two? And yet in very truth it is so. For this very permanent water is the stone, but while it is water it is no stone.

The motto of alchemy is **solve et coagula**, dissolve and solidify, and mercury is an archetypal example of the tendency of things to dissolve and coagulate, for it exists as water, and as vapour, and may be fixed or solidified by sulphur to become the solid red sulphide cinnabar.

# The Mercury-Sulphur Theory of the Generation of Metals

When pure red sulphur comes into contact with quicksilver in the earth, gold is made in a short or a long time, either through persistence [of the contact] or through decoction of nature subservient to them. When pure and white sulphur comes into contact with quicksilver in pure earth, the silver is made which differs from gold in this, that sulphur in gold be red, whereas in silver it will be white.

Attrib: Albertus Magnus, *Libellus de alchimia*

> . . . It is of the one part,
> A humid exhalation, which we call
> *Materia liquida*, or the unctuous water,
> On th'other part, a certain crass and viscous
> Portion of earth; both which, concorporate,
> Do make the elementary matter of gold:
> Which is not, yet, *propria materia*,
> But common to all metals and all stones.
> For, where it is forsaken of that moisture,
> And hath more dryness, it becomes a stone;
> Where it retains more of the humid fatness,
> It turns to sulphur, or to quicksilver,
>     Who are the parents of all other metals.

Ben Jonson, *The Alchemist*, II, iii. 143ff

Ben Jonson in his brilliant play presents a classic statement of a classic doctrine, which underpins all transmutatory **alchemy** in the West. Medieval alchemists adopted from the Arabs the theory that all **metals** were a synthesis of **mercury** and **sulphur,** whose union might achieve varying degrees of **harmony**. A perfectly harmonious marriage of the mother and father of metals might produce **gold**. All other metals were in varying degrees imperfect, corrupt and subject to corrosion:

> Nature doth, first, beget th'imperfect; then
> Proceeds she to the perfect. Of that airy,
> And oily water mercury is engender'd;
> Sulphur o' the fat and earthy part: the one,
> (Which is the last) supplying the place of male,
> The other of female, in all metals.
> Some do believe hermaphrodeity,
> That both do act, and suffer. But these two
> Make the rest ductile, malleable, extensive.
> And, even in gold, they are; for we do find
> Seeds to them, by our fire, and gold in them:
> And can produce the species of each metal
> More perfect thence, than nature doth in earth.

op cit., II. iii.

In *The Forge and the Crucible* Mircea Eliade has shown how primitive thought believed in the organic growth of metals in the womb of the earth. Many texts use quite explicit sexual language about the marriage of male and female principles which produces metals in the earth: a *conjunctio*, or mystic marriage, is vital to producing the **elixir** or **Stone** of transmutation.

Jung's monumental work, *Mysterium Conjunctionis*, explores the depth and complexity of the symbolism of the sexual opposites and their union or marriage in alchemy. Mercury and sulphur correspond also to the **King and Queen**, and to **Sol and Luna** (sun and moon) as primal sexual principles of generation and **creation** in the world. Citing an Italian poem of the seventeenth century by Fra Marcantonio Crasselame, Jung provides a very illuminating account of the mystical aspect of the generation of metals:

> If I clearly understood, your unknown Mercury is nothing other than a living innate universal Spirit which, ever agitated in aerial vapour, descends from the Sun to fill the empty Centre of the Earth; whence it later issues forth from the impure Sulphurs and, from volatile, becomes fixed and having taken form, imparts its form to the radical moisture.

Jung comments that 'through his descent Mercurius is made captive and can be freed only by the art':

> But where is this golden Mercury, this radical moisture, which, dissolved in sulphur and salt, becomes the animated seed of the metals? Ah, he is incarcerated and held so fast that even Nature cannot release him from the harsh prison, unless the Master Art open the way.

Here we find the most primitive concepts of the organic growth and incubation of metals, from seeds within the depths of the earth.

**Thomas Vaughan** speaks of the generation of metals in *Magia Adamica* (Rudrum edition, p.146):

> . . . thou wilt find the Earth surrounded with the water, and that water heated, and stirred by the Sun and his starrs, abstracts from the Earth the pure, subtil, saltish parts, by which means the water is thickened, and coagulated as with a Rennet: out of these two Nature generates all things. Gold and Silver, Pearls and Diamonds are nothing else but water, and salt of the Earth concocted.

# Metals

According to the doctrine of **transmutation**, all metals are basically of the same constitution and nature (*see* **The Mercury-Sulphur**

Theory of the Generation of Metals), and we know from research on
Sir **Isaac Newton**'s alchemy that, even after **Robert Boyle**'s *Sceptical
Chemist*, alchemists still believed that they could 'extract' a living
liquid **mercury** from any metal. The **tree** of metals is a common
symbolic icon.

Mircea Eliade (*The Forge and the Crucible*), traces much alchemical
**myth** and symbolism to primitive beliefs about mining and
metallurgy. Gold and copper were mined as early as the fourth
millennium BC. Long before that, stone-age craftsmen discovered
meteoric iron and fashioned this into weapons and tools. The
discovery of techniques of smelting and moulding metals was a
landmark in the history of mankind. The crafts of smith and metal-
worker naturally were given special significance, and myths and
magical theories arose concerning the origin and birth of metals.
Metals were believed to actually grow organically within the earth,
and Islamic alchemists handed on to their European successors the
theory that mercury and **sulphur** were the parents of metals. Thus the
idea arose of the seeds or semen of metals lying within the womb of
the earth, and the recovery of metals being like a process of birth, of
emergence from the dark womb.

**Zosimos** gives an account of the secrecy and restrictions upon the
mining and working of precious metals under the Egyptian Pharaohs.
There can be no doubt that the idea of a secret craft tradition, with its
own theories and myths, lies at the root of our alchemical tradition.
A vital technique of metallurgy was the use of **acids** to separate and
purify metals from their state within mines. Nitric acid or sulphuric
acid was used to dissolve silver and other metals. Much alchemical
myth concerns the death or dissolution of metals and minerals in
waters or acids.

Alchemists say little about the individual metals, a surprising fact!
(But *see* **Gold**.) But lead was vital as **Prime Matter** of all metals.

## Lead

It was not so easy to distinguish metals from one another, and much
confusion could be caused by terminology. Thus tin was called white
lead (*plumbum candidum*), whilst our lead is called black lead
(*plumbum nigrum*). The Egyptians called lead 'the mother of metals',
just as later alchemists called mercury 'the mother of metals'. Lead
was often regarded as the Prime Matter, the starting point of the opus,
its black colour being well suited to the **nigredo** stage of
commencement.

The planet of lead is Saturn, the god who is supposed in Greek myth
to have devoured his own children, and there are alchemical

illustrations of this gory process, corresponding to the process of putrefaction and **mortification** (*see also* **Metals and Planets**):

# Metals and Planets

Nothing could be more basic to **alchemy** than the equation of metals and planets, which dates from very early times. In Mithraism and Hermetic philosophy there is a concept of liberation or **redemption** of the soul, which rises through the planetary spheres. Thus there is a spiritual gradation of planets and **metals**. At the lower end of the scale is Saturn – lead, then Mars – iron; Jupiter – tin; Venus – copper; Mercury – **mercury**; the moon – silver and the sun – **gold**. **John Dee** in his *Monas Hieroglyphica* (1564) makes great play of the significance of the actual planetary symbols, which he considers inventions of the ancient magi, full of magico-cabalist significance: for him each point, line or circle in the planetary symbols has Pythagorean meaning.

There is also the wealth of classical **myth** surrounding the planetary gods, and the correspondence of the planets with metals is fundamental to the Hermetic world view. Early gnostics and Hermetic philosophers were obsessed with **astrology**, gripped by the belief that every aspect of the material and spiritual world was under the sway of stars and planets. To quote from **Chaucer**'s Canones Yeomans Tale:

> The bodies seven eek, lo! hem heer anoon:
> Sol is gold, and Luna silver we thrape,
> Mars yren, Mercurie quicksilver we clepe,
> Saturnus leed, and Jupiter is tin,
> And Venus coper, by my fader kin!

John Dee considers the symbols for the planets and metals to have mystic significance in themselves, being the invention of the ancient magi. He created his Monas symbol as synthesis of the planetary-metals symbols.

In the time of **Zosimos** Saturn was regarded as a Hebrew god: Saturday, the Sabbath, actually means 'Saturn's day'. In his essay on 'Transformation Symbolism in the Mass', Jung provides an explanation of the significance of Saturn-lead:

> The parallel between the Hebrew god and Saturn is of considerable importance as regards the alchemical idea of transformation of the God of the Old Testament into the God of the New.

The alchemists naturally attached great importance to Saturn, for, besides being the outermost planet, the supreme archon . . . and the demiurge Ialdabaoth, he was also the *spiritus niger* (black spirit) who lies captive in the darkness of matter, the deity or that part of the deity which has been swallowed up in his own creation. He is the dark god who reverts to his original luminous state in the mystery of alchemical transmutation.

Of the alchemical metals, gold, silver, mercury and lead are by far the most important: tin, copper and iron are less vital.

# Microcosm-Macrocosm

This doctrine of man as a 'lesser world', reflecting in himself the Hermetic **harmony** of the greater world, is the key to esoteric **alchemy**, which is concerned with the **redemption**, the liberation of man from the dark prison of the elemental world.

It is clear that the Hellenistic, Graeco-Egyptian tradition of alchemy is best characterized as a gnostic tradition (*see* **Gnosticism**). Early gnostic thinkers were also subject to Platonist and other philosophical influences (*see* **Neoplatonism**). The doctrine of the microcosm-macrocosm analogy permeates the **Hermetic texts**, and it may be found in Plato's *Timaeus*, a work which was available in part during medieval times. According to the *Timaeus*, when the universe was formed, God decided to rescue it from disorder and lack of harmony by implanting reason and a world soul, thus rendering the cosmos 'a living being with soul and intelligence'. This concept of an *anima mundi* is vital to the Hermetic tradition, and provides the rationale for the microcosm-macrocosm analogy.

Marie-Louise von Franz advances clear evidence that the Philosophers' **Stone** was made analogous to the **Creation** or cosmos. The earliest evidence dates from the third century AD, which was a time when the heretical gnostic and Hermetic cults and communities flourished. The gnostic alchemist Olympiadorus says that 'Hermes calls man the small cosmos' (which is the literal translation of *mikro-kosmos*), for man reflects the processes of the great cosmos. Just as the greater world has animals in land and sea, so man nourishes fleas, lice and worms. Man's intestines correspond with the rivers, wells and oceans. His breath is like the winds, and his two eyes correspond to the sun and the moon, the right eye to the sun, the left to the moon.

**Zosimos of Panoplis** provides a rare insight into the gnostic theology underlying third-century alchemy as a gnostic tradition.

Although not a Christian in any sense, he makes clear that the alchemical work must be performed upon man himself, as the *terra Adamica*, the Adamic earth (i.e. man's Adamic body).

In this conception of alchemy, **Adam** is compared to the cosmic **egg** of the philosophers, being composed of the four **elements** with animating **spirit**. The egg is a classic symbol for the cosmos, not only in Greek Orphic tradition, but also in the Chinese Taoist and the Indian Tantric schools of alchemy (*see* **Chinese alchemy; Indian alchemy**). Zosimos likes the whole opus to a process of hatching a cock from an egg, the **Prime Matter** being often described as the egg, or the cock, of the man 'accursed by the sun', i.e. man after the Fall.

The microcosmic notion of man was influential in the Middle Ages, but it did not accord too well with the Aristotelian world view of scholastic theology. There remained, however, an undercurrent of mystical **Neoplatonism** and the **Cabala**.

During the Renaissance there was a burgeoning of occult philosophies (*see* **Magic**), incorporating Platonist mysticism and Hermetic magic. In this climate, **Paracelsus** introduced the idea of man as endowed with inner heavens or *astra* governing his health (*see* **Astrology**). *See* Jolande Jacobi, *Paracelsus*, p.21, for the following citations from Paracelsus' vast corpus of writings:

> Since man is a child of the cosmos, and is himself the microcosm, he must be begotten, each time anew, by his mother. And just as he was created by the four elements of the world even in the beginning, even so he will be created in the future again and again. For the Creator created the world once, and then He rested . . . . Thus life in the world is like life in the matrix [i.e. in the womb]. The child in the maternal body lives in the inner firmament and outside the mother's body it lives in the outer firmament.
>
> The inner stars of man are in their properties, kind and mature, by their course and position, like his outer stars and different only in form and in material. For as regards their nature, it is the same in the ether and in the microcosm man . . . . Just as the sun shines through glass – as though divested of body and substance – so the stars penetrate one another in the body . . . . For the sun and moon and all planets, as well as all the stars and the whole cosmos, are in man . . . the body attracts heaven . . . and this takes place in accordance with the great divine order.

The following passage comes from the *Secretum secretorum* (***The Secret of Secrets***), a work treasured by **Roger Bacon**. This work existed in a variety of medieval **manuscript** versions, and came via the Arabic Hermetic tradition. The text leaves no doubt as to the identification of the microcosm with the Philosophers' Stone and the philosophers' egg, all of which are typical of the kind of symbols which circulate around the core of the philosophy, intimating at mysteries rather than stating clear explanations:

> . . . take the animal, vegetable, and mineral stone, the stone which is neither a stone, nor has the nature of a stone, although it is created resembling some stones of mountains and mines, for it also resembles vegetables and animals. And it exists in every place and time, and with every man. And it has all colours, and in it there are present all the elements. It is the microcosm. I shall name it to thee according to its common names. Take the egg, I mean the philosophers' egg. Divide it into four parts, each part being a nature (or element). Then compound it equally and temperately in such a way that the various parts should join but one counteract each other.

*See also* Marie-Louise von Franz, 'The Idea of the Macro- and Microcosmos in the Light of Jungian Psychology', *Ambix*, 1965.

# *Monas Hieroglyphica*

This is the title of a cabalist, alchemical work of Dr **John Dee** (1527–1608), published by Willem Silvius of Antwerp in 1564. It contains a long prefatory letter addressed to Maximilian II of Habsburg, full of cabalist learning, and the entire work is a structure of cabalist **numerology**, whose real significance eludes us today, as it did most of Dee's bewildered contemporaries. Renaissance **magic** knew of three cosmic dimensions: the natural, the celestial and the supracelestial. Dee claims that one in a thousand philosophers will understand his *Monas*, but only one in a million will understand God's **Creation** on celestial as well as supracelestial levels.

Meric Casaubon, a seventeenth-century scholar and editor of Dee's **angel magic** communications, says that Dee was 'a Cabalistical man, up to the ears, as may appear to any man by his *Monas Hieroglyphica*, a book much valued by himself'.

The Monas symbol itself is compounded of the standard alchemical-astrological symbol for **Mercury** with the sign for Aries added at its foot, Aries being the spring sign, the first sign of the zodiac, belonging to the fire triplicity. The upper part of the symbol comprises the circular symbol of the sun (*see* **Sol and Luna**), with a semicircle representing the moon, suggesting a marriage, a *conjunctio*, of sun and moon – this being the fundamental concept of **alchemy**, the union of active and passive, male and female, universal principles:

Our hieroglyphic monad possesses hidden away in its innermost centre, a terrestrial body. It teaches without words, by what divine force that [terrestrial body] should be actuated. When it has been actuated, it [i.e. the terretrial centre] is to be united (in perpetual marriage) to a generative influence which is lunar and solar, even if previously they were widely separated.

> See 'Prefactory Letter to the *Monas Hieroglyphica*' (*Ambix* 1964)

Dee calls the **conjunctio** of Sol and Luna by the magic name 'Gamaaea', composed of two Greek words meaning 'earth of marriage': this may well refer to the well-known Adamic earth of the opus. Using this magical symbol, the magus can go through a metamorphosis, attaining the invisibility of the magus. There can be no doubt of the magical nature of Dee's alchemy, practised in the prestigious tradition of Renaissance *magia naturalis*:

> The scryer may here see most exactly in a crystal lamin all sublunary things that are on the earth, in the water, and, in a carbuncle or ruby stone, he will explore the entire regions of air and fire.
>
> op. cit

Dee cites the mysteries of **Hermes**, **Ostanes**, Pythagoras, **Democritus** and Anaxagoras, and to explain his cabalist numerology, he uses a series of theorems in imitation of Euclid's *Geometry*. There are 24 theorems, the last of which is apocalyptic (*see* **Prophecy**):

Theorem III explains that the central point of the Monas is the earth, the centre of orbit of sun and moon in pre-Copernican astronomy.
Theorem VI says that sun and moon rest upon a rectilinear cross which represents the four elements – and Dee detects not only the quaternary, but also the mystic ternary, in this cross.
Theorem X refers to Aries as a fire sign, added at the foot of the cross: 'The sun and moon of this monad desire their elements, in which the Denarian proportion will be strong, to be separated, and that this be done with the aid of fire.'
Theorem XII claims that the ancient magi designed all five planetary signs from the sun and moon.

# Morienus
## Or Marianus; seventh century

Prince Khaled ibn Yazid, of the Umayyad dynasty, is said to have been the first Arab to follow the alchemical quest; he died in 704 AD. He is said to have commissioned the translation of works from Greek and Syriac, and to have sought the company of philosophers and alchemists from Egypt. After consulting many alchemists, however, Prince Khaled achieved nothing, and is said to have ordered the execution of fraudulent alchemists who promised **transmutation** but were unable to perform this.

This led him to seek out the Christian hermit and alchemist Morienus, who lived the life of an ascetic mystic, refusing even the comfort of a monastery or hermitage, and living in the mountains near Jerusalem. Jung quotes a long and revealing tract from Morienus, which indicates that he espoused a form of gnostic **alchemy**, seeking mystical goals rather than material wealth (*see* **Gnosticism**). He is said to have sought to convert the Arab prince to Christianity.

The tenth-century biographer Ibn al Nadim lists various works attributed to Prince Khaled which were the fruit of his consultations with Morienus. These include a book of amulets and an alchemical testament – many alchemists composed testaments of faith in the art. The prince also wrote lengthy treatises in verse, the longest being 'The Paradise of Wisdom'.

However, there is some doubt as to the truth of the legend of Khaled's consultation with Morienus.

# Mortification
## The Theme of Death and Resurrection

As Jung has so abundantly proven, the themes of life, death, resurrection, rebirth and **redemption** are really the key to alchemical **myth**. Mortification is strongly associated with the *nigredo* and the putrefaction, all referring to the blackness and death encountered early in the opus. The idea of 'killing' **mercury** is familiar in **Indian alchemy** as it is in western alchemy, where the myth of the killing of the **dragon** or serpent is always cropping up. The dragon announces boldly:

> 'I announce therefore to all you sages, that unless ye slay me, ye cannot be called sages. But if ye slay me, your understanding will be perfect, and it increases in my sister the moon according to the degree of our wisdom, and not with another of my servants, even if ye know my secret.'
>
> Cited by Jung, *Mysterium Conjunctionis*, p.138, from the *Rosarium*, and oft-quoted in other texts

Jung associates the slaying of the dragon with the stage where the spirit mercury is freed from the prison of the **Prime Matter**, and it is analogous to the slaying of the **King**, so frequently illustrated, who is the symbol of Sol (see **Sol and Luna**). 'The idea that the dragon or Sol must die is an essential part of the mystery of transformation' (*Mysterium Conjunctionis*, p.142).

> The alchemists understood the return to chaos as an essential part of the opus. It was the stage of the *nigredo* and mortificatio, which was then followed by the 'purgatorial fire' and the *albedo*. The spirit of chaos is indispensable to the work, and it cannot be distinguished from the 'gift of the Holy Ghost' any more than the Satan of the Old Testament can be distinguished from Yahweh. The unconscious is both good and evil and yet neither, the matrix of all possibilities.
>
> Jung, op. cit., pp.197

# Multiplication and Projection

The **elixir** or **Stone** of the Philosophers is often likened to a ferment, which is introduced to a liquid. Thus a tiny portion of a 'powder of projection' is thought to start a process of **fermentation**, or transformation, which leads to production, by 'multiplication', of an ever-increasing amount of **gold** or silver.

These concepts of multiplication and projection are most brilliantly explained by Ben Jonson in his brilliant play, *The Alchemist*. He refers to the power of the 'great Medicine', which is the elixir which heals to corruption or imbalance of the baser **metals** when it is projected onto these metals:

> But when you see th'effects of the great Medicine,
> Of which one part projected on a hundred
> Of Mercury, or Venus, or the Moon.
> Shall turn it, to as many of the Sun;
> Nay, to a thousand, so *ad infinitum*.

**Mercury**, Venus and the moon here designate the metals mercury, copper and silver, the sun being gold (see **Metals and Planets**).

In another grandiloquent speech, the alchemist Subtle emphasizes the phenomenon of multiplication, which is the result of projecting the elixir or 'great Medicine' onto various metals:

> For look, how oft I iterate the work,
> So many times, I add unto his virtue.

As, if at first, one ounce convert a hundred,
After his second loose, he'll turn a thousand;
His third solution then; his fourth, a hundred;
After his fifth, a thousand thousand ounces
Of any imperfect metal, into pure
Silver, or gold, in all examination,
As good as any of the natural mine.

Ben Jonson is ridiculing the gullibility of the adepts of his time. Hundreds of years of failure to discover any reliable method of **transmutation** did nothing to dim the enthusiasm of the early seventeenth century, when stories of the success of **John Dee, Edward Kelley** or **Sendivogus** were on everyone's lips. Even Lord Burleigh, trusted adviser and minister of Elizabeth I, was inclined to take Edward Kelley seriously. This suggests that besides the mystical aspect of the art, transmutation really was an aim.

# Mylius, Johann
*floruit* **1620s**

Johann Mylius was a student of philosophy and **medicine** at Wetterau in Hesse, whose well-known *Philosophia Reformata* (Philosophy Reformed) was published by Luca Jennis in Frankfurt in 1622. This work amounts to 700 pages. The first volume concerns the origin and generation of **metals** as well as the 12 **stages** of the opus, with a general account of **alchemy,** and the second volume provides quotations. The work contains 60 illustrations, which were also used by **Daniel Stolz** with full acknowledgement. As an epilogue, Mylius included an earlier work by Johann Bringer: *Azoth, sive Aureliae Occultae Philosophorum* (Frankfurt, 1613).

Mylius' work is another example of the passion for alchemical writing and symbolism which swept across Europe through the early seventeenth century. This was the period of lavish emblem books, such as those published by **Michael Maier.** This was also the period of the spread of fervent interest in the philosophy of the **Rosicrucians**, with its strong emphasis on the immense value of medical and mystical alchemy.

# Myth in Alchemy

**The Jungian theory of alchemy** is based upon Jung's vast research into the interrelationship between **dreams** and archetypal myth symbolism. In searching for the psychological meaning of the alchemical opus, Jung revealed a whole network of myths and mythic images which have the deepest psychological significance, above all myths to do with death and rebirth, with descent to the underworld and ascent to the highest realization of spiritual life.

Ben Jonson's play *The Alchemist* provides a range of myths current in the alchemical writing of his day:

> I have a piece of Jason's fleece, too,
> Which is no other, than a book of alchemy,
> Writ in large sheepskin, a good fat ram's vellum.
> Such was Pythagoras' thigh, Pandora's tub,
> And all the fable of Medea's charms,
> The manner of our work: the bulls, our furnace,
> Still breathing fire; our *argent-vive*, the dragon;
> The dragon's teeth, mercury sublimate,
> That keeps the whiteness, hardness, and the biting;
> And they are gathered into Jason's helm.
> Th'alembic, and then sow'd in Mars his field,
> And thence, sublim'd so often till they are fix'd.
> Both this, th'Hesperian garden, Cadmus's story,
> Jove's shower, the boon of Midas, Argus' eyes,
> Boccace his Demogorgon, Thousands more,
>     All abstract riddles of our stone . . .

*The Alchemist*, II. i. 89-104

These lines beautifully convey the interplay of classical myth and chemical operation. The golden fleece made a natural allegory for the opus, as did the **Grail** legend.

From its earliest roots, **alchemy** drew upon the Egyptian mysteries of Isis and Osiris for mystic names for chemicals: Osiris represented lead. The astral associations of **metals and planets** involves alchemists in a whole network of pagan myths (*see* **Beasts; Pelican; Phoenix; Sol and Luna**), while Sir **Isaac Newton** puzzled for decades over the chemical meaning of arcane mythic symbolism, which Jung interprets as projection of the unconscious mind and its archetypal conflicts.

# Nature

From earliest times alchemists were aware that their art was distinct from nature, being an attempt to use artificial means to alter the natural state of things. The motto of the early Greek texts is: 'Nature helps nature, nature rejoices in nature, nature conquers nature.' This suggests a philosophy of nature, and one of the earliest alchemical texts is that attributed to the pseudo-**Democritus**, entitled *Phusika kai mustika*. This does not mean simply 'physical and mystical things' – *phusis* is the Greek word for nature, and *mustika* denotes things associated with initiation into the mysteries. Thus the alchemist is initiated as adept into the realm of natural and secret mysteries.

**Thomas Thymme**, an Elizabethan commentator and student of **John Dee**'s writings on **alchemy**, gives this lucid and coherent account of the adept's relationship with nature:

> As Nature worketh effectually allone in this manner, so much more effectually, when Art is joyned with Nature. For Art prepareth for Nature, and ministreth unto it the·matter in the last preparacion, and Nature prepareth and disposeth for herself unto the end with the help of Art; and afterwards bringeth in the forme, even Golde Chemicall, better than that which is simply naturall because it is mixed with a burning Sulphur, corrupting and wasting. Nature (with Arte) hath congealed and hardened some things, with weake and faint heate, and hath left them half digested as Leade and Tynne, and some thinges hath hardened with a sufficient temperate heate, as Silver. Some things it hath not hardened, by reason of the want of heate, and for the want and separation of silver, as Quicksilver. And some things it hath hardened with a convenient temperature, as Gold. Imperfect metals are in fact Silver and Gold, but their sickness and imperfections do hide their properties . . . .
>
> From Thomas Thymme, *A light in darkness, which illumineth for all the* Monas Hieroglyphica *of the famous and profound Dr. John Dee*, ed. S.K. Heninger

# Neoplatonism

A whole range of scholarship has now cast light upon the rise of

Renaissance Neoplatonism and its connections with the tradition of religious Hermetic philosophy which illuminated the work of the alchemists.

Medieval philosophy and science, derived directly from Islam, was dominated by **Aristotle**, although Plato's cosmological *Timaeus* was also known. During the 1460s, Marsilio Ficino established a school of Platonist philosophy, which supplanted Aristotle for many Renaissance humanists and magi. Ficino was asked by his patron Cosimo dei Medici to translate from Greek the entire Hermetic corpus, before embarking upon Plato, Plotinus and Iamblichus. His work established a Renaissance tradition of astral **magic** and **astrology** which strongly influenced men like Dr **John Dee** and **H.C. Agrippa**. His successor was Pico della Mirandola, whose *Oration on the Dignity of Man* dispelled medieval ascetic visions of man, substituting a grand vision of man in commerce with angels and demons. The Renaissance tradition of natural magic, which involved **Trithemius**, Dee, **della Porta**, **Fludd** and **Thomas Vaughan**, as well as the Paracelsians, owes much to the Platonising influence of Ficino and Pico. Though neither were actually alchemists, their work influenced the philosophy of all who worked with alchemical theories.

Modern historians of science are increasingly ready to admit the influence of traditions like alchemy, magic, Neoplatonism and Hermetic philosophy upon the rise of modern experimental science which took off with the founding of the Royal Society in England. Certainly **Isaac Newton** was under the influence of Platonising and Hermetic theories of his time, derived from the Renaissance.

*See* F.A. Yates, *Giordano Bruno and the Hermetic Tradition.*

# Newton, Sir Isaac
## born Christmas Day 1642, died 1727

One of the startling revelations to emerge from recent research into Newton's work and personality is the importance he gave to alchemy in study and in experimental practice. There is still controversy over possible links between Newton's mathematical work (his 'respectable' science) and his alchemical work, which had its 'respectable' chemical aspect, but also involved delving into ancient myth and symbol. Maynard Keynes, a collector of Newton's alchemical notes and writings, described him as not being 'the first of the age of reason', but rather 'the last of the magicians, the last of the Babylonians and Sumerians'. This he felt justified in thinking 'because he looked on the whole universe and all that is in it as a riddle'. The alchemist sought 'mystic clues' which are part of the Lord's **Creation**. Newton was a deeply religious man, and his vast researches into biblical chronology are not out of tune with mystical alchemy.

The chronology of Newton's achievements in science is well known to historians, but where does alchemy fit, and how could a rational genius like Newton engage in the adept's 'Huntyng of the Grene Lyon'?

The son of a Lincolnshire yeoman, Newton entered Trinity College, Cambridge, in 1661 and graduated BA in 1664–5. During the plague epidemic of 1665 he abandoned Cambridge, to return in 1667 with the fruits of his *annus mirabilis*. His three great scientific, mathematical achievements were his discovery of white light as being composed of the colours of the spectrum, his theory of fluxions (the basis of calculus), and his first mathematical law of gravity. Proceeding MA, he was elected Fellow of Trinity College, and in 1669 Isaac Barrow resigned his Lucasian professorship in mathematics to make room for the young genius. In 1672 Newton was elected a Fellow of the Royal Society, mainly on the basis of his optical discoveries. It should be remembered that **Elias Ashmole** was also an FRS, and his world view was dominated by **astrology**, alchemy and **magic**.

Newton's greatest work was the *Principia* (The Mathematical Principles of Natural Philosophy) and it should emphasized that science and philosophy were not distinguished at this time. In 1696 he was appointed Warden of the Royal Mint, where he was involved with the massive project of renewing the coinage, and in 1699 he was Master of the Mint, responsible for persecuting forgers and clippers of the coinage.

The problem of Newton's alchemy is a vast subject for research. He was certainly a diligent and skilled experimenter with a well-equipped laboratory, and he was involved with the complex chemical philosophy emerging from the work of men as diverse as **Robert Boyle** and Sir **Kennelm Digby**. He also has much in common with the alchemical work of John Locke. A thorough-going study by Betty Jo Dobbs, *The Foundations of Newton's Alchemy*, is essential reading. A vivid portrait of the intensity of his work is given by his nephew and laboratory assistant, Dr Humphrey Newton:

> He very rarely went to bed till two or three of the clock, sometimes not until five or six, lying about four or five hours, especially at spring and fall of ye leaf, at which time he used to spend about six weeks in his elaboratory, the fire scarcely going out either night or day.
>
> *The Foundations of Newton's Alchemy*, p.34

Newton is said to have written an alchemical text book from the experimental work which he carried, but unfortunately this was burnt.

Keynes classified Newton's **manuscripts** as follows (quoted op. cit., p.21):

1) The more or less complete exact transcripts of others' works, the largest group.
2) Translations of others' writings, probably by Newton himself.
3) A group of summaries, indexes and comparisons.
4) A very small group of Newton's own contributions.

It is important to emphasize that Newton entered wholeheartedly into the forefront of the alchemical movement of his day. Under the influence of Boyle, Digby and others, alchemy was becoming increasingly experimental and chemical. But these men were still fascinated by the symbolic and mythic language of alchemy, and Newton's endeavours and labours at the **furnace** seem to show a complete fascination with these riddles. Betty Jo Dobbs comments that:

> He had read Greek alchemists, Arabic alchemists, the alchemists of the medieval Latin West, of the Renaissance and of his own period. He had read Aristotelian alchemists, medical alchemists, Neoplatonic alchemists, and mechanical alchemists. He had read the most mystical and the most pragmatic.
>
> op. cit., p.19

We are left to speculate that natural magic and alchemy, which inspired so many sixteenth-century Renaissance scientists, exerted its sway over Newton, especially in his attitude to the divine Creation as a system of riddles and mystic clues, accessible only to the adept.

# *Nigredo*
## Greek: *melanosis*, meaning literally 'blackening'

Again and again in his profound psychological account of **alchemy**, Jung returns to the *nigredo*, which is the initial **stage** of blackness and melancholy (*see* **Colours**). This is also involved with the *putrefactio* and the *mortificatio*, confronting us with the death and rebirth theme so fundamental to the quest (*see* **Mortification; Redemption**). The stage is followed by that of the *albedo*, the whitening or purifying, baptism and washing. On an experimental level, this refers to the *calcinatio*, the burning and blackening, and also to dissolution.

In the *Aurora Consurgens*, 'the golden hour of dawn shines yellow and red (*citrinitas* and *rubedo*) midway between night (*nigredo*) and day (*albedo*)'. Olympiodorus is cited on this: 'To the North they assigned the *nigredo*, to the East the *albedo*, the white substance which is called silver.'

**George Ripley**, in his *Book of the Twelve Gates* describes the stage thus (the head of the crow is the famous *caput corvi*, crow and **dragon** being archetypal symbols of the **Prime Matter** in its *nigredo* state):

The head of the Crowe that token call wee,
And some men call it the Crowes bill;
Some call it the ashes of Hermes tree,
And thus they name it after their will;
Our toade of the earth which eateth his fill,
Some nameth it by which it is mortificate
The spirit with venome intoxicate.
But it hath names I say to thee infinite,
For after each thing that blacknes is to sight,
Named it is till time it waxeth white,
Then hath it names of more delight,
After all things that been full white,
And the red likewise after the same,
Of all red things doth take the name.

The **uroboros** or the dragon are classic symbols for the *nigredo* stage, representing as they do the Prime Matter (*Prima materia*) in its blackened state of **mortification** and putrefaction. The slaying of the dragon is vital to the progress of the opus: the *Rosarium* has the oft-quoted maxim, 'The dragon dieth not, except with his brother and his sister.' As Jung shows,

> . . . the idea that the dragon or Sol must die is an essential part of the mystery of transformation. The *mortificatio*, this time only in the form of mutilation, is also performed on the lion, whose paws are cut off, and on the bird whose wings are clipped. It signifies the overcoming of the old and obsolete as well as the dangerous preliminary stages which are characterized by animal-symbols.
>
> Jung, *Mysterium Conjunctionis*, p.142

# Norton, Thomas
## Dates and exact identity uncertain; *floruit* 1470s

All that is known of this famous author comes from his long poem,

'The Ordinall of Alchimy', which has pride of place in the *Theatrum Chemicum Britannicum* of **Elias Ashmole**. Norton and **Ripley** are the two major contributors to the genre of English alchemical poetry, which was a lively tradition in the Middle Ages. We know that Norton came from Bristol and the **manuscript** illustration of a neat laboratory, with a chemical balance, suggests he may have been a man of means (*see* Fig. 2, p.**49**). His father was probably the Norton who was Sheriff and then Mayor of Bristol in 1413, and thereafter MP for the city.

The 'Ordinall' was written in 1477 and Norton tells us that he studied for 40 days with his master George Ripley in Yorkshire to learn the 'secrets of Alkimy'. The tale of dejection and depression following the theft of his red **elixir** is all too typical, and he relates the story of another unfortunate alchemist, Thomas Daulton, a monk in an abbey in Gloucestershire. Daulton was forced to attend the court of Edward IV, and the nobility were clearly interested in **alchemy**. One manuscript of the 'Ordinall' bears the arms of George Nevill, Archbishop of York, and this prelate seems to have offered patronage to Ripley as well.

Norton attests the rampant craze for **gold**-making alchemy which afflicted his time, and his own work was influential, being treasured by Ashmole and his alchemical Master **William Backhouse**, and even by Sir **Isaac Newton**. Alchemy was clearly rife in Church and state, amongst rich and poor alike:

> Popes with Cardinalls of Dignity,
> Archbyshopes with Byshopes of high degree,
> With Abbots and Priors of Religion,
> With Friars, Heremites, and Preests manie one,
> And Kings with Princes and Lords great of blood . . .
> For every estate desireth after good.

> 'The Ordinall of Alchimy'

# Numerology

The whole secret of the art of **alchemy** may be attributed to numerological formulae. The mystical 'shriek' of **Maria Prophetissa**, the Jewish gnostic, speaks of the derivation of the entire opus from the primal **unity**, through duality, to triad or trinity, and thence to quaternity.

The earliest Greek philosophers were preoccupied with the problem of 'the One and the many' (*see* **Unity**), and already in the writings of Stephanus of Alexandria in the sixth century we see gnostic ideas of numerology. The source and origin of such speculation is the philosophy of Pythagoras, and the Pythagoreans founded a mystical cult which attributed all kinds of symbolic functions to numbers. Their belief was that the entire cosmos, in a sense, consists of numbers, or even is constructed from numbers, numbers being a sort of **Prime Matter.**

The whole problem of medieval philosophy, as derived from both Hellenistic and Islamic sources, was to account for the mystery of **Creation** as the process of birth of the cosmos from the Creator, the ineffable, mystical unity of God (*see* **Harmony; Hellenistic Alchemy; Islamic Alchemy**). God creates the universe in six days and rests on the seventh, and the numerology of seven is everywhere in alchemy and Hermetic or cabalist mysticism and **magic.**

In most **myths** of Creation, the primal act is to create a duality, a pair of opposites, and Jung's vast researches in *Mysterium Conjunctionis* are devoted to deciphering the problem of the opposites which derive from unity. *The Emerald Tablet*, the ancient **Hermetic text**, suggests a concept of Creation in which meditation on unity produces all things, and the parents of all things are the primal opposites **Sol and Luna.** The dual opposites in alchemy, then, are sun and moon or Sol and Luna, **mercury** and **sulphur,** which are the father and the mother of **metals** (*see* **Mercury-Sulphur Theory of the Generation of Metals**). In Christian alchemy, the Trinity or 'Ternary' was increasingly important. The **Stone** of the Philosophers is in its nature a Trinity composed of body, soul and **spirit**, as well as being animal, vegetable and mineral.

With the advent of the Paracelsians and the Renaissance *magia naturalis*, the universe is increasingly conceived as founded upon the Trinity: in natural magic there is the trinity of the terrestrial, celestial and supra-celestial worlds, within which the magus seeks to operate. Dr **John Dee** tells us that the quaternary of the four **elements** actually rests on the ternary or trinity (*see* **Monas Hieroglyphica**). **Paracelsus** worked out the theory of *Tria Principia*, the three cosmic principles which are named as **salt**, sulphur and mercury. This triad does not displace the four elements, rather it provides the mystic structure of the cosmos. **Joachim of Fiore** divides the prophetic structure of history into a trinity of 'status' or **stages**: the Old Testament is the status of the Father, the New Testament epoch is the age of the Son, and an eagerly awaited millennarian, spiritual realization of human history is the monastic age of the spirit.

Numerology reaches its zenith in sixteenth-century alchemy, where John Dee's famous *Monas hieroglyphica* (1564) is a sophisticated working out of a system of the **Cabala** and the mathematical Pythagorean philosophy of numbers. **Thomas Thymme**, strongly influenced by this work, on which he made a commentary, discusses the numerological significance of a version of *The Emerald Tablet*:

> True it is without a lye, certaine and most true, by the affinity of Unity. That which is superiour is like to that which is inferiour, and that which is inferiour is like that which is superiour, because all Numbers consist of Unites, for the working of many miracles of one thing. Do not all things flow from Unitie through the goodness of the One? Nothing that is varying, and in discord can be ioyned to Unity, but the like that by simplicity, aptacion, and fitness of one, it may bring forth fruite; what else springeth from Unitie, but the Ternary it selfe. The Unarie is simple, the Binarie is compound, and the Ternary is reducible to the simplicity of Unitie. His father is the Sun, his Mother is the Moone. The Wind carrieth the seede in his Wombe, the Earth is the Nourse. Thou shalt separate the Earth from the Fire, the thick from the thin, and the Ternary being now brought to it selfe with witt, it assendeth upward wiyth greate sweetness, and returneth againe to Earth adorned with virtue and greate beauty, and so it receiveth superiour and inferiour force, and it shall be from henceforth potent and orient in the brightness of Unitie, to produce all apt number, and all obscurity shall flee away.

The passage shows how the text of *The Emerald Tablet*, attributed to **Hermes Trismegistus**, acquired a somewhat incongruous Christian significance. Alchemists were always keenly aware in the Christian tradition that the 'Ternary' really means the Trinity, while **unity** naturally means God as Creator, from whom emanates all numbers, i.e. the full multiplicity of the universe. However, the pagan text makes the sun and moon (*see* **Sol and Luna**), the father and mother of the miraculous unity of the mystical **stone**.

Marie-Louise von Franz quotes the following passage from the writings of the sixteenth-century Paracelsian writer, **Gerard Dorn**:

> The whole world has its form from the holy ternarius number three in its order and measure, because one is no number but is the union of peace. Number two, on the contrary, is the first number, which can be counted and is the source and origin of strife and conflict. Through accepting or taking on a material form, two has cut itself off from the original oneness and can only be made to return into that through a completely solid unbreakable bond. As one can only mate similar things with similar things, and because God has pleasure only in odd numbers, the one unites, with its simplicity, the two into a three, and gives them a soul.

> Cited p.33, Marie-Louise von Franz, *Alchemical Active Imagination*

These passages give insight into the vital importance which numerology plays all through the alchemical tradition.

Regarding the significance of specific numbers, the number four is always associated with the four elements and their opposing qualities. This is the quaternary. Jung has explored the universal, archetypal symbolism of this in alchemy and comparative religion: the fourfold structure forms the basis of most western **mandala** symbolism in alchemy and religious art.

Five is associated with the **quintessence**, the mystic fifth or spiritual 'element' of which the heavens are composed.

The number six figures very little in western numerology, but seven is a number with vast implications. The seven planets correspond to the seven metals (see **Metals and Planets**). The number has supreme significance in the obsessive astral mysticism of the Hermetic, cabalist and early magical philosophies which flourished during the Hellenistic emergence of alchemy. Not only is seven a supremely biblical number, but the seven seals of the book of Revelations were especially significance in millennarian speculation (see **Joachim of Fiore; Prophecy**). Seven is also magical and pagan.

The number eight, the ogdoad, is to be found in Paracelsian theory, with the concept of the 'eight mothers' or matrices of the universe, probably derived from the Cabala.

Twelve is naturally vital, with the twelve signs of the zodiac, and many alchemical works are based upon a twelve-fold arrangement: **Ripley**, for instance, in his *Book of the Twelve Gates*, divides the **processes** or stages of the opus into twelve, as do many other authorities.

Numerology is a universal 'science', relevant to every aspect of magic and divination, and we find a great deal of astral numerology in **Chinese alchemy**, which has a system of five elements, and which, of course, owes no debt to the Bible, or to millennarian speculation, so influential in the West.

# Ostanes
## Persian magus; third century BC

Ostanes is one of the names which appears regularly amongst Greek alchemical texts of the Hellenistic period, and various tracts were attributed to him. He was one of the Persian magi who influenced the Hellenistic alchemists in Egypt, and he appears in the well known work, the *Physika kai mustika* (Natural and Initiatory Things), attributed to **Democritus** (*see* **Bolos of Mendes**). This is to be found in the transcript of St Mark's, Venice. It is well known as an early alchemical text, including various recipes for dyeing, but also passages concerning the quest for the secret of 'harmonizing the natures', an alchemical concept. Ostanes appeared as the main teacher of a group of frustrated alchemists. He is said to have communicated wisdom in **dreams**, and Jung cites a text where Ostanes instructs adepts to visit the Nile, to seek there a stone with a **spirit**, and to 'draw out its heart, for its heart is in its soul'; this may be a reference to the process of heating cinnabar to release the vapour or spirit **mercury** (*see* Jung, *Psychology and Alchemy*, p.356).

Persian magi belonged to a priestly tribe of the Medes, and they were influenced by Chaldaean **astrology**. Herodotus names one Ostanes as brother of Xerxes who accompanied that emperor in his disastrous invasion of Greece. Pliny blames this Ostanes, along with Zoroaster, for the epidemic craze for Persian **magic** which swept the Greek world. He says that Ostanes 'disseminated there germs of this monstrous art and so infected all parts of the world'.

An Ostanes is also named as the magician who accompanied Alexander the Great on his conquests, and he is said also to have instructed Democritus of Abdera.

There is the story that when he died, his disciples used necromancy to summon up his spirit, in order to discern the secret of the 'harmonizing of the nature', the key to the alchemical sacred and magical art. The spirit of the magus directed them to a temple in Egypt, saying only that 'the books are in the temple', but they found only the enigmatic inscription, which became the motto of **Hellenistic alchemy**: 'One nature rejoices in another nature, one nature conquers another nature, one nature rules another nature.'

# P

## Paracelsus
### Latin name adopted by Dr Theophrastus Bombastus von Hohenheim; born Einsiedeln c. 1493, died 1541

Paracelsus seems to be intended to mean 'beyond Celsus', for this powerful reformer in the history of **medicine** boasted that his form of alchemical-medical philosophy transcended the learned medicine of the Galenist physicians of his day. Our word 'bombastic' derives from his dynamic attacks upon the contemporary authorities.

Paracelsus came of a family of Swabian noblemen and his father was a physician. He was born at Einsiedeln, a mountain place of pilgrimage in Switzerland, and was early initiated into **alchemy** and natural **magic** (*magia naturalis*) by **Trithemius**, Abbot of Sponheim. Much of his enthusiasm for alchemical remedies seems to originate from his work in famous mining districts. He studied in Vienna (1509–11) and at Ferrara in Italy (1513–16). After his university training, he spent seven years wandering the length and breadth of Europe, and it is difficult to know whether his own catalogue of countries visited is an exaggeration: between 1517 and 1524 he says that he journeyed to Russia, Turkey, the Balkans and the Middle East, not to mention Scandinavia, England and Spain.

Paracelsus may have been army surgeon in Scandinavia from 1518 to 1521, and he served as military surgeon to the Venetians in 1522. This work gave him a contempt for academic physicians who had no experience of surgery: he dismissed them as 'painted monkeys' and all his life he attacked classically trained Galenist physicians, advocating that they abandon their studies to consult 'The Book of Nature', using as their guide not academic authorities, but the very light of **nature**, the *lumen naturae*, provided by God's **Creation**.

During 1525-6 he served as radical physician in Salzburg, then in Strassburg, and in 1526 his reputation reached its zenith. In that year he apparently succeeded in treating Johannes Frobenius, the Basle humanist publisher and friend of Erasmus. Following this success he was appointed as town physician (*Stadt Physicus*) of Basle, a prestigious appointment carrying with it the duty of lecturing in the university there. He soon caused outrage in the establishment, for not only did he lecture in German in an era of academic Latin, but he preached that physicians should abandon their textbooks and consult 'The Book of Nature'. He was finally driven out in 1528, and during the 1530s his life became hopelessly unstable. He made a bid for the patronage of the Habsburg Emperor Ferdinand I, but failed to secure his position, and was left to wander through Switzerland, Germany and Austria composing a range of unique books, not only on medicine but also on theology, which did not see publication until after his death in 1541.

He published very little at all during his lifetime, although the books *Der Grosseren Wundartzney* (Books of the Greater Surgery) appeared in 1536-7, establishing a distinguished medical reputation.

## The Theories and Writings of Paracelsus

Paracelsus is the most important and consistent philosopher in the history of the alchemical tradition, and it is still unclear whence he derived his integrated system of theories and ideas. Dr W. Pagel suggests that **Gnosticism** as well as **Neoplatonism** provided a foundation, and if he studied with Abbot Trithemius, he would have been introduced to natural magic, which, with the **Cabala**, was so much in fashion during this theological age.

Paracelsus regards nature not as a system of laws, but as a dynamic, autonomous, creative flow, its vital force more magical and mystical than rational and law-bound. The source of everything created is not the divine intellect of a father-figure God: it is the Great Mystery (*Mysterium Magnum*), a concept which closely resembles that of the mystical Tao (*see* **Chinese Alchemy**).

Paracelsus evolved in his philosophical and theological tracts a complete vision of the cosmos, of the divine process and miracle or mystery of the Creation, and his philosophy is truly alchemical in the highest sense of the word. His idea of man, in health and sickness, is the ancient **microcosm-macrocosm** analogy: medieval medicine assumed that the stars ruled the body (*see* **Astrology**), but Paracelsus teaches that within man there are inner planets or constellations, the *astra*, in fact an inner heaven. This inner heaven corresponds to the outer heavens which we observe, and it is the inner *astra* which govern health and sickness.

In assessing his vast output, there is still much research to be done. His earliest writings are medical books or tracts which are remarkably clear and concise. Following his lectureship at Basle, he embarked on the large-scale philosophical works which were collected by his followers after his death, edited and published.

## Publications:

Paracelsus' account of the Creation and constitution of the world is expounded in the *Philosophy to the Athenians*.

The *Paragranum* and the *Opus Paramirum*, dating from the period 1530-4. These lay the foundations for Paracelsus' revolutionary concept of an alchemical system of medicine. The *Paragranum* rests the edifice of medicine upon four pillars: 1) philosophy; 2) astronomy; 3) alchemy; 4) virtue.

The *Opus Paramirum* gives an account of five entities (*entia*, from the Latin word *ens*) which give rise to sickness in the body:

1) *ens veneni* (poison);
2) *ens naturale* (natural entity);
3) *ens astrale* (the astral entity or factor);
4) *ens spirituale* (spiritual entity);
5) *ens deale* (from Latin *deus*, meaning the divine or God-given entity).

The *Volumen Paramirum* (to be distinguished from the *Opus Paramirum*) explains the best known aspects of Paracelsus' medical theory. Above all there is the doctrine of the **Tria Prima**, the three principles of **mercury, sulphur** and **salt** which Paracelsus regards as the ultimate trinity of principles underlying the phenomenal world. These are not to be conceived as **elements**, and the ancient system of four elements remains: rather they are the active principles of creation. Jolande Jacobi explains that 'the *Paragranum* and the *Paramirum* are a complete exposition of ideas that had matured for a long time; they conclude a period in Paracelsus' development'.

The *Books of the Greater Surgery* were published in 1536-7, the only major works which were published during Paracelsus' short lifetime.

*Astronomia Magna* (1537-9), a work which fills 500 printed pages; this huge work concerns the microcosmic nature of man.

*See* W. Pagel, *Paracelsus*, and Jolande Jacobi, *Paracelsus: Selected Writings*, which gives a valuable chronology of the works of the master.

## Paracelsians

Paracelsus was one of the great scientific revolutionaries in the history of medicine, and his influence still needs to be more fully researched. His writings and lectures inspired a whole movement, which involved searching in 'The Book of Nature' for new medical remedies from chemical, metallic and mineral sources. His leading apostles included **Oswald Croll, Gerard Dorn, Joseph Duchesne** (Quercetanus), **John Dee, Heinrich Khunrath**, Adam von Bodenstein, Alexander Suchten, Michael Toxites and **Leonhardt Thurneysser zum Thurn**. These men collected, edited and published his works, which appeared in central Europe during the 1560s and 1570s.

In 1571 **Petrus Severinus**, physician to the Danish king, published his *Idea of Philosophical Medicine*, an important defence of Paracelsus. This work urged the physician to sell books and possessions and to plunge into 'The Book of Nature', studying animal, vegetable and mineral cures, and building **furnaces**, rather than frequenting libraries. This sums up the vigorous new aims of this powerful scientific and spiritual movement.

Physicians like Thomas Erastus, however, sought to reinstate the authority of the classical Galenist tradition against this dangerous radical innovation in medicine. In 1572–3 Erastus published *Disputations on the New Medicine of Paracelsus*, a savage attack on Paracelsus and all his works which sought to demolish Paracelsian medicine, attacking its cures as dangerous and toxic, and its theories as erroneous, especially the doctrine of the three principles (*see* **Tria Prima**). In spite of this, however, the Paracelsian movement continued its advance.

### Paracelsians, English

England was rather slow to produce budding Paracelsian physicians, but after a sluggish start in the reign of Elizabeth, Paracelsian medicine gained ground during the seventeenth century.

In 1559 Conradt Gesner, the Swiss naturalist and physician, provided a book on pharmacy translated into English as *Treasure of Euonymus*, a work with many chemical or mineral cures, then in 1585 R. Bostocke published *Difference between the auncient Phisicke . . . and the latter Phisicke*. Little is known of Bostocke, but he provides a vigorous defence of the Paracelsian doctrines of the microcosm and the three principles.

John Hester was another Elizabethan Paracelsian, an apothecary by trade. He translated a work of Dr Leonardo Fioravanti, called *A Ioyfull Iewell* (1579). Dr Thomas Moffett defended chemical medicines in a work of 1584 and was involved with a project for a Pharmacopoeia, under the auspices of the Royal College of Physicians. George Baker, Master of the Company of Barber-Surgeons, lent his authority to the new chemical medicine, and a distinguished surgeon, John Woodall, threw much light on Paracelsian medicine. In 1617 he published *The Surgions Mate*, which concerned primarily the problems of serving as ship's surgeon. **Thomas Thymme**, a friend of John Dee's, was also a translator of Paracelsian works.

John Dee's great library at Mortlake contained a whole section of 'Paracelsian books'.

# Peacock
## Peacock's tail = *cauda pavonis*

Meanwhile she of the Peacocks Flesh did Eate
And Dranke the Greene-Lyons Blood with that fine Meate,
Which Mercurie, bearing the Dart of Passion,
Brought in a Golden Cupp of Babilon.

From Ripley's *Cantilena*, verse 17 (cited in Jung, *Mysterium Conjunctionis*, p.285)

Ripley's song describes the nuptials of a **King and Queen**, and the Queen during pregnancy feeds upon peacock's flesh. The peacock was renowned in legend for its ability to consume and neutralize poisons: in medieval **medicine**, viper's flesh was a vital ingredient, since it was supposed to contain an antidote to poison. The peacock figures in alchemical art because of the multi-coloured **stage** in the opus called *cauda pavonis*, peacock's tail (*see also* **Colours**). Jung locates this stage before the *albedo* or *rubedo*:

Immediately before the *albedo* or *rubedo* 'all colours' appear, as if the peacock were spreading his shimmering fan. The basis for this phenomenon may be the iridescent skin that often forms on the surface of molten metal (e.g. lead). These *omnes colores* are frequently mentioned in the texts as indicating something like totality. They all unite in the *albedo*, which for many alchemists was the climax of the work.

Jung argues that eating the peacock's flesh is equivalent to 'integrating the many colours' of the opus. He also says:

The *cauda pavonis* announces the end of the work, just as Iris, its synonym, is the messenger of God. The exquisite display of colours in the peacock's fan heralds the imminent synthesis of qualities and elements, which are united in the 'rotundity' of the Philosophical Stone.

The peacock is sacred as the bird of Juno, mother of the gods.

# Pelican

The pelican is familiar in alchemical art as wounding itself in order to feed its young with its own blood; thus, like the **phoenix**, it is an archetypal symbol for Christ whose blood redeems mankind (*see* **Redemption; Stone**).

The pelican was also a familiar piece of medieval **apparatus**, its function being 'the digestion of substances by long steeping in hot fluid to extract the essence'. The apparatus works by reflux **distillation**: the substance under treatment is boiled and the vapour condenses in the glass head, then flows back, establishing a **process** of circulation.

# Philalethes, Eirenaeus
### Pseudonym for author of mid-seventeenth century alchemical tracts

Eirenaeus says that he wandered the world and discovered the Philosophers' **Stone** in 1645, in his twenty-third year. He claims to be a friend of **Robert Boyle**, and there is a long list of works attributed to him. The mystery of his true identity is one of the great problems in the history of **alchemy**. The remarkable metaphysical alchemist **Thomas Vaughan** used the pseudonym 'Eugenius Philalethes', but Eirenaeus is generally thought now to be **George Starkey** (1627–65). Starkey arrived in England during November 1650, bringing with him a series of tracts on alchemy which he attributed to a New England adept. It has been suggested that the tracts were in fact the work of a New England physician, Dr Childe, but the evidence favours attribution to Starkey himself. The **manuscripts** were circulated within the 'Invisible College', of which **Samuel Hartlib** was the presiding genius. Starkey also brought with him an **elixir**, consisting of some sophic **mercury** which was to be used for **multiplication** of his supply of the white elixir.

The Philalethes tracts are a determined bid to revive interest in the medieval alchemy of **George Ripley**, also drawing upon Paracelsian sources (*see* **Paracelsus**), above all **Sendivogius** and D'Espagnet.

### Publications:
*The Marrow of Alchemy, being an Experimental Treatise discovering the secret and most hidden mystery of the Philosophers' Elixer* (London, 1654).

*Introitus appertus ad occlusum regis palatium* (Open Entrance to the Locked Palace of the King) (Amsterdam, 1667).

*Ripley Reviv'd: or an Exposition upon Sir George Ripley's Hermetico-poetical Works* (1678). This work contained the following tracts by 'Philalethes':

1) *An Exposition upon Sir George Ripley's* Epistle
2) *An Exposition upon Sir George Ripley's* Preface
3) *An Exposition upon the First Six Gates of Sir George Ripley's* Compound of Alchymie.
4) *A Breviary of Alchemy; or a Commentary upon Sir George Ripley's* Recapitulation.
5) *An Exposition upon Sir George Ripley's* Vision.

*A Breviary of Alchemy; or a commentary upon Sir George Ripley's recapitulation; being a paraphrastical epitome of his* Twelve Gates.

*Opus tripartitum de philosophorum arcanis* (A Triple Work concerning the Secrets of the Philosophers) (1678). This is in three parts: the first includes a section on method; the second part concerns experiments on preparation of sophic mercury; and part three is an alchemical *vade mecum.*

*Enarratio methodica trium Gebri medicinarum in quibus continetur lapidis philosophici vera confectio* (Methodical Account of Three Medicines of **Geber** in which is contained the True Making of the Philosophers' Stone) (1678).

*The Secrete of the Immortal Liquor called Alkahest* (1683).

*See* R.S. Wilkinson, 'The Problem of the Identity of Eirenaeus Philalethes', *Ambix*, 1964; *also* **George Starkey.**

# Phoenix

Of all the mythic **beasts and birds** of the alchemists, the phoenix deserves special attention as the classic symbol of the sacrifice, of the death and resurrection of Christ (*see also* **Pelican**). Medieval legend has it that the phoenix dwells in Arabia, but flies to Egypt, the home of **alchemy**, to undergo its death and rebirth. The phoenix is an archetypal sun symbol (*see* **Sol and Luna**), being burnt to ashes to rise anew, and it is ideal for the death-rebirth symbolism of the *nigredo* **stage** of the opus. In *Symbola aureae mensae* **Michael Maier** goes in quest of the phoenix in Egypt, and Jung discusses its alchemical significance in *Mysterium Conjunctionis* (pp.211–17). Maier identifies the phoenix with the alchemical bird called 'Ortus', which had 'a red head with streaks of gold reaching to its neck, black eyes, a white face, white forepaws, and black hindpaws'. The **colours** represent the alchemical panacea which is a remedy for all ills and corruption in this material world, and Maier begs the bird to give its feathers to the wise man.

# Porta, Giambattista della
## born Naples, 1535, died 1615

Although not well known as an alchemist, della Porta belongs to the distinguished tradition of *magia naturalis*, which was popularized by **H.C. Agrippa**. Natural **magic** was a vital influence upon alchemists and a worked-out philosophy of magic dominated the minds of men like Dr **John Dee**, and later **Elias Ashmole**. It was believed that the universe was pervaded by magical forces of sympathy and antipathy, and that divine **harmony** pervaded the cosmos: this made it easy to believe in alchemical miracles.

Porta belonged to a noble family and is said to have been so gifted that he produced *Magiae Naturalis*, his influential book on natural magic, at the age of 15. Four volumes of this project appeared in 1558: Book One dealt with magic, spiritualism and magical sympathy in the universe; Book Two was mainly a practical study of fruits, with experiments on improving them, and items like fireworks, different kinds of ink or poisons also featured; Book Three was alchemical, dealing with production or extraction of waters and oils, and covering also **metals**, glass and imitation gems; Book Four contained optical experiments – which were classed as magic in these naïve times. The work was an instant success and passed through many editions. In 1589 there appeared an enlarged version, with 20 books. Book Five was devoted to chemical things, including **transmutation**. In a Preface, della Porta strove to defend himself against superstitious attack. He explains magic as involving sympathy and antipathy, and emphasizes the practical science of fruits and bread.

**Publications:**
*Magiae Naturalis, sive de miraculis rerum naturalium* (four books, Naples, 1558).

*See* J.R. Partington, *A History of Chemistry.*

# Prime Matter
## *Prima materia*; first matter

As with all the key concepts in **alchemy**, this is supremely difficult to define in any useful manner. However, various alchemical philosophers do present a coherent view. **Chinese alchemy** was not faced with the conceptual and scientific problems inherent in the hybrid western tradition, and Taoism provides a view of **nature** which is quite lucid. The primal intuition that the universe must have some unborn origin takes verbal form in the *Tao te Ching*:

> There is a thing confusedly formed,
> Born before heaven and earth.
> Silent and void,
> It stands alone and does not change,
> Goes round and does not weary.
> It is capable of being the mother of the world.
>
> *Tao te Ching*, XXV, tr. D.C. Lau

In seeking to reach the essence of the material world, the true nature of matter and of phenomena, western alchemists found themselves in possession of a tradition of fiendish complexity. They inherited from Islamic philosophers a tradition which was firmly monotheistic: God was the sole Creator of the world, and therefore ultimately everything in the world must be traced back to God's ineffable unity of being (*see* **Islamic Alchemy; Numerology; Unity**).

Jung analyses the resulting confusion of the texts concerning the meaning and nature of the *prima materia*:

> The basis of the opus, the *prima materia*, is one of the most famous secrets of alchemy. This is hardly surprising since it represents the unknown substance that carries the projection of the autonomous psychic content.
>
> *Psychology and Alchemy*, p.304

It was common to regard **mercury** as the essence of all things, the prime substance, although Jung cites an entry in the *Lexicon* of Martin Rulands, published in 1612, which gives 50 synonyms for prime matter. Early Greek philosophers sought to derive the universe initially from one single **element**: Thales chose water as the ultimate constituent of everything, and **Joan Battista van Helmont** revived this ancient and obvious notion. Herakleitos, however, made fire the basis of everything: 'Everything is an exchange for fire.' Since both water and fire are such vital principles in alchemy, they sometimes qualify as prime matter too.

Stephanus of Alexandria, writing in the sixth century, suggests that by his day the Pythagorean concepts of **numerology** were accepted as fundamental to alchemy and to understanding matter and prime matter:

> The multitude of numbers compounded together has its existence from one atom and natural monad. This, which itself exerts a mutual condition, comprehends and rules over the infinite as emanating from itself. For the monad is so-called from its remaining immutable and unmoved. For it displays a circular and spherical contemplation of numbers like to itself.
>
> F. Sherwood Taylor, 'The Alchemical Works of Stephanos of Alexandria' *Ambix*, 1937

For the purposes of practical alchemy, as opposed to theoretical philosophy, the adept has to start with something, and the **nigredo stage** may be identified with the *prima materia*: the *nigredo* or blackness is the initial condition present from the beginning as a quality of the *prima materia*, also described as the chaos or *massa confusa*.

Most texts explain that in order to achieve **transmutation**, the adept must reduce his **metals** to their prime matter. The theory is that as physically existing metals, **gold** and silver are dead, inert, lacking in **spirit**, the spagyric art revives them by means of the spirit, to make the gold and silver of the philosophers. Transmutation can never take place without reducing metals to their prime matter, so that they may yield their seed, the active ferment which leads to creation of the healing **elixir**. There is little controversy over the alchemical doctrine that the first matter of metals must be mercury.

Most alchemists were content to dabble and experiment with 101 ingredients as the starting point for the transmutatory opus. However the true philosophers of the tradition are concerned with the secrets of the universe, with the true state of the divine **Creation**. In his *Philosophy to the Athenians*, **Paracelsus** shows himself a profound mystical philosopher, and his account is not so far from the Taoist conception of Tao as mother of all things:

> Of all created things the condition whereof is transitory and frail, there is only one single principle. Included herein were latent all created things which the aether embraces in its scope. This is as much as to say that all created things proceeded from one matter, not each one separately from its own peculiar matter. This common matter of all things is the Great Mystery (*Mysterium Magnum*). Its comprehension could not be prefigured or shaped by any certain essence or idea, neither could it incline to any properties, seeing that it was free at once from colour and from elementary nature . . . . This Great Mystery is the mother of all the elements.

**Thomas Vaughan** has this to say about the *prima materia* in his *Aula Lucis* – writing during the seventeenth century, he is nevertheless fully consistent with the ancient tradition, which sees the mercurial *prima materia* as the beginning and end, the **alpha and omega** of the opus:

> First, that the first matter of the stone, is the very same with the first matter of all things.
>
> Secondly, that in this matter all the essential principles, or ingredients of the Elixir, are already shut up by Nature, and that wee must not presume to add anything to this matter, but what wee have formerly drawne from it; for the stone excludes all extractions, but what distill immediately from its owne chrystalline universal Minera.
>
> Thirdly, and lastly, that the philosophers have their peculiar secret metals, quite different from the metals of the vulgar, for where they name Mercury they mind not quicksilver; where Saturn, not lead, where Venus and Mars, not Copper and Iron.

# Processes or Operations

A whole series of chemical, laboratory processes are involved with **alchemy**, and it is as usual difficult to relate **myth** to experimental practice. A number of operations have specific entries, but they are summarized here. **Distillation** is probably the most important, for it involves the alchemical **mercury**, and it is profoundly significant at a symbolic level as a process of purification, of separating the subtle, **spirit** from the gross matter or body.

The motto of alchemy was *Solve et Coagula*, dissolve and coagulate, and texts which give recipes for experiments show how processes of dissolving solids, especially **metals**, were vital – a range of **acids** was used, above all nitric acid, to separate out **gold**, while the search for a universal solvent or **alkahest** was essential. Coagulation was known from the operation of fixation of mercury: **sulphur** + mercury led to coagulation, it being supposed that metals were created in the very earth by this process of uniting sulphur and mercury (*see* **Mercury-Sulphur Theory of the Generation of Metals**).

*See also* **Stages**, where the symbolic, mythic progression to the **Stone** or **elixir** is summarized. Here some of the chemical processes are outlined:

1) Normally, *calcination* comes first, involving reduction of the solid metal or mineral to a powder. This is usually achieved by roasting, which leads to oxidation and blackening, hence the stage of *nigredo*.

2) *Solution*: The blackened earth or powder thus produced is next dissolved in the philosophers' **bath**: 'Until all be made water, perform no operation' was a maxim of the philosophers. This is a stage of washing and purification.

3) *Separatio* is traditionally next, involving the release of the spirit or watery vapour from the body or earthy matter.

4) **Conjunctio**, which follows, involves 'a combination of qualities, equalisation of principles, a putting in order of contrariety'. This is the mystic marriage of **Sol and Luna**, of sophic sulphur and mercury, of the **King and Queen** of the opus. The hot dry fiery principle (sulphur) is married to the cold moist, watery principle (mercury). Alchemical illustrations show rainstorms as a symbol of fertility.

5) The marriage is followed by the stage of *putrefaction*, which involves the death of the product of the mystic marriage (also called *mortificatio, calcinatio*).

6) *Ablutio*, washing or baptism (*see* alchemical **bath**), is next, leading to the vital stage of *albedo*, the whitening. This is the first major achievement, or *magisterium*: it is the white elixir or Stone. This may be preceded by the many-coloured tail of the **peacock**, the *cauda pavonis*.

7) The final stage is always the red, *rubedo* stage, which creates the red elixir. The 'Red Magisterium' is the culmination of the opus.

## Textual Evidence and Citations

This all sounds fine in theory, but how does it work in practice?

First, it is vital to appreciate the variety of instructions: *there is no standard procedure* followed in alchemy. A good example of the complex elaboration of basic processes is shown in an illustration from **Thomas Norton**, of the Philosophical **Tree**. This recommends as many as seven preparatory stages before the first major goal of the opus, the mystic *conjunctio*, the union or marriage of opposites, including purgation, sublimation, calcination, fixation, solution and separation. The ninth stage is the putrefaction in sulphur which follows the *conjunctio*. Then there is solution, the dissolving of the sulphur body, leading to the important stage of **fermentation** (in fact the Stone or elixir is often described strictly as a *ferment*). This is followed by **multiplication**. The culmination of this tree is the production of the white elixir (though of course this is only the first stage, before achieving the red). The white elixir is credited with powers of healing and **transmutation**.

Norton was a sophisticated alchemist with a well-equipped laboratory in Bristol. Other alchemists followed a simpler outline of processes.

Another interesting text concerning alchemical processes is the printed edition of **Paracelsus'** *The Secrets of Alchemy* (probably spurious). This instructs the adept to prepare two sorts of mercury ready for the *conjunctio*. First, philosophical mercury is to be dissolved in quick mercury to kill it or fix it (i.e. solidify or coagulate it). To this end glass **vessels** and a moderate fire are to be prepared. The heat will create blackness in the first matter, and then the dryness will begin to work on the humidity:

> . . . there will likewise arise in the Glass, varrious flowers of divers colours, such as appeare like the taile of a Peacocke, and such as no man ever saw before.

Sometimes, apparently, it seems as though the glass 'were drawn into Gold', indicating that 'the seed of the Male doth rule and operate upon the seed of the Female'. This text strongly emphasizes the growing, vegetative nature of the opus. Slowness is vital, and the stage of whitening, or *albedo*, must grow naturally: what is quickly born will hastily perish! 'For so soon the Sun and the Moon do cause Maturity, and bring to birth, as the infant from the belly of his Mother, so the grain from the bowels of the Earth.'

The transition to the invincible red elixir sounds childishly simple. The adept slowly heats the whiteness, producing a yellow colour (*citrinitas*). This 'Yellow and Saffron-like Colour' may then reach perfect redness, with the right heat. 'Then is the substance of Gold prepared, and there is born an oriental King sitting in his Throne, and ruling over the Princes of the World.'

This stage was followed by **multiplication**.

# Prophecy

From its inception, **alchemy** was strongly associated with the religious concepts of **redemption** of the soul and/or **spirit** of man and **nature**, with liberation of the spiritual realm from the dark cave or prison of the material world, and by the time the tradition was fully established, from the third to the fourth centuries AD, it was rooted in **Gnosticism**. This was a prophetic, apocalyptic religious movement, and the religious aspect of the tradition continued through **Islamic alchemy** into the Middle Ages, where **Petrus Bonus of Ferrara** discovered that esoteric alchemy was essentially prophetic.

**Thomas Thymme**, the Elizabethan disciple of **John Dee's**

cabalist alchemy, gives the following eloquent account, but it should not be assumed that this is an Elizabethan invention in the tradition. **George Ripley**, John of Rupescissa and others were strongly prophetic in their approach, and **Joachim of Fiore** was an influence upon esoteric alchemy. Thymme expresses himself like this:

> This noble Science is the way to caelestiall and supernaturall things, by which the ancient wisemen were led from the worke of Arte and Nature to understande, even by reason, the wonderfull powre of God in the Creation of all things and their final purification by alteracioun through fire in the day of doome. At which time God will separate all the unclean faeces, and corrupcion that is in the foure Elements and bring them to a Christalline cleereness . . . .

> Thus we see, that the heavenly contemplacion of this Scyence, is no common ascending, nor for every mans pitch, neither is it to be gotten of them which are carried upward with one winge only, but is familiar to very few, namely to them which have seriously reduced themselves to Unitie.

# Quintessence

This is one of those all too universally applicable alchemical concepts which covers a multitude of sins.

It is common in eastern and in early western philosophy to equate **spirit** with breath: in Greek *pneuma* has this significance, as does the idea of *prana* in Sanskrit, which combines the idea of physical breath with that of spiritual energy. Early Greek speculation identified *pneuma* with spirit, and this tended to be regarded as a fifth **element**, which is the root meaning of 'quintessence', or fifth essence. The signs are that the Greek texts edited by Berthelot, relating to early **Hellenistic alchemy**, are based on a theory of using the spirit or *pneuma*, identified with rising vapours, as a **tincture**, to tinge **metals** by penetrating them: clearly the best **colour** dye must penetrate the substance, and only a strong spirit or essence can achieve this. **Distillation** separates and frees the spirit-vapour from the body, and this spirit must be reunited with another body, on which it can work as an active spiritual principle. The quintessence extracted by the alchemist from **nature** is regarded as equivalent to that incorruptible quintessence of the which the stars are made, as eternal luminaries.

A **manuscript** in the British Library gives a good idea of the whole concept of quintessence. Its title: 'The Book of Quinte Essence or the Fifth Being; that is to say, Man's Heaven. A tretise in englisch brevely drawne out of the book of quintis essenciis in latin that hermys the prophete and kyng of Egipt, after the flood of Noe, fadir of philosophris, hadde by revelacioun of an aungil of god to him sende'. This shows the classic need to foist texts upon ancient prophets: here **Hermes Trismegistus** is classed with biblical prophets. The text concerns the **elixir** of life, which, it soon emerges, is actually distilled alcohol. Distillation was constantly interpreted as separation of a spirit from the body. When the distillation of alcohol was discovered in the fourteenth century, this was given various names: *aqua ardens*, or burning water, 'the soul in the spirit of wine', and *aqua vitae*, water of life, as well as *quinte essence*.

The concept developed of 'extracting' the quintessence, a spiritual essence, from various bodies. Thus quintessence sometimes appears as synonymous with spirit, with elixir or **medicine**, and even with the **Stone** itself. Sometimes all of these words are assumed to be quite synonymous.

*See* F. Sherwood Taylor, 'The Idea of the Quintessence; in Science Medicine and History' in *Essays in Honour of Charles Singer.*

# Redemption

The great achievement of the **Jungian theory of alchemy** is the discovery of the soteriological significance of its **myth** and symbolism, and above all the proof that the mystic *Lapis*, the **Stone** of the Philosophers, was constantly equated with Christ as Redeemer. Gnostics were concerned with the liberation of the **spirit** or soul from the dark prison of the material world (*see* **Gnosticism**), and **Hellenistic alchemy** became completely gnostic, as may be seen with **Zosimos** (third century AD), who expounds the doctrine of the gnostic *anthropos*, the man of light in the prison of the flesh, the redeemer being the gnostic Son of Man. Zosimos was a non-Christian gnostic, but later alchemists use the Christian doctrine of the redemption by Christ. In an interesting passage from the *Aurora consurgens*, attributed to Sir Thomas Aquinas, Christ is called the second **Adam**, born to redeem the Fall of the first mortal Adam (*see* **Adam and Eve**). An illustration from **Ripley** shows how medieval alchemists identified the true Stone of the Philosophers with the figure of Christ as Redeemer. In this way the all-pervasive symbolism of death, torture and rebirth, which is expressed in the pagan myth of **alchemy**, becomes Christianized.

Jung also relates the themes of ascent and descent in alchemy to the doctrine of Christ the Redeemer. *The Emerald Tablet* suggests the **unity** of the **processes** of ascent and descent as the key to alchemy. Jung cites **Mylius** as saying that the earth cannot ascend unless heaven comes down first (i.e. Christ the Redeemer must descend to earth). The earth can only be redeemed by dissolution in its own spirit. He quotes the Paracelsian Penotus, who identifies Mercurius with Christ, the Son of Man:

> As to how the son of man is generated by the philosopher and the fruit of the virgin is produced, it is necessary that he be exalted from the earth and cleansed of all earthliness; then he rises as a whole into the air and is changed into spirit. Thus the word of the philosopher is fulfilled: He

ascends from earth to heaven and puts on the power of Above and Below, and lays aside his earthly and uncleanly nature.

Penotus, cited Jung, *Mysterium Conjunctionis*, p.222

**Khunrath** identifies the Stone with Christ as the *filius macrosmi*, the Son of the Macrocosm. The Paracelsians were thus responsible for a tremendous impetus towards the kind of spiritual alchemy espoused by **Jacob Boehme**, an alchemy in which all laboratory or chemical vestiges have disappeared, submerged in a new form of Christian revelatory mysticism. What is astonishing is that the pre-Christian gnostic roots of alchemy are true to the similar concept of redemption, as found in medieval and sixteenth-century texts.

The ideas of purification and redemption are universal, archetypal notions, and it becomes obvious that the kind of yoga tradition of alchemy popular in India has this basic motif, this concept of liberating the spiritual nature of man through the purification of suffering (*see* **Indian Alchemy**).

Jung summarizes the theme like this: the key concept of ascent/descent in alchemy involved 'the freeing of the soul from the shackles of darkness, or unconsciousness; its ascent to heaven, the widening of consciousness; and finally its return to earth, to hard reality, in the form of the tincture or healing drink, endowed with the powers of the Above' (Jung, op. cit., p.224).

# Reusner, Hieronimus

An example of a fine sixteenth-century book:

*Pandora, das ist die edelste Gab Gottes, oder der werde und heilsame Stein der Weisen mit welchem die alten Philosophi, auch Theophrastus Paracelsus, die unvolkommene Metallen durch Gewalt des Fewrs verbessert.*

'Pandora, that is the most worthy Gift of God, or the noble and healing Stone of the Philosophers, with which the ancient Philosophers, including also Theophrastus Paracelsus, improved the imperfect metals through the power of Fire.'

A book with beautiful illustrations, printed in Basle in 1582, reprinted Basle 1598 and Frankfurt 1706. It illustrates the great popularity of **alchemy** with sixteenth-century readers.

# Rhazes
## Abu Bakr Muhammad ibn Zakariyya al-Razi, 'The Man from Ray'; famous Persian physician; born 866, died 925 AD

Known to the West as Rhazes, this Arabic physician practised **medicine** and lectured at Ray and at the hospital in Baghdad. He was a celebrated doctor in the Hippocratic tradition, and he praised men like Hippocrates and Euclid as men of science, in contrast to religious leaders who deceive their people. Religious fanaticism, he believed, leads to wars.

His **alchemy** lacks the imagery and mysticism of the Jabirian school, but there are 21 books on alchemy ascribed to him. His *Kitab Sirr al Asrar* (Book of the Secret of Secrets) deals with **apparatus** as well as chemicals, which are classified as animal, vegetable and mineral. His work on **salts** and alums, *De salibus et alumibus*, was famous in the Middle Ages, including chapters on **elixirs** or medicines of **transmutation** of **metals**. Minerals are arranged as **spirits** and bodies, vitriols, boraces and salts. Rhazes expounds a doctrine of spirits: two are combustible and volatile, namely salammoniac and **mercury**. **Sulphur**, arsenic, realgar and orpiment are divided according to these four spirits. Stones and metals are classified as 'bodies'. 'Vitriols' include ferrous sulphate and alum. Apparatus includes beakers, flasks, phials, basins, glass crystallizing dishes, jugs, casseroles, pots with lids, and porous cooking jars. For heating, the physician recommends candle lamps, **athanors**, smelting **furnaces** and bellows. His tools include hammers, ladles, shears, tongs, forceps, moulds and crucibles.

Like **Avicenna** and **Jabir**, al-Razi was a philosopher of eminence. He criticized **Aristotle**'s idea of space, affirming a concept of absolute space and absolute matter which existed before the **Creation**. He was an atomist, believing in indivisible particles of matter. Like so many Islamic philosophers, he held gnostic doctrines about the fall of the soul into the body: gnosis is achieved through the intellect which is the Creator's gift to awaken the slumbering spirit. *The Dictionary of Scientific Biography* tells us that hostile tradition accused him of ruining wealth through alchemy, destroying the body through his medicine and corrupting the soul by defaming the prophets (Vol. XI, pp.323-6).

*See also* R. Steele, 'Practical Chemistry in the Twelfth Century: *Rasis de aluminibus et salibus*', *Isis*, 1929.

# Ripley, George
## Dates uncertain, died *c.* 1490

Ripley was probably the most influential alchemist in the English poetical tradition, and he was the master who communicated the secrets of the art to **Thomas Norton** of Bristol – Norton was happy to travel 100 miles to see him. He was born in the Yorkshire village of Ripley, and by the 1470s he was securely established as Canon of Bridlington Priory in Yorkshire, an Augustinian foundation. He is said to have studied theology at Rome and Louvain, and his continental travels brought him into contact with alchemists who perhaps had more sophisticated notions of the art than their English counterparts: **Geoffrey Chaucer** in the Canones Yeomans Tale paints a picture of the blind leading the destitute in ruinous expense in experimental work to find **gold**. Ripley studied the arcane arts with the Knights of St John on the island of Rhodes, and legend has it that he eventually was able to contribute vast sums of money to their crusade. The Knights of St John were strongly suspected of practising **magic** and witchcraft, and there is every reason to suppose that Rhodes was exposed to influence from throughout the Middle East.

Ripley was strong enough to secure patronage from royalty and nobility alike at a time when, according to Thomas Norton, **alchemy** was all the rage at every level of society, throughout the Church, at court and amongst the nobility. Like Norton, he dedicated a work to George Neville, Archbishop of York. This was the *Medulla alchimiae* (The Marrow of Alchemy) (1476). His *Compound of Alchimie* dates from 1471 and was dedicated to King Edward IV. His strange work, the *Cantilena*, has been subjected to analysis by C.G. Jung: it is a legend of a king who seeks an heir (*filius philosophorum*, Son of the Philosophers). He seeks return to the maternal womb by dissolving himself in the *prima materia* (**Prime Matter**). His mother (i.e. the alchemical matrix) becomes pregnant and feeds herself on **peacock**'s flesh and drinks the blood of the Grene Lyon. The result is the birth of the Son of the Philosophers who changes from moonlike radiance to splendour of the sun (*see* **Sol and Luna**). He becomes a great healer and reformer of sins.

Apart from this **myth**, composed in verse, Ripley is famous for his vision of a toad, which passes like a chameleon through the **colours** of the opus:

> When busy at my books I was upon a certain Night,
> This vision here expressed appear'd unto my dimmed sight:
> A Toad full ruddy I saw, did drink the juice of Grapes so fast,
> Till over-charged with the broth, his Bowels all to brast . . .

The theme is the death of the toad, imbibing its own poisonous venom: the dying toad becomes 'like coal for colour black' - clearly an allusion to the *nigredo* (*see* **Processes; Stages**). Next follows the putrefaction. Heating the rotting carcass, the alchemist perceives the colours of the *cauda pavonis*, the peacock's tail. From the venom he creates a **medicine** or **elixir**, which is precisely the poisonous **mercury** which, when properly treated, becomes the healing elixir which is both the elixir of life and the medicine of **metals** in a mystical sense.

**Publications:**

*The Compound of Alchymy. Or, the ancient hidden Art of Alchemie: conteining the right . . . means to make the Philosophers Stone, Aurum potabile, with other excellent Experiments* (1591). This is a translation completed by Ralph Rabbards, who mentions **John Dee**'s *Monas* in his Preface. The work is called in Latin: *Liber duodecim portarum*, or 'The Book of Twelve Gates', and sets out a sequence of twelve stages or processes. There is a dedicatory letter to King Edward IV, and the English edition includes the poem of Ripley's toad as well as his **mandala** diagram, 'Ripley's Wheele'.

Sir **Isaac Newton** was strongly influenced by a work published by **Eirenaeus Philalethes** - a pseudonymous translator:

*Ripley Reviv'd: or an exposition upon Sir George Ripley's Hermetico-poetical Works* (1678). The work boasts that the most arcane secrets from ancient philosophy are revealed within.

## The Ripley Scroll

The 'Ripley Scrowle' may derive from an original work of George Ripley, but surviving copies date from the end of the sixteenth century. There are two copies extant in the British Library and one in the Fitzwilliam Museum in Cambridge. Adam Mclean comments, 'It was influential upon the explosion of emblematic symbolism during the first decades of the seventeenth century, and many copies of it must have been in circulation.' He dates the scroll to the latter sixteenth century, making it contemporary with the *Splendor solis* (The Sun's Splendour) and the *Rosarium* illustrations.

The first emblem in the Scrowle is that of a bearded old man with a Hermetic **vessel** in which a circulatory process is in motion, the rising of vapours within the vessel being symbolized with feathers. This is supposed to represent the arising of the **elements**, one from another. An inscribed ribbon refers to the hidden **Fountain** of the Philosophers, from which is born the ferment or **Stone**. Conspicuous in the vessel is the form of the black toad, reminding us of Ripley's verse on the colour changes of the toad. Beneath the toad is a wheel or mandala figure representing the progress of the opus.

The second emblem shows a castle with four towers displaying a **dragon** emblazoned on one wall with a black toad. Within the castle is an alchemical **bath**, and from this rises a pillar which supports an astonishing structure in the form of a castle with seven towers, which is once more an alchemical bath. King Sol and Queen Luna are bathing therein (see **King and Queen; Sol and Luna**), and a philosophical **tree** rises from the bath.

# Rosicrucians

The Rosicrucian movement is one of the great enigmas of history, and Dr F.A. Yates has provided the groundwork for study of what she terms the 'Rosicrucian Enlightenment of the early seventeenth century'. This was a period of intense millennarian anxiety, with grim forecasts of the end of the world, so the announcement of the existence of a reforming, humanitarian brotherhood of secret learning was greeted with tremendous enthusiasm. The eponymous hero of the movement was Christian Rosencreutz whose supposed birthdate was 1378, and who was said to have lived for 106 years. He was said to have founded the original Order or Brotherhood of the Rosicrucians, but the first dated documents we have are two Rosicrucian manifestos, the *Fama Fraternitatis*, published in 1614, and the *Confessio Fraternitatis*, 1615. The authors of these tracts are not known, but in 1616 there appeared a worked called *The Chemical Wedding of Christian Rosencreutz*, by **Johann Valentin Andreae**, which Yates calls 'a strange alchemical romance'.

The *Confessio* of 1615 was published with a pamphlet called *A Brief Consideration of the More Secret Philosophy*, and Dr Yates points out that this is a précis of some of the theorems of **Dee's Monas Hieroglyphica**. 'The strangely exciting suggestion is that the Rosicrucian movement in Germany was the delayed result of Dee's mission in Bohemia over twenty years earlier . . . ' (*The Rosicrucian Enlightenment*, p.69). She suggests that the 'more secret philosophy' of the Rosicrucians is in fact based on Dee's spiritual, cabalist **alchemy**.

The manifestos of 1614 and 1615 are vibrant in their optimism about man's nobleness and worth, his title of *microcosmus* (see **Microcosm**). The *Fama* gives the story of the wanderings of Brother Rosencreutz, who was a physician who conversed with Turks and Arabic wise men during his travels in the Middle East. Most dramatic was the account of his vault. The manifesto affirms that in 1604 his tomb was discovered, being built as a heptagon (seven-sided building). The tomb was not lighted by the sun, but was nevertheless illuminated by an inner sun, and instead of a tomb there was an altar.

The manifesto also pays brief tribute to **Paracelsus**, whose works dominated *fin de siècle* alchemy.

The Rosicrucians proclaimed the 'General Reformation of the whole wide World' by their Brotherhood, and it is made clear that this reformation was to be accomplished by men of cabalist, magical wisdom. They warned against fraudulent alchemy, which had brought the subject into disrepute, but we are left in no doubt as to the existence of an honest alchemy, concerned with truth. The Brotherhood was founded by only four men, who created the magical language and writing with the help of a large dictionary – this reminds us of the Enochian language with which Dee and **Kelley** sought to converse with angels.

A series of rules for the fraternity leaves little doubt that those involved were medical men, concerned with healing the sick, probably in **harmony** with Paracelsus above all.

*See* F.A. Yates, *The Rosicrucian Enlightenment.*

# Rulands, Martin
**Father and son both called Martin; father died 1602, son died 1611**

Dr Martin Rulands the elder was a Paracelsian physician who compiled several dictionaries as well as medical works. Like **Paracelsus** himself, and in tune with the style of alchemical works of the period, he was interested in theology.

Dr Martin Rulands the younger was a physician at Regensburg during the 1590s and he later moved to Prague. He was one of the retinue of personal physicians who surrounded Emperor Rudolf II, and he described himself as a 'chemical physician' (*chymiatrus*). The court of the Habsburg Emperor Rudolf II was legendary for its involvement with **alchemy, astrology** and every form of Natural **Magic**. Nobility was conferred upon Martin Rulands the younger in 1608, as an indication of the favour in which he was held. He acted as editor of his father's published works.

**Publications:**
*Lapidis philosophici vera conficiendi ratio* (The true method for

completing the Philosophers' Stone) (1606).

*Defence of Alchemy* (1607), dedicated to one of Rudolf's most feared advisors.

*Progymnasmata alchemiae sive problemata chymica* (Frankfurt, 1607).

*Lexicon alchemiae sive dictionarium alchemistarum* (Frankfurt, 1612). The *Lexicon* of alchemy was a valuable work for relating alchemical concepts, but with a strong practical bias, including the treatment of metallic ores.

# S

## Salt

Like the other mysteries in **alchemy**, salt may at first seem familiar to modern science, but it soon emerges as a more mercurial substance. Salt was given prominence by the Paracelsians (*see* **Paracelsus**), who base the universe upon the *Tria Prima*, the trinity of mystic principles underlying all matter: salt, **sulphur, mercury.** **Paracelsus** expounds the theory of a natural **balsam**, which he conceives as a salty preservative which shields the body from corruption, decay and old age. Thus salt is easily interpreted as a magical preservative **elixir.**

In his *Mysterium Conjunctionis*, which provides us with a light in the labyrinth of alchemical symbolism, Jung cites **Gerard Dorn**, who makes salt analogous to the inner, invisible sun in man which provides the light of **nature**. Jung relates the symbolism of salt to that of salt water, with its baptismal quality, and to the 'Red Sea' which figures prominently in alchemical **myth**. For him, salt belongs to the lunar symbolism of the unconscious. In the *Tria Prima*, sulphur appears as masculine and solar, salt as feminine and lunar, and mercury is ambivalent and **hermaphrodite**: salt thus appears not as a substance, but as a cosmic principle in alchemy. Jung cites the *Turba Philosophorum* (The Crowd of Philosophers), one of the most popular medieval alchemical works, as identifying salt-water with *aqua permanens* (*see* **aqua**), and Mercurius is sometimes derived from salt. He also quotes **Arnald of Villanova**: 'Whoever possesses the salt that can be melted, and the oil that cannot be burned, may praise God'; and the *Rosarium*, which states that the 'whole secret lies in the prepared common salt'.

Salt is also often identified with ash, and with the earth-**dragon**, the self-devouring **uroboros**, while the salt of **metals** is the *Lapis*, the **Stone** itself. Salt may be dissolved, then coagulated in crystalline form, bringing to mind the alchemists' motto 'Dissolve and Coagulate'. **Khunrath** calls salt the 'physical centre of the earth' (Jung, op. cit., p.190). Salt may appear as ash at the *nigredo* **stage,** then appear in its white crystalline form in the *albedo* (*see* **Colours**).

# The Secret of Secrets
## Secretum Secretorum

*The Secret of Secrets* was one of the most popular medieval works expounding natural philosophy as being equivalent to natural **magic**. The text will be discussed here as it appears in the **manuscript** edited carefully and lovingly by **Roger Bacon**. There were, however, many manuscripts of the work in different forms.

Steele comments that from his first to his last works, Roger Bacon cites the *Secretum* 'as an authority, and there can be no doubt that it fortified, if it did not create, his belief in astrology and natural magic'. Bacon believed for certain that the work was by **Aristotle**, and it appears in the form of a letter written by Aristotle, addressed to his pupil Alexander the Great, the ostensible topic being kingship and the wisdom of being a ruler. Steele says it is a product of the interaction of Syriac and Persian culture from the seventh to the ninth centuries AD, the period of the flowering of **Islamic alchemy**.

An Arabic authority, al-Makin, says that 'Aristotle translated the books of Hermes, an ancient sage of the country of Egypt, out of the Egyptian into the Greek tongue, and he explained in his translation the sciences, and wisdom and knowledge . . . .' Aristotle was often credited with magical, astrological, or alchemical ideas, as many medieval manuscript attributions will testify.

The *Secretum* opens with a discourse on justice and wisdom as keys to success as a ruler or king – the king is likened to the rain which harms some and benefits others – but the treatise progresses into the area of magical wonders, including in Bacon's version a section on physiognomy, and alchemical ideas.

Bacon's notes on the *Secretum* include the following:

> All writers, because of the greatness of the secrets, conceal the science of alchemy in words and metaphors and figurative work, and God inspires them to this so that only the most wise and good men perceive it achieving the good of the republic. So the *Lapis* is to be taken first of all metaphorice, for all that upon which the *operacio alchimica* works. And this can be mineral things, like sulphur and arsenic, but better is the vegetable realm, like fruits and parts of trees and herbs, and especially parts of man, amongst these blood, in which four humours are distinguished to the eye: flegm, cholera, blood and melancholia. The alchemist, then, seeks to separate these humours in turn and to purge one from the other. And when through difficult works they are reduced

to their pure simplicity, then they are mixed in a secret proportion and most certain; to which is added quicksilver after it is mortified and sublimated several times. Similarly calx or pulvis of baser metal from which it becomes nobler. And the same with nobler metals. And after this they are incorporated in turn until they become one body. And then it is projected onto the baser metals liquefied and becomes nobler. But in all this are most difficult works and of great expenses, to which works only the wisest and happiest can attain.

See *Secretum Secretorum, Opera hactenus inedita*, V, ed. R. Steele.

# Sendivogius, Michael, and Sethon, Alexander
## Sendivogius: 1566–1646; Sethon: *floruit* 1600s

The story of these two men belongs to a category of legends of the achievement of actual **transmutation. John Dee** and **Edward Kelley** toured the Continent during the 1580s and were supposed to have used a powder for actual transmutation, and the story of Sethon and Sendivogius similarly identifies the transmuting agent as a powder of projection. A.E. Waite, in his *Lives of the Alchemystical Philosophers* (1888) tells the tragic story, in order to defend his thesis that alchemists really were concerned with actual transmutation, not just with some mystical quest, which is the Jungian thesis about **alchemy**.

The story goes that Alexander Sethon was a Scot who was responsible for rescuing a Dutch seaman who was wrecked off the Scottish coast in 1601. In 1602, Sethon visited the pilot Jacob Haussen in Holland, and whilst residing as his guest, demonstrated before his very eyes the secret of transmutation: he changed a piece of lead into **gold**. Sethon subsequently toured Italy, Switzerland and Germany and encountered Professor Dienheim of Fribourg, who refused to believe in transmutation. Sethon arranged a demonstration in Basle with witnesses, and convinced everyone by apparently using a powder to produce gold from lead. There are several documented instances of supposed transmutation in Germany, and Sethon even used lapis lazuli in a demonstration in Cologne which convinced many sceptics. Many charlatans and frauds had brought alchemy into disrepute here as everywhere, at a time when the Paracelsian movement was in full swing. Eventually the story of Sethon's miraculous powers reached the ears of Christian II, Elector of Saxony, and he arrested and cruelly tortured the Scottish alchemist, but without success in extracting any Hermetic secrets.

*These two sets of four emblems show the image of the King and Queen, representing Sol and Luna, in the mystic marriage or* conjunctio. *They are shown standing on a double lion with a single head, then like Adam and Eve, beside the furnace. There is the charming image of the alchemical bath, with the spiritual bird, and sun and moon symbols for the King and Queen.*

*From Mylius,* Philosophia reformata *(Frankfurt, 1622), from the presses of Luca Jennis. Mylius does not explain his emblems, which appear to be copies from manuscripts. There was a craze for such emblem books, as occult learning spread around the time of the Rosicrucians.*

*By kind permission of The Bodleian Library, Oxford.*
*BB33, Art. p.17 and p.224.*

Michael Sendivogius (Sensophax) is supposed to have exploited Sethon and his published work, *Novum Lumen* (A New Light of Alchymie), is said to be a compilation of Sethon's own writings. Sendivogius was an expert chemist and he arranged the escape of Sethon from prison. The latter lived only two more years after his ordeal, but left some powder to Sendivogius, whose fame was enormously enriched as a result of his helping the unfortunate Scot.

Sendivogius was born in 1566 and a fictional biography by an anonymous German pupil connects him with the court of Emperor Rudolf II and with an imperial mission to the East to seek arcane

secrets from a Greek adept. He is said to have married Sethon's widow and to have used a dialogue between Mercury and an alchemist, which was actually the work of his master: it was published in his *Novum Lumen*. He convinced the court of Rudolf II by a demonstration of apparent transmutation and was rewarded with an imperial appointment. He suffered ambush and imprisonment by the Duke of Wurtemberg, but was able to gain imperial protection. His fame did not outlive his supply of transmuting powder. A.E. Waite tells us that he died in Parma in 1646, at the age of 84 years, having served as Counsellor of State under four successive emperors. He refers to the treatises in the *Novum Lumen* as being the work of Sethon-Sendivogius, and he quotes one passage in which the authors affirm that only the man who can achieve true transmutation of base metals into real gold by philosophical rather than fraudulent means can claim the title of true alchemist.

**Publications:**

*A New Light of Alchymia, taken out of the fountaine of Nature and Manuall Experience to which is added a Treatise of Sulphur; also Nine books of the Nature of Things, written by Paracelsus, viz. of the*

*Generations, Growths, Conservations, Life, Death, Renewing, Transmutation, Separation, Signatures of Natural Things* (1650). Also *A Chymical Dictionary explaining hard places and words met withall in the writings of Paracelsus and other obscure authors,* translated by John French (London, printed by Richard Cotes for Thomas Williams).

# Severinus, Petrus
## Sorenson; born Jutland, 1542, died Copenhagen, 1602

Severinus was a Danish Paracelsian physician whose writings had a strong influence in the Paracelsian movement of the latter sixteenth to the early seventeenth century (*see* **Paracelsus**). He became Canon of Roskild, and served for 30 years as physician to the King of Denmark.

Severinus taught the Paracelsian doctrines of man as **microcosm**, who has within himself an inner *astra* in the human body corresponding to the stars in heaven. The stars of things are their seeds (*semina*). This doctrine of seeds was very important in Paracelsian theory.

Severinus' main publication was *Idea medicinae philosophiae fundamenta continens totius doctrinae Paracelsicae, Hippocraticae et Galenicae* (Basle, 1571).

# Sol and Luna
## Sun and Moon

This is the primal duality in **alchemy** and Sol and Luna are generally shown as crowned figures, often quite naked, as in the famous *Rosarium* series. They are brother and sister, representing sun and moon, corresponding to the duality of **gold** and silver (*see* **Metals and Planets**), but also to **sulphur** and **mercury**. Sulphur as the fiery element, being hot and dry, with mercury as the feminine, watery, cold and wet polarity. They represent what Taoists would call the yin and yang polarity in the cosmos.

**Thomas Vaughan** gives fine literary expression to the pair:

> The sun and moon are two Magicall Principles, the one active, the other passive, this Masculine, that Feminine. As they move, so move the wheeles of Corruption and Generation: they mutually dissolve and compound, but properly the moon is *Organum transmutationis inferioris materiae*. These Two Luminaries are multiplied and fructifie in every one particular generation. There is not a compound in all nature but hath in

it a little Sun, and a little Moon. The little Sun is *Filius solis coelestis*. The Little Moon is *Filia lunae coelestis*.

What offices so ever the two great luminaries perform for the conservation of the great world in general, these two little luminaries perform the like for the Conservation of their small Cask, or Microcosm in Particular.

From the most ancient times, the sun has been worshipped as a radiant, immortal god. In Greek **myth**, Apollo is the brother of Artemis, the moon goddess. The sun god as hero is often doomed to a short life, as Baldur for example, in Norse mythology. Under the Roman Empire a number of cults, including the popular cult of Mithras, worshipped the sun god, of whom the Emperor was thought to be a personification, Sol Invictus. There can be no doubt that the archetypal myth of the death and resurrection of the sun god is a vital aspect of alchemical myth. One of the most impressive alchemical **manuscripts**, with brilliant illustrations, is called the *Splendor solis* (The Sun's Splendour).

The significance of sun and moon in every aspect of the human psyche is a universal archetype. The sun represents the radiance of life-giving energy and warmth, and is the **King** or ruler of the world and the planets, while the moon is associated with **magic**, with the realm of darkness and shadows, indeed with witchcraft.

In the types of yogic alchemy which evolved in the Chinese, Indian and Tibetan traditions, the sun and moon are associated with the system of chakras and channels which carry the circulation of spiritual energy: *chhi* in Chinese, *pneuma* in Greek, *prana* in Indian. The right and left channels in yoga are the channels of sun and moon. In **Chinese alchemy**, the principles of active, masculine, and receptive feminine, which rule the universe and man, are abstracted in the theory of yin-yang.

# Solve et Coagula

The motto of the alchemist from earliest times was the injunction to 'dissolve and coagulate'. An archetypal image of this process is the metal **mercury**, which is normally a liquid, subject to being dissolved, but which is fixed or solidified when united with **sulphur**. In general alchemists were always using waters (*aquae*): they had no modern way of distinguishing the various types of solvents, **acids**, or cleaning and purifying solutions. It was generally believed that **metals** were actually a product of the coagulating union of mercury and sulphur (*see* **Mercury-Sulphur Theory of the Generation of Metals**).

In the many allegories of the **King and Queen** in **alchemy**, there is a common image of the King drowning, crying desperately for help, and this is an image of the alchemical process of solution: dissolving is a form of death, by drowning. Jungian interpretation sees water as a symbol for the unconscious mind, in which the incautious ego personality may easily dissolve, suffering a form of psychic death and disorientation (*see* **Jungian Theory of Alchemy**). *Solutio* in alchemy is very much involved with the **stage** of *nigredo*, with putrefaction and **mortification**.

There are the oft-repeated images of the King in his **bath**, generally the heat bath.

Jung cites **Gerard Dorn** in a remarkable interpretation of what *solutio* means:

> The chemical putrefaction is compared to the study of the philosophers, because as the philosophers are disposed to knowledge by study, so natural things are disposed by putrefaction to solution. To this is compared the philosophical knowledge, for as by solution bodies are dissolved, so by knowledge are the doubts of the philosophers resolved.
>
> Jung, *Mysterium Conjunctionis*, pp.270--1

He further defines dissolution as knowledge, as being the *conjunctio* stage in which there occurs a 'spagyric marriage'. The copulation of **Sol and Luna** is frequently portrayed as a couple dissolving in the waters of the alchemical bath.

# Spagyric

A word supposed to be derived by **Paracelsus** himself from the Greek words *spao* and *ageiro*, which means 'tear apart and gather together'. It is universally used from the sixteenth century to describe **alchemy**, which is said to be the 'spagyric art' or science.

# Spirit

## Spirit and Matter

Of all the riddles in **alchemy**, the relationship of body, soul and spirit is most baffling. This stems from alchemy's very roots in the gnostic philosophy of the world, which is a radical dualism between the spiritual world and the dark prison of materiality and corruption which man inhabits (*see* **Gnosticism**). According to this philosophy, although inhabiting a mortal body, subject to all manner of disease or injury, there is in man also a spark, a spirit of immortal life. This is reflected in the alchemical opus on the level of chemical experiment in liberating the active spirit from passive matter. The active spirit is then reunited with matter. In other words, the adept releases the life-giving, energizing essence, and uses this to transform or redeem matter (*see* **Redemption**). Such a philosophy is in fact prehistoric, and is expressed in **Chinese alchemy** the concepts of yin and yang. Yang, as the active, masculine principle, is especially strong in certain substances, such as **cinnabar** or **gold**, and such yang substances may therefore be used to prolong and enhance the vital principle in man. **Elixirs** are supposed to be especially rich in yang.

Here is what the Paracelsian alchemist **Thomas Thymme** says about the problem of body-soul-spirit continuum:

> The philosophers have called that the Body which, according the naturall power, may be fixed and, with continuall perseverance, can constantly abide the tryall of fire. And they have called that soule, which according to her naturall power hath no stedfastness or perseverance to abyde the trial of fire. Also they have called that Spirit which, being subtiled, dissolved, or moulten with fire, according to the naturall power thereof, hath ability to *resoule* the body with the soule into vapour or of retayning the soule with the body to the fiery triall, if it vapour not.
>
> *A Light in Darkness, which illuminateth . . .*
> *the* Monas Hieroglyphica, ed. S.K. Heninger

The spirit, then, is higher than body and soul and without the spirit 'the soule tarieth not with the Body, neither is it separated from the Body, because it is the Bond of them both'. This helps to explain the mythology and symbolism of **mercury**, for this mystic principle is in fact 'Body, Soule and Spirit, in divers respects'.

We always have to bear in mind here the Jungian concept of projection. The adept is projecting into matter his own psychic preoccupations, fears, anxiety, longing for health, purity of spirit and redemption from a world which is rendered a prison by the rule of death and disease.

### Spirit and Soul

The entire alchemical quest is based upon the duality of spirit and matter, and there are some signs of shamanistic origins to the art, with men like **Ostanes** and **Zosimos**. Shamanism rests on the idea of freeing the soul, either to ascend the world **tree**, or to embark on journeys of the soul. Alchemy, eastern or western, is deeply embedded in animism and **magic**. The Philosophers' **Stone** was from earliest times credited with having body, soul and spirit, and an early text attributed to Ostanes instructs the adept to go to the Nile to seek a mystic stone with a spirit. Mercurius is always described as a spirit, and the liberation of liquid mercury from its solid ore cinnabar may from earliest times have been a mythic allegory for the liberation of spirit from matter. Alchemists relied upon the Genesis myth of **Creation** for inspiration, and the Hermetic **vessel** is a **microcosm** for the process of Creation, which begins with the spirit of God moving upon the waters.

Hellenistic alchemists were strongly gnostic, and Zosimos discusses at length the spiritual nature of man, the man of light, as being imprisoned in the body, the dark prison of the four **elements** ruled by the star daimons. The gnostics had many myths of the imprisonment of mind, spirit or *pneuma* in the embrace of **nature**, or 'phusis', and there can be little doubt that originally there was an alchemical cult of the ascent of the soul through the planetary spheres, as also in Mithraic ritual.

The alchemical opus, involving the seven planetary **metals**, necessitates liberation of the soul, and progress in the opus involves liberating the soul from the body, then reuniting it. The initial *nigredo* **stage** represents the putrefaction, **mortification** and torture of the body (the theme also of the 'Visions' of Zosimos) (*see also* **Processes or Operations**). Early alchemists may have regarded **colours** or **tinctures** as being active spirits of metals. Hence **transmutation** is achieved using the spiritual powers liberated from matter.

The most prominent feature of alchemical **myth** is also the theme of death and rebirth, with the state of spiritual renewal and regeneration being represented by gold.

The body-soul-spirit trinity itself corresponds to the structure of the Hermetic-Neoplatonist cosmos, with its terrestrial, celestial and supercelestial dimensions (*see* **Neoplatonism**). According to this view, the four elements are material, and the adept must seek the **quintessence**, the fifth mystic, spiritual-celestial element of the stars.

Here is **Thomas Vaughan** on the spirit:

> . . . there is in Nature a certain Spirit which applies himself to the matter, and actuates in every Generation. That there is also a passive Intrinsecall principle where he is more immediately resident than in the rest, and by meditation of which he communicates with the more gross, materiall parts. For there is in Nature a Certain Chain, or subordinate proximity of Complexions between visibles and invisibles, and this is it by which

the superiour, spirituall Essences descend and converse here below with the Matter. I speak not in this place of the Divine Spirit, but I speake of a certain Art by which a particular Spirit may be united to the universall, and Nature by consequence may be strangely exalted, and multiplyed.

Vaughan, *Anima magica abscondita*, Rudrum's edition, p.108

In his *Magia Adamica*, Vaughan speaks of 'the practice or operation of the Divine Spirit working in the matter, uniting Principles into Compounds, and resolving those compounds into other Principles' (p.155, Rudrum's edition), and also states:

The Lawes of the Resurrection are founded upon those of Generation, for in all these God works upon one, and the same Matter, by one and the same spirit. Now that it is so, I mean that there is a Harmonie between Nature and the Gospell.

Vaughan, op. cit., p.185

# Stages

## Stages of the Alchemical Opus

The main spiritual and mystical systems of the world have each worked out a concept of the graded path towards spiritual enlightenment. In Tibetan mysticism this graded path to liberation of the mind is called *lam rim*, and Tibetan meditators often use the idea of **alchemy** as a metaphor for purification of the lower levels of the mind. Sufism also has an idea of an ascent to enlightenment or liberation, and we find that Sufism kept alchemy alive in the Islamic tradition (*see* **Islamic alchemy**).

Western alchemy has its roots in **Gnosticism**, and Hellenistic alchemists like **Maria Prophetissa** or **Zosimos** worked with a system of stages designated by **colours**. First came the *melanosis*, the stage of blackening called **nigredo** in Latin. This was followed by *leukosis*, or *albedo* in Latin, the whitening. Next came the *xanthosis*, or yellowing stage, which was later dropped, and finally there was the **iosis**, the stage of the purple, which represents the perfection of the opus:

1   *melanosis* = **nigredo** = blackening. This is sometimes the result of an operation like calcination (*see* **Processes or Operations**). But blackening or *nigredo* may be produced by various conditions: *mortificatio* and *putrefactio* are vital to the opus. There are endless images of death and melancholy in alchemical

pictures, and the whole drama of the opus is one of death and rebirth or **redemption**. In this stage the soul departs from the body.

2) *leukosis* = *albedo* = whitening. Following the stage of blackening, of calcination or putrefaction, there is a need for a purifying process of whitening and cleansing, often called the washing (*ablutio*, baptism). The *opus album* (= the white work) is the first major stage in the opus. The white **tincture** or **elixir** is associated with the moon (*see* **Sol and Luna**), and the white elixir transmutes to silver.

This whitening stage is often equated with the reuniting of the soul with the body. Jung makes clear that the white is the colour which contains all other colours, hence the image of the peacock's tail (*see* **Peacock**) indicates the burgeoning of the work.

3) Hellenistic alchemists then sometimes posit a *xanthosis* stage = *citrinitas* = yellowing, but Jung tells us that this colour lapsed from the list, and is seldom mentioned.

4) The perfection of the work for Hellenistic alchemy is achievement of *iosis* = purpling, but the corresponding phase in the Latin tradition is the *rubedo*, which is the stage of the red magisterium or elixir.

This early scheme of stages was intended to represent the movement from the stage of **Prime Matter**, through the calcination or blackening, to the purification which was the prelude to **transmutation**. There can be no doubt that the white and the red elixirs constitute the goal of the opus, the former being supposed to make possible transmutation to silver, the latter being the perfection of the **Stone, medicine**, or elixir.

There are many variations on this kind of scheme, and it is important to realize that the alchemical opus involved a circulatory sequence, with processes like **distillation**, sublimation, separation and conjunction being repeated over and over again, with the aim of purifying the Prime Matter or mercurial substance of the Stone.

Once the tincture or elixir is produced, then the processes of **multiplication** and projection can take place. Alchemists toiled for many years in their efforts to decipher this mysterious sequence, the secret of secrets, and we cannot hope to come to any easy definition or understanding.

However, in general the initial aim of the opus was to reduce **metals** to their Prime Matter in order to create the conditions for transmutation to occur. At an early stage separation takes place, and this is interpreted in the context of the idea of the divine **Creation** as set out in the Book of Genesis. The alchemical opus is a **microcosm** of the majestic process of God's Creation, which involved the initial separation of the four **elements**. In all alchemical illustrations the **myths** of death and rebirth are repeated over and over again.

## The Tree of Stages and Processes

The progress of the opus is often shown in the form of a philosophical **tree**.

One example of this, which adorns Jung's *Psychology and Alchemy*, is the illustration from Samuel Norton's *Catholicon physicorum* (1630, Frankfurt) which appears on p.390. At the root of this tree, the **Prime Matter** of the opus is **antimony**, or Lead of the Philosophers. The stages listed are:

1) *matrimonium corporale* (= **conjunctio**, bodily marriage)
2) *solutio*
3) *calcinatio*: *calcinatio* naturally causes blackening of **metals**, *nigredo*
4) *hylatio*: this is the concept of reducing metals to their Prime Matter, *hyle* being the Greek word for prime matter
5) *separatio*: here the tree branches or separates between body (*corpus*) and soul (*anima*).

After this branching or separation of soul from body, the alchemist ascends to the final celestial and mystical stages:

6) *matrimonium coeleste*: this is the celestial mystic marriage (*see* **Conjunctio**) of body and soul, which are reunited after their previous separation.
7) As Jung points out, the *conjunctio* is regularly followed by death of the offspring, the Son of the Philosophers. Hence we have a putrefaction stage. This precedes the summit of the tree, where is the *Lapis* or Stone itself, the mystic goal of the entire opus.

From the variety of diagrammatic illustrations which we find in alchemical **manuscripts** it is very clear that the stages or **processes** are jumbled in endless variations. There is no single, standard path to the summit.

Another illustration of an alchemical tree from Samuel Norton, *Mercurius redivivus* (1630), shows 12 stages reaching the goal of the opus in the form of the philosophical tree (*see* Jung, *Psychology and Alchemy*, p.229). At the root of the tree the Prime Matter is given as *Mercurius: Argentum vivum* – in other words mercury alone is the basic matter for making the elixir.

The stages are:

1) purgation
2) sublimation
3) calcination
4) exuberation (not a usual term)
5) fixation
6) solution
7) separation
8) conjunction (marriage)
9) putrefaction in sulphur
10) solution of bodily sulphur
11) solution of sulphur of white light
12) fermentation in elixir
13) multiplication in virtue
14) multiplication in quantity.

At the summit of the tree is 'elixir of the third order of medicine of life'. This was the alchemists' final goal.

# Starkey, George
## New England alchemist; 1627–1666

George Starkey is most famous for his involvement in propagating the **manuscripts** which he attributed to a New England alchemist whom he calls **Eirenaeus Philalethes**. He was born in 1627 and spent his childhood in the Bermudas, where he was interested in the entomology and botany of the islands, and he performed experiments on spontaneous generation. He entered Harvard at the age of 16, in 1643, gaining his BA in 1646 and MA in 1650, and became a close friend of **John Winthrop**, who amassed an impressive alchemical library. It appears that Winthrop introduced him to adeptship in 1644, the date he gives for commencement of his study of 'Chemical Philosophy'. He studied **medicine**: not only the Galenist classical tradition, but also the new Paracelsian chemical medicine, becoming known as a disciple of **Joan Battista van Helmont**. He then practised in the English colonies in America, where he claims to have met Eirenaeus Philalethes and been initiated into the mysteries of transmutatory alchemy.

In 1646 he travelled to England, joined **Samuel Hartlib**'s 'Invisible College', which included **Boyle** and chemical philosophers, and became involved with producing various medicines and panaceas. He styled himself 'a philosopher made by the fire' – alchemy was often called 'pyrotechny', or skill in use of fire – and succeeded in extracting silver from **antimony** and **gold** from iron. His conclusion: that he could achieve **transmutation** of tin to silver, then silver to gold. He circulated the Philalethes tracts which he had brought from New England and worked with Boyle on **elixir** preparations. He claimed to have brought from America a potion of sophic **mercury**, a white elixir to transform metals into silver. Starkey also engaged in the search for the mystic **alkahest**, the universal solvent in which both **Paracelsus** and van Helmont passionately believed.

He posed as an enthusiastic Royalist on the Restoration of Charles II, and continued his practice, but fell victim to the plague of 1665. Believing that chemical medicines could combat plague, he died after a cooperative venture to dissect the body of a plague victim.

**Publications (under the name of Philalethes):**
*The Marrow of Alchemy* (London, 1654–5).
*Nature's Explication and Helmont's Vindication, or a Short and Sure Way to a Long and Sound Life* (1657), a strong assertion of Starkey's adherence to the new chemical medicine of van Helmont. (In 1648 van Helmont's works had been published as the *Ortus medicinae*.)
*Pyrotechny Asserted and Illustrated by the help of Vulcan to know how to unlock Natures secrets* (1658).
*The Admirable Efficacy of Oyl which is made of Sulphur-vive* (1660).
*George Starkey's Pill vindicated from the unlearned Alchymist 'The Admirable Efficacy, and almost incredible Virtue of true Oyl, which is made of Sulphur-vive'* (1663–4). This recommended van Helmont's remedy of sulphur-oil.
*A Smart Scourge for a Silly Sawcy Fool* (1664).
*A brief Examination and Censure of several medicines* (1664).
*Liquor Alkahest, or a Discourse of that Immortal Dissolvent of Paracelsus and Helmont* (1675).

*See* R.S. Wilkinson, 'George Starkey, Physician and Alchemist', *Ambix*, 1963; *see also* **Alkahest**; **Paracelsus**; **van Helmont**.

# Stibnite
*See* **Antimony**.

# Stolz, or Stolzius, Daniel
**floruit 1620s**

The family of Daniel Stolz von Stolzenberg came from Kutna Hora in

Hungary, which was a silver mining area. He went to Prague University, gaining a BA in 1618 and MA the following year. For his MA, he debated an astrological question concerning the propitious motion of stars. He also studied at Marburg University from 1621.

In 1624 his *Viridarium Chymicum* (Chemical Garden) was published in Latin – this is now a very rare book. There was a German edition of the same year. The work was the product of collaboration between the eager publisher, Luca Jennis of Frankfurt, and Stolz. This was an age when lavishly illustrated emblem books were bound to cause great public excitement, and Jennis commissioned Stolz to write Latin epigrams for his own collection of copper engravings. John Read, in his *Prelude to Chemistry* describes this precious book, with its 107 copperplate illustrations and brief Latin epigrams, as an alchemist's *vade mecum*. Stolz also studied with **Michael Maier**, who was experienced in publishing emblem books.

# Stone, Philosophers'
*Lapis Philosophorum*

There are thousands of texts giving accounts of the mystic Stone. The following gives a marvellous wealth of imagery:

> Thou shalt see the Stone of the Philosophers (our King) go forth of the bed-chamber, of his Glassy Sepulchre, in his glorified body, like a Lord of Lords, from his throne into the Theatre of the World. That is to say, regimented and more than perfect, a shining carbuncle, most temperate splendour, whose most subtile and depurated parts are inseparably united into one, with a concordial mixture, exceedingly equal; transparent like crystal, compact and most ponderous, easily fusible in fire, like resin or wax before the flight of quicksilver yet flowing without smoke; entering into solid bodies and penetrating them like oil through paper, dissoluble in every liquor and commiscible with it; friable like glass in a powder like saffron, but in the whole mass shining red like a Ruby, (which redness is a sign of a perfect fixation and fixed perfection); permanently colourating and tingeing, fixed in all trials, yea in the examination of the burning sulphur itself and the devouring waters and in the most vehement persecution of the fire, always incom-bustible and permanent as the Salamander.
>
> Heinrich Khunrath, *Amphitheatrum* (1609)

This is a fitting, eloquent tribute to the ultimate goal of the opus, always described in terms of paradox and enigma: Ben Jonson captures the authentic spirit of the concept in *The Alchemist*:

Tis a stone and not,
A stone; a spirit, a soul, and a body,
Which if you do dissolve it, it is dissolv'd,
If you coagulate it, it is coagulated,
If you make it flie, it flieth.

An ancient concept is the idea of the 'touchstone' which transmutes **metals** to **gold**, and this is variously described as a powder or an **elixir** or **tincture**. Often such words seem interchangeable, but there is a common legend of a red powder which is said to be the Stone (*see* stories of **Thomas Charnock, John Dee** and **Helvetius**). In **alchemy** there is a bewildering translation of everything into everything else, and most texts equate the Stone directly with **mercury**, with its volatile **spirit** and yet its tendency to coagulate and form a stone or powder with supposed miraculous effects.

The touchstone of the philosophers is closely associated, and often identified, with the elixir, the tincture, the Mastery. **Islamic alchemy** used the word *kimiya* to mean both alchemy and the substance making **transmutation** possible. This was a pure substance which could transform, transmute or perfect gross matter. At the same time, the Stone is the one which the builders reject, yet becomes the corner-stone. It is found in the vilest places, and its redemptive power is so often equated with Christ.

Alchemists like Thomas Charnock or John Dee had miraculous powders (of which the red was the strongest), which dissolved to form the elixir or **medicine** of metals. The Stone was a solid, to be powdered and dissolved, hence the idea that it is a stone when solid and yet not a stone in solution.

The loose and confusing use of the word to cover every alchemical mystery is admirably illustrated in a poetic passage by **Elias Ashmole** in his *Prologomena* to his *Theatrum Chemicum Britannicum*. First there is the Stone of transmutation:

It is wrought up to the degree onely that hath the Power of Transmuting any Imperfect Earthy Matter into its utmost degree of Perfection; that is to convert the basest of Metals into perfect Gold and Silver; Flints into all manner of Precious Stones . . . and many other Experiments of the like manner.

However, transmutation is only one aspect of the quest, and according to Ashmole, God is a 'goodly light' and we gaze upon him as children at the bird of Juno (*see* **Peacock**). Ashmole therefore repeats the age-old refrain, that spiritual enlightenment is the true goal of the philosophers:

And certainly he to whom the whole course of Nature lies open, rejoyceth not so much that he can make Gold and Silver, or the Divells to become Subject to him, as that he sees the Heavens open, the Angells of God Ascending and Descending, and that his own Name is fairely written in the Book of Life.

Besides this philosophical Stone, Ashmole describes a 'Vegetable Stone', by which 'may be known perfectly the Nature of Man, Beasts, Foules, Fishes, together with all kinds of Trees, Plants, Flowers, &c, and how to produce and make them Grow, Flourish and bare Fruit'. This Stone is a sort of union, a *conjunctio* of opposites, having a solar and lunar part, being both masculine and feminine (*see* **Hermaphrodite**).

Besides this 'Vegetable Stone' for transforming growth, there are magical Stones in which Ashmole had the keenest interest, for it was he who collected many of John Dee's papers. The 'magical or prospective Stone' is an all-seeing Stone, enabling the scryer to seek out the location of a person anywhere in the world, no matter how secretive or concealed they may be. This Stone is able to make 'strict Inquisition' into hiding places like chambers, closets, or even the very caverns of the earth. Another interesting property is to enable man to know languages and to understand animals or birds. Ashmole must surely have the Dee-**Kelley** séances in mind when he speaks of conveying a spirit into the Stone, assuming an image which may observe heavenly or stellar influences and thus becomes an oracle. This, however, Ashmole assures us, is in no sense necromancy. Thus the Philosophers' Stone links some of the variegated activities of many alchemists: for men like Dee, spiritualist angelic scrying was part of the alchemical quest for magical wisdom.

There is much evidence that the Stone is regarded as synonymous with the medicine or the elixir of the philosophers, as a transmuting agent. The Paracelsian **Gerard Dorn**, for example, regards the Stone as an 'incorrupt medicament', to be found only in Heaven. He exclaims in an inspired moment: 'Transmute yourselves from dead stones into living philosophical stones.'

For Jung, however, the Stone represents the ultimate union of opposites, being the symbol of the inner unity and balance of the matured self: 'The stone is the projection of the unified self' (*Aion*, p.170).

Of the all the deep mysteries of the alchemical opus, its final goal, the *Lapis* or Stone is the strangest. Here all concepts turn to paradox: in Ben Jonson's play *The Alchemist* we hear that this is the 'stone that is not a stone'. John Read remarks: 'To most of its seekers . . . the

Grand Magisterium and Elixir was merely a magic source of wealth, health and long life.'

### The *Lapis-Christus* Parallel

Perhaps the most significant discovery made by Jung was the tendency for alchemists during medieval and Renaissance times to equate the alchemical *Lapis*, the Stone of the Philosophers, with the figure of Christ the Redeemer (*see* **Redemption**), thus destroying the notion of greedy gold-seeking as the motive for alchemy.

Jung cites valuable evidence for his parallel or equation of the fabled Stone with the Redeemer. There can be no doubt that western alchemy has its roots in Hellenistic **Gnosticism**, and gnostic philosophers were concerned above all with redeeming the **spirit** from the dark prison of the material world, ruled by grim fate.

Jung's evidence is strongly confirmed by 'George Ripley's Wheele mentioned in his worke'. The wheel is a **mandala** symbol of the divine, microcosmic nature of the opus, displaying signs of the zodiac at the four corners under their retive **elements**, seasons, directions and bodily humours.

Jung also cites **Ramon Lull**, **Bonus of Ferrara**, **Zosimos** and **Ripley** as medieval alchemists who compare the Stone or *Lapis* to the Redeemer:

> As Christ from earth to heaven did ascend,
> In cloudes of clearnes up to his throne,
> And raigneth there shining without end,
> Right so our Sunne, now made our Stone,
> Unto his glory againe is gone,
> His fire possessing here in the South,
> With power to heale leapers and renewe youth.
>
> Ripley, *The Compound of Alchymy*, Rabbard's translation, 1591

Another verse of the same work speaks of the Stone descending into the womb of 'our Virgin Mercuriall', exactly as Christ descended into the womb of the Virgin Mary, while another two verses speak of the death and resurrection of Christ as analogous to the death and burial of the Stone which 'upriseth from darknes and colors variable/appearing in the East with clearenes incomparable'.

# Sulphur

Sulphur in **alchemy** has a complex role, being eclipsed very much by the omnipresent, polyvalent **mercury**. In Islamic theory, mercury and sulphur are the parents of **metals** (*see* **Mercury-Sulphur Theory of Generation of Metals**). According to this theory, mercury is generally regarded as cold and moist, being the liquid component of metals, whilst sulphur is hot and dry, being the solid, material component.

The motto of alchemy was *Solve et Coagula*, dissolve and coagulate, and sulphur was important in chemical symbolism as the substance which coagulates liquid mercury, or fixes it: thus the two principles are masculine and feminine, and when they are conjoined in mystic marriage (*see* **Conjunctio**), the sulphur is the masculine principle, 'fixing' the feminine. Sulphur and mercury are also equivalent to **Sol and Luna** – sulphur, being fiery and active, represents the sun, whilst mercury, being liquid and passive, is the moon. Thus the idea arises that sulphur may be identified with **gold**, or treated as the **Prime Matter** of Sol, of the solar gold-making principle.

Some alchemists, for example **Bernard of Trevisa**, were inclined to emphasize the polyvalence of mercury as the Prime Matter of metals, but sulphur might also be regarded as such. Jung points out in his *Mysterium Conjunctionis* (p.111), that the situation can be as ambivalent with sulphur as it often is with mercury: sulphur is 'duplex', there being a white sulphur (likened to the moon) and a red sulphur (representing the sun). It is also ambivalent as to its alchemical value in that it is burning and corrosive, explains Jung, and is thus 'hostile to the matter of the stone', yet if it is 'cleansed of all impurities, it is the matter of our stone'. 'Altogether, sulphur is one of the innumerable synonyms for the *prima materia* in its dual aspects, i.e., as both the initial material and the end-product.'

In fact, by pursuing the portrait of sulphur we get new insight into the true meaning of the alchemist's conception of mercury. Sulphur is an earthly substance, coming from the fatness of the earth, and as such it may be designated by the **dragon**, which is called 'our secret sulphur'. In that form it is also the mercurial water, whose symbol is the **uroboros**. Jung suggests that this makes the distinction between the opposites of mercury and sulphur very difficult.

**Paracelsus**' view was that sulphur and salt are the parents of mercury, the child of sun and moon. Sulphur is found 'in the depths of the nature of Mercurius', or it is 'of the nature of Mercurius', or 'Sulphur and Mercurius' are 'brother and sister' (cited Jung, *Mysterium Conjuncionis*, p.112). Just as mercury is a healing elixir, so too sulphur is credited with the 'power to dissolve, kill, and bring metals to life' (op.cit., p.113).

# T

## Thurneysser zum Thurn, Leonhardt
### born Basle 1531, died Cologne 1596

Thurneysser was the son of a Basle goldsmith, and was soon bitten with enthusiasm for the works of **Paracelsus**, which he encountered whilst gathering **herbs** for a physician; he was later to publish an astrological **herbal** himself. He got into trouble in 1548 after fraudulently selling a gilded lead brick to some Jews. This forced him to travel to England in that year, and then to France the following year and we find him joining the army of the Markgraf of Brandenburg in 1552. He was taken prisoner by the Saxons after a battle, but was released to exercise his skills in mining and metallurgy. He worked in Germany, the Tyrol, Scotland, Spain and Portugal.

Thurneysser firmly adhered to the Paracelsian cause and his output of esoteric books was colossal, showing a deep involvement with the **Cabala**. He became one of the most famous Paracelsian physicians: after settling in Frankfurt an der Oder in 1571, he became physician to the Elector of Brandenburg, whose wife he cured. In 1584 he travelled to Italy, becoming a Roman Catholic. He had many pupils who paid him to impart the mystic secrets of his art, but in the end he died in poverty in Cologne.

### Publications:

His works include some colossally obscure cabalist productions, some herbals and a work on mineral waters and spas, so fashionable at this time:

*Quinta Essentia, das ist die höchste Subtilitet, Krafft und Wirkung . . . der Medicina und Alchemia* (1570).
*Pison*, a work on warm and cold spa waters, both mineral and metallic waters (Frankfurt, 1572).
*Historia sive descriptio plantarum* (Berlin, 1578).
*Megale chumia, vel Magna Alchymia, das ist ein Lehr und Unterweisung von den Naturen allerhandt wunderlichen Erdtwechssen, als Ertzen, Metallen &c* (Berlin, 1583).

# Thymme, Thomas
### died 1620

Thymme was a fairly prolific Elizabethan writer and translator, who was one of those enthusiasts for Paracelsian **medicine** who translated a work into English. He translated **Duchesne**'s *The Practice of Chymicall and Hermeticall Physicke, by Quercetanus* (= Duchesne) (1605) from the Latin. This was a work of some significance in encouraging English Paracelsian medicine, which was so strongly 'chymicall' in its orientation. Thymme seems to have been a friend of **John Dee**, for he also produced an explication of the formidable problems of understanding Dee's masterfully obscure book, *Monas Hieroglyphica* (1564): *A light in darkness, which illumineth for all the Monas Hieroglyphica of the famous and profound Dr. John Dee.* (See **Numerology**; **Spirit** for quotations from this brilliant elucidation of Dee's *Monas*).

Thymme may have studied at Pembroke Hall, Cambridge – what is certain is that he became a clergyman, holding various rectories during his life. During the 1590s he was rector of St Antholin in Cornwall.


# Tincture

The concept of a tincture for tingeing **metals** exists from the very inception of the alchemical tradition. In Hellenistic times there was extensive literature on dyeing and colouring metals, and collections of recipes are extant (*see* **Hellenistic Alchemy**; **Manuscripts**). Tingeing metals might give the superficial appearance of **gold** or silver, but the true tincture must act like a penetrating **spirit**, lending new **colour** throughout the substance of the metal. **Transmutation** was equated with the use of such a penetrating tincture, and so the word itself became equated with the **elixir** and **Stone** of the Philosophers as transmutatory agent.

We see what a crucial part the concept of tincture plays in the whole opus from Ibn Sina **Avicenna**'s introductory remarks in his *Kitab al-Shifa*, or 'Book of the Remedy', a study of minerals, chemistry and geology:

> After thinking the matter over [of alchemy] I said: 'If this is possible what makes it so? And if it is a thing that cannot be, why is this the case?' Now I knew that if it were possible for us to impart the colour of Gold to Silver, and of Silver to Copper, we should require a Red Tincture, capable of

imparting redness, and a White Tincture, capable of imparting whiteness. We also know that the mingling of tinctures with hard stone-like bodies is out of the question unless the latter be first softened and converted into the fluid state.

As regards the White Tincture, we see that Mercury whitens while in addition to its whitening power we see that it clings to metals and penetrates into them. For example, when Copper is made into thin plates and Mercury is vigorously rubbed on it for some time, after digestion with Mercury in Vinegar and other medicines, whiteness will soon penetrate to such an extent into the interior of the Copper that both its interior and its exterior, its visible and its inward part, will become as white as Silver. One can thus imagine that, if it were to undergo still further treatment with Mercury, the effect and action of the latter would be even greater.

Mercury flees from fire, not being damaged by combustion, because of its volatility (fugitive Mercury!). If treated with fused substances, it will remain in them with its natural whiteness unaffected.

We get a good idea here how **mercury** becomes revered as the penetrating spirit or tincture.

The author is, however, aware that he is creating a colouring or dyeing agent, not transmuting the metal itself:

Having done this, we obtain a tincturing and penetrating virtue, a Tincture indeed of unsurpassed power and penetration, so much so that its colour differs in no respect from that of pure Silver, nay more, its colour is deeper and its whiteness more vivid.

Having dealt with the white tincture, which tinges metals to silver, he then passes to the red tincture, which is the same as the red elixir or *magisterium*, usually regarded as the tincture of gold (*see also* **Colours**):

We do not find any natural substance which imparts a red colour; we actually find that all things which penetrate into Silver and other metals and impart a colour to them, have a tendency to turn them black. In the case of Sulphur, when a small quantity of it is passed over Silver, we see that it turns yellow; but if its remains in contact with the Silver, the Silver is blackened.

These quotations give unique insight into the alchemical arts of dyeing metals. Avicenna appears to have denied the reality of actual transmutation of one metal into another, rather he admitted only that the species, the appearance, might be transformed by dyes and tinctures.

*See* H.E. Stapleton, R.F. Azo, M. Hidayat Husain, and G.L. Lewis, 'Two Alchemical Treatises attributed to Avicenna', *Ambix*, 1962.

# Transmutation

For most people, **alchemy** means essentially the art of transmuting or transforming base **metals** into **gold**, although the alchemical tradition of Christian Europe, inherited from its Hellenistic and Islamic predecessors, is the only continuous tradition which relies on ideas or **myths** of transmutation. Indian and Chinese alchemists believed in the reality of transmutation, of the perfecting of metals by more or less magical means, however the main aim of eastern alchemy has always been to prolong and enhance life, vitality and youth, using alchemically prepared panaceas and elixirs, rather than to effect transmutation.

In the western tradition, however, the forging of gold must already have become a serious problem by *c.*300 AD when a decree of the Roman Emperor Diocletian forbade the art of *chemeia*. Islamic writers debated the possibility of transmutation by alchemical arts, some arguing strongly for it, others like **Avicenna** categorically denying there was even a remote chance of it ever occurring. The theory that metals were born through the harmonious marriage of the principles of **mercury** and **sulphur** was helpful to the cause of alchemists, and led them to argue that, if metals could grow to perfection in the womb of the earth as combinations of mercury and sulphur, the alchemist might by his art speed up the process of metallic incubation: this possibility is explicitly what Avicenna denied (*see* **Conjunctio**; **Mercury-Sulphur Theory of the Generation of Metals**).

The most popular theory of the possible physical transmutation of base metals was that metals inferior to gold are in fact diseased metals. Curing their infirmity is possible using the **medicine** of metals, which means the same as the **elixir**. The **Stone** of the Philosophers, called the 'stone that is not a stone' is generally considered synonymous with the elixir. However, a number of circumstantial narratives of purportedly successful transmutation, speak of a 'powder of projection'. Success of the overall alchemical opus would produce two elixirs: the white elixir or tincture would transmute base metals to silver, while the red elixir would change metals to gold.

This search for gold led in medieval Europe to papal decrees becoming necessary to ban alchemy as an attempted gold-making art. The story of Chaucer's Canones Yeoman shows how even churchmen indulged in the dubious chemistry which was involved with 'vulgar' alchemy. There are many circumstantial narratives of actual transmutation, and men like **John Dee** and **Edward Kelley** used a powder which they believed achieved true transmutation (*see also* **Helvetius; Sendivogius and Sethon**).

The concept of alchemy as the art of metallic transmutation was argued by A.E. Waite in his fascinating book, *The Lives of the Alchemystical Philosophers*. However, **Jungian theories about alchemy** have strongly argued that this 'extrovert', material aspect concealed and obscured the true inner purpose, the 'introvert' meaning of alchemy as a mystical, adept tradition. Jung strongly asserts the spiritual, gnostic roots of the alchemical tradition in viewing it as one involving the **redemption** of man and **nature**, liberation from the dark prison of mortality and corruption. In this interpretation, the Stone of the Philosophers (*Lapis philosophorum*) or the mystic elixir are not to be given material meaning: they are mythical and mystical concepts.

The present author finds room for an intermediate assessment: men like John Dee and Sendivogius were *believed* to have achieved true transmutation, and the myth of true transmutation was an inspiration to many to practise alchemy. Those who lacked wisdom or honesty often brought themselves and others to ruin – Ben Jonson's play *The Alchemist* is a superb satire on the simple-minded 'vulgar alchemist'. However, the classic texts repeatedly emphasize secrecy in order to convey an atmosphere of mystic wisdom. The earliest alchemists had a system of initiation and **Hellenistic alchemy** may have been virtually a mystery religion. The roots of the alchemical tradition undoubtedly lie in gnostic religion, which sought the inner transformation of man, the achievement of spiritual liberation, by the understanding of matter, of birth, death, redemption and resurrection, of **spirit**, body and soul.

# Tree
## *Arbor Philosophica*, Tree of the Philosophers

One of the most ancient primordial spiritual symbols is the tree, which so often in **myth** and ritual has a numinous character: the oracle of Zeus at Dodona was centred upon an oak tree, and one thinks also of the golden bough and the ceremonies of the Druids. The shamans have the legend of the world or cosmic tree. In **alchemy** the tree is most readily associated with the Tree of Knowledge and Life in the Garden of Eden. There are many illustrations of trees: often the tree is shown with the symbols for the planets-**metals** amidst its branches. The *Museum Hermeticum* displays trees with chemical symbols amidst their leaves. The central tree bears the sun sign which touches the heavens.

**Michael Maier**, in *Atalanta fugiens*, refers to the golden apples: 'In the garden of wisdom stands a tree, which produces golden apples.' In his *Symbols of the Golden Table*, Maier shows a garden with a tree which has fruit in the shape of moons, suns and Saturn, with the instruction that the first stage of the opus involves sprinkling its roots.

The *Rosarium sapientiae* (Rose Garden of Wisdom) shows a tree of life, which brings life and happiness to those who lay hold upon her. (*see* de Jong edition of *Atalanta fugiens*).

Jung has explored the symbolism of the alchemical tree in a study devoted to the subject, for he considers the tree a natural archetypal symbol of the spiritual growth within the human psyche. He refers to the numerous sun and moon trees in illustrations. One work is entitled 'On the tree of Aristotle' (*Super arborem Aristotelis*) which shows the moon's orb perched 'in the form of a stork on a wonder-working tree by the grave of Hermes' (cited Jung, *Mysterium Conjunctionis*, p.133).

A *Book of Secrets* attributed to Galen contains a description of the moon tree or **herb**, 'whose roots are metallic earth, whose stem is red, veined with black, and whose flowers are like those of the marjoram; there are thirty of them corresponding to the age of the moon in its waxing and waning. Their colour is yellow.' Jung also cites a reference in **Khunrath** to the tree of the sun and the moon, which is a red and white coral-tree of 'our sea', growing from a salty **fountain** (Jung, op. cit., p.133).

There are many medieval illustrations of allegorical trees, and **Joachim of Fiore** conceives of a tree of apocalyptic history and prophecy. In the **Cabala** the tree of the Sefiroth is the central key.

# *Tria Prima*
## Three Principles: Mercury, Salt, Sulphur; Paracelsian theory

The three principles were introduced by **Paracelsus** as the trinitarian basis of all phenomena. According to his theory, God created a universe with the quaternity of the four **elements**. But this quaternity was founded upon the trinity of three principles, **mercury**, **salt** and **sulphur**. This does more than add salt to the Islamic **mercury-sulphur theory of generation of metals**. These principles constitute the properties and qualities of all material things. The macrocosm or greater world of stars and planets consists of the three principles, as does the lesser world of man, the microcosm (*see* **Microcosm-Macrocosm**).

The doctrine is by no means mystical and arcane in significance. *Mercury* is conceived as the 'vaporous principle of the body', being 'by itself a boundless, humid, liquid vehicle of natural balsam'. The philosophers' mercury is, of course, the ambivalent liquid-vapour substance, the very essence of metals, and Paracelsus says metals arise from liquid. *Sulphur* is the inflammable principle of bodies, 'fatty, light, uniform, a fomentation of vital balsam'. *Salt* is 'truly the fixed principle of a body, weighty, solid, and uniting the greatest strength, yielding neither to iron nor fire'. Thus, salt and mercury represent solid, or earth, and liquid, or water.

**Duchesne**, an ardent Paracelsian, gives this explanation:

> Mercury is a sharpe liquor, passable and penetrating, and a most pure & Aetheriall substantiall body: a substance ayrie, most subtill, quickning, and ful of Spirit, the food of life, and the essence or terme, the next instrument.
>
> Sulphur is that moyst, sweet, oyly, clammy, original, which giveth substance to itself; the nourishment of fire, or of natural heat, endiued with the force of mollifying and of gluing together.
>
> Salt, is the dry body, saltish, meerely earthy, representing the nature of Salt endued with wonderfull vertues of dissolving, congealing, clensing, emptying, and with other infinite faculties which it exerciseth in the individuals, and separated in other bodyes, from their individuals.

Here mercury and salt emerge as antithesis of **spirit** and matter, so vital in alchemy. Sulphur plays a mediating role, as an oily substance, glueing the solid and spirit together.

This alleged confused thinking was attacked by anti-Paracelsian propagandist Thomas Erastus. However, the theory exercised tremendous influence, being a vital inspiration to men like **van Helmont** in stimulating chemical inquiry. Like all Paracelsian ideas, it is profoundly mystical and magical in significance.

# Abbot Trithemius of Sponheim
## 1462–1516

This mysterious figure is regarded by some as a key figure in the history of natural **magic**. He was born near Trier on the River Moselle and seems to have had prophetic **dreams and visions** from an early age – these he interpreted as divine revelation. Having received instruction in magic while studying in Heidelberg, he soon decided to become a monk in the monastery of Sponheim. Ordained in 1482, he became abbot of the monastery in the following year and in this position he amassed one of the most impressive libraries in Europe. This astonishing collection of over 2,000 **manuscripts** included priceless works on the sciences and philosophy, with a good collection of Greek texts. He remained abbot until 1505, as his reputation for humanist learning and philosophy spread throughout Europe. His reputation for being a Faustian magician and alchemist comes largely from the story that he instructed both **Agrippa** and **Paracelsus** in esoteric knowledge. He was known as an alchemist, but his most famous book was concerned with **angel magic**: this was the *Steganographia*, which **John Dee** valued most highly, as a work worthy of the attention of princes. Men like Dee believed that Trithemius had discovered vital secrets about magical or psychic communication. There can be no doubt that the old abbot was something of an expert in cryptography and codes, and this subject came under the heading of magic at this time.

Although accused of sorcery and necromancy, Trithemius always insisted that he was a devout Christian and he was certainly a prominent humanist philosopher. His magical interests were typical of many devout philosophers of the Renaissance Hermetic tradition.

**Publications:**

The *Steganographia* circulated in manuscript. It was printed in Frankfurt in 1606.

# U

## Unity

True it is without a lye, certaine and most true, by the affinity of Unity. That which is superior is like to that which is inferiour, and that which is inferiour is like that which is superiour, because all Numbers consiste of Unites, for the working of many miracles of one thing. Do not all things flow from Unitie through the goodness of the One? Nothing that is varying, and in discord can be ioyned to Unity, but the like by simplicity, adaptacion, and fitness of one, it may bring forth fruite; what else springeth from Unity, but the Ternary itself. The Unarie is simple, the Binarie is compound, and the Ternary is reducible to the simplicity of Unitie. His father is the Sun, his Mother is the Moone. The Wind carrieth the seede in his Wombe, the Earth is the Nourse. Thou shalt separate the Earth from the Fire, the thick from the thin, and the Ternary being now brought to itself with witt, it assendeth upward with great seetenes, and retorneth againe to Earth and adorned with virtue and greate beauty, and so it receiveth superior and inferiour force, and it shalbe from henceforth potent and orient in the brightnes of Unitie, to produce all apt nomber, and all obscurity shall flee away. Thus Hermes.

This passage comes from **Thomas Thymme**, friend of **John Dee**, whose *Monas Hieroglyphica* he is commenting upon in his *A light in darkness, which illumineth for all the* Monas Hieroglyphica *of the famous and profound Dr. John Dee*. It is an eloquent Elizabethan paraphrase of **The Emerald Tablet**, the Hermetic *Tabula Smaragdina*, revered by Islamic and Christian alchemists alike as a manifesto of the mystic doctrine of **Creation** from divine unity and perfection.

**Thomas Vaughan** in *Anima magica abscondita*:

The first principle is One in One, and One from One. It is a pure, white Virgin, and next to that which is most pure and simple. This is the first created Unity. By this all things were made, not actually but Mediately, and without this, Nothing can be made either Artificial or Natural. This is the *Uxor Dei et Stellarum* [wife of God and the stars]. By mediation of this, there is a descent from One into Four, and an ascent from Three by Four to the invisible, supernatural *Monas*. The diameter line in the circle creates the *Ternarius*. The second principle is the *Binarius* which fell from its first Unity by adhesion to Matter, which rendered it impure. This third [principle] is properly no principle, but a product of Art. It is a various Nature, compounded in one sense, and Decompounded in another, consisting of Inferiour and Superiour powers. This is the Magicians fire, this is *Mercurius Philosophorum, Celeberrimus ille Microcosmus, et Adam*. This is the Labyrinth and Wild of Magick where a world of students have lost themselves.

This is a cabalist view of the world, as being a process of emanation from divine unity. The third principle, the *Ternarius*, is the key to reuniting impure **nature** with the purity of divine unity. Thomas Vaughan again:

> This *Ternarius*, being reduced *per Quaternarium* ascends to the Magicall Decad, which is *Monas Ultissima*, in which state *quaecumque vult potest*; for it is united then *per Aspectum* to the first, eternall, spirituall unity.

# Uroboros-Serpent

The uroboros-serpent is the true archetypal emblem of **alchemy**; it is portrayed in the form of a serpent devouring its own tail, and in this it resembles the alchemical **dragon** of later times which is the symbol for Mercurius and for the **Prime Matter**. In early pictures, it bears the motto in Greek *hen to pan*, everything is one (*see* **Numerology**).

The significance of the serpent is vividly portrayed by **Thomas Vaughan**:

> The Body of the Serpent tells you it is a fierie substance, for a Serpent is full of heat and fire, which made the Egyptians esteem him divine: this appears by his quick motion without feet or finns, much like that of the Pulse, for his impetuous hot spirit shoots him on like a Squid. There is also another Analogie, for the Serpent receives his youth, so strong is his natural heat, and casts off his old skin. Truly the matter [i.e. Prime Matter] is a very Serpent, for she renews herself in a thousand ways.
>
> Vaughan, *Magia Adamica*, Rudrum's edition

In explaining the mysteries of the Egyptians, Vaughan delivers this fascinating account of the uroboros-serpent:

> First of all then, they draw a Circle, in the Circle a Serpent not folded, but Diameter-wise, and at length; her head resembles that of a Hawke, and the Tayle is tyed in a small knot, and a little below the head her wings

are Volant. The circle points at Emepht, or God the Father being Infinite, without Beginning, without End. Moreover it comprehends, or Conteines in it self the Second Deitie Phtha, and the Egg, or Chaos out of which all things were made. The Hawke in Egyptian symbols signifies Light, and Spirit; his head annexed here to the Serpent represents Phtha, or the Second Person, who is the first Light, as wee have told you in our *Anthroposophia*. He is said to forme all things out of the Egg, because in him, as it were in a Glasse, are certain Types or Images, namely the Distinct Concepts of the Paternall Deities, according to which by Cooperation of the Spirit, namely the Holy Ghost, the Creatures are formed.

The passage shows how in Egyptian mysteries the Serpent has divine significance, symbolizing the Creator and the **unity** of the cosmos, which is also symbolized by the philosophical **egg**.

The uroboros-serpent represents Mercurius, the universal spirit of **transmutation**. The serpent impregnates and feeds upon itself, being thus an ideal symbol for the unity (*see* **Monas**, **Unity**) underlying the diversity of the cosmos. Jung comments:

In the age-old image of the uroboros lies the thought of devouring oneself and turning oneself into a circulatory process, for it was clear to the more astute alchemists that the *prima materia* of the art was man himself. The uroboros is a dramatic symbol for the integration and assimilation of the opposite, i.e. of the shadow. This feedback process is at the same time a symbol of immortality, since it is said of the uroboros that he slays himself and brings himself to life, fertilizes himself and gives birth to himself.

Jung, *Mysterium Conjunctionis*, p.365

# Valentine, Basil
**Apparently a legendary figure, said to have lived
1394–1413**

Like Christian Rosenkreutz (*see* **Rosicrucians**), legend has it that
Valentine was a fifteenth-century monk, a Benedictine of St Peter of
Erfurt. No one has established the historical existence of such a man,
although many churchmen did practise **alchemy**. It seems likely that
the name is a fiction, to lend religious and medieval authority to the
published works. J.R. Partington comments that Basil Valentine
'probably represents the literary forgery which has misled and
perplexed chemists for the longest period'. The works were published
in German at the height of the craze for Paracelsian medical alchemy
and they show an expertise in chemistry which could only have come
in the wake of the Paracelsians. Those who disliked **Paracelsus**
claimed that Valentine invented the theory of the *Tria Prima*, the
three principles of **salt**, **sulphur** and **mercury**, and that Paracelsus
stole these ideas from him.

In his works Valentine claims his travels took him to Belgium,
Holland and Britain, even as far as Egypt. He was also said to have
made a pilgrimage to St James Compostella in Spain. There are no
fifteenth-century **manuscripts** of his work, however, and he includes
anachronistic references to America, tobacco and printing.

It is probable that Valentine's works are actually composed by
Johann Tholde, who edited them. He was a salt-boiler of
Frankenhausen, who published an account of salts and their mining.
His connection with the Rosicrucians seems to have been strong, and
he was probably involved with a circle of experimenters who were
exploring the reactions involving **antimony**, as well as observing
**acids** and **salts**.

The great work attributed to Valentine was the *Triumph wagen
antimonii* which was an important survey of the properties of
**antimony**, a metal which fascinated **Isaac Newton**. We now know
that Newton used this work of Valentine, and was fascinated by the

crystalline formation of the *Star Regulus* of antimony.

The Preface to the *Triumph wagen* contains a typical Paracelsian salvo against the ignorance of doctors and apothecaries. Antimony, a highly poisonous metal, is declared to be one of the seven wonders of the world, whose toxicity may be removed by alchemy. It should be noted that the Indian system of **medicine**, *ayurveda*, makes use of poisonous substances, which are combined, purified and treated to work as effective medicines. In the Preface, antimony is allowed to speak for itself, and declares itself to contain all the Paracelsian *Tria Prima*, the three principles of salt, **sulphur** and **mercury** which underlie the universe.

**Publications:**
*Von dem grossen Stein der Uralten* (Of the Great Stone of the Ancients) (1599).
*De Microcosmo von der grossen Heimlichkeit der Welt* (On the Microcosm of the Great Secret of the World) (1602).
*Von dem natürlichen und übernatürlichen Dingen. Auch von der ersten Tinctur, Wurtzel und Geister der Metallen und Mineralien.* (Of Natural and Supernatural Things. Also concerning the First Tincture, Root and Spirits of Metals and Minerals) (1603). This work was published in English in 1671: *Of Natural and Supernatural Things*).
*De occulta philosophia, oder von der heimlichen Wundergeburt der sieben Planeten und Metallen* (Occult Philosophy, or the Secret Generation of the Seven Planets and Metals) (1603).
*Letztes Testament* (Last Testament) (subtitled 'Opening of Heavenly and Earthly Secrets') (1626).
*Basil Valentine, Friar of the Order of St Benedict: His Last Will and Testament. The Last Will and Testament of Basil Valentine, Monke of the Order of St Bennet. Which being alone, He hid under a Table of Marble, being the High Altar of the Cathedral Church in the Imperial City of Erfurt* (1657).

# Vaughan, Thomas
**Brother of the metaphysical poet Henry Vaughan; 1621–65**

Thomas was the twin brother of the metaphysical poet Henry Vaughan, both being born 'at Newton in the parish of St Briget's in the yeare 1621'. He entered Jesus College, Oxford, in 1638, and remained at Oxford for the next decade, despite the unsettling conditions of the English Civil War. Thereafter he became rector of the Welsh parish of Llansanffraid (= St Briget) and it was here that he took up medical studies, motivated by the lack of doctors in Wales. He was evicted from the parish, however, in 1650 because of his Royalist sympathies. He married his wife Rebecca in 1651 (she died in 1658), and spent the next period of his life in London.

It would seem that, although he did not practice **medicine**, Vaughan sought to apply his chemical skills to preparing medicines in the way recommended by **Paracelsus**. He corresponded with **Samuel Hartlib**, establishing a reputation with his book *Anthroposophia*, a magico-mystical work, very difficult to get to grips with.

Vaughan later became involved with a plan of Dr Robert Child to form a chemical club, with a laboratory and library, the main aim being to translate and collect chemical works. In the course of litigation with one Edward Bolnest, he was accused of spending 'most of his tyme in the studdy of Natuall Philosophy and Chimicall Phisick'. He is reported as having confessed that he had 'long sought and long missed . . . the philosopher's stone'. He died on 27 February 1665.

It now seems clear that Thomas Vaughan was the author of tracts published under the name of Eugenius Philalethes (*see* **Philalethes** for other pseudonymous works).

As a writer, he shows a literary quality rare in the history of **alchemy**, being animated with a metaphysical passion for his subject. He clearly had the deepest religious belief and commitment to the esoteric, deeper truths of the alchemical, Hermetic tradition.

**Publications:**

Anthroposophia theomagica, *or A Discourse of the Nature of Man and his State after Death; grounded in his Creator's Protochimistry* (1650).

Anima magica abscondita *or A Discourse of the Universal Spirit of Nature, with his strange, abstruse, miraculous ascent and descent* (1650).

Magia Adamica abscondita, *or The Antiquity of Magic, and the descent thereof downwards, proved* (1650).

The Man-Mouse taken in a Trap, and Tortured to Death for Gnawing the Margins of Eugenius Philalethes (1650).

Lumen de lumine *or A New Magicall Light Discovered or Communicated to the World* (1651).

The Second Wash, or the Moore Scour'd once more (1651).

Aula lucis, *or the House of Light* (1651).

The Fame and Confession of the Fraternity of R.C., commonly of the Rosie Cross (1652).

*Euphrates or the Waters of the East* (1655).

The works are available in an excellent edition: ed. Alan Rudrum, *The Works of Thomas Vaughan*.

# Vessel, Hermetic
## Vas Hermeticum

We still use the term 'hermetically sealed', which arises from the need for securing the seal on the philosophical vessel. This vessel is the scene from the **stages** or **processes** of the alchemical opus, and it is here that the adept observes the **colour** changes which lead from the *nigredo* to the production of the red **elixir** or **Stone**. Our illustration (opposite) shows four key stages, commencing with the ashes (*cinis*) produced in calcination, with the *conjunctio* or mystic marriage of **King and Queen** representing the fruition of the opus. The *conjunctio* taking place in the vessel is a very common alchemical illustration, and from this union is born the Son of the Philosophers (*filius philosophorum*) who represents the Stone or *Lapis* of transformation. The *Aurora consurgens* refers to the *vas naturale* (the natural vessel) which is a womb or matrix for incubating the Stone.

Many texts speak with religious reverence of the sacred vessel of **transmutation**. The religious emphasis may originate with the gnostics (*see* **Gnosticism**). A **Hermetic text** speaks of a divine vessel, the *Krater*, which God has filled with *nous* (mind) or *pneuma* (**spirit**), and mankind can be baptized in mind and spirit, thus attaining mystic gnosis. **Zosimos** refers to this Hermetic Krater.

From the very beginning of the tradition, the vessel is a kind of **Holy Grail**; it is generally shown as being circular in shape, to show that it is a **microcosm** of the heavens which govern the progress of the opus.

**Maria Prophetissa** already attached vital importance to the dimensions of the vessel, which was a deep secret: 'The philosophers teach everything except the Hermetic vessel, because that is divine and is hidden from the Gentiles by the Lord's wisdom, and those who know it not, know not the true method, because of their ignorance of the vessel of Hermes.'

Throughout the tradition the vessel was equated with the philosophical **egg**, which represented the microcosm of heaven and earth. As the egg itself is equated with **mercury**, so is the vessel.

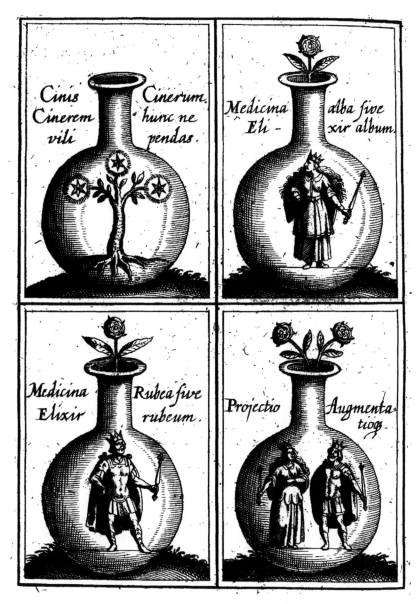

*The Hermetic vessel of transformation.*
  *The alchemical tree is shown in the first vessel, then the white medicine or elixir (feminine, representing Luna), followed by the red medicine or elixir (masculine, representing Sol). Finally, the goal or the projection and multiplication is achieved, symbolized by the mystic union of the King and Queen, the* conjunctio *of* Sol and Luna.
  *Mylius,* Anatomia Auri, sive Tyrocinia *(Frankfurt, 1622).*
  *By kind permission of The Bodleian Library, Oxford.*
  *4°S. 5 (3) Med.V. p.20.*

**Philalethes**, in the seventeenth century, says that mercury is not only a two-edged sword, guarding the way to the **Tree** of Life, but is also 'our true, hidden vessel, the Philosophic Garden, wherein our sun rises and sets'.

## Water
*See* **Elements**.

## Wei Po Yang
**Chinese alchemist; *floruit* 120–40 AD**

The two fathers of **Chinese alchemy** are Wei Po Yang and Ko Hung, both of whom are remarkable personalities, imbued with Taoist natural philosophy. It is said that Wei was summoned to the imperial court in 121 AD, but he wisely refused the invitation, preferring the reputation of hermit and holy man. His famous work, dated 142 AD, was the *Ts'an T'ung Ch'i*, in which he tells us that he leads a quiet life in a remote valley, with no interest in the acquisitive values of his society. The text is the oldest Chinese work devoted fully to **alchemy**, and is written in the form of a commentary on the *I Ching*. It is evident that it is a work of **elixir** alchemy, being an account of the preparation of the mystic pill of immortality.

A famous story is told of Wei Po Yang and his white dog. In the company of three disciples, Wei went into the mountains to try out his pills, his elixir of life. He decided to perform an unkind animal experiment, and gave the dog a pill. The animal expired, and the disciples at once lost faith. In spite of this, Wei felt it would be an impossible humiliation to return without trying his own **medicine** – but having taken one of his pills, he too fell down apparently dead. One loyal disciple followed suit, but the other two returned to arrange a funeral. In the meantime, Wei revived from the apparently lethal dose, and gave medicine to his dog and disciple, whereupon the three became immortals, achieving the state of the *Hsien*.

*See* Tenney L. Davis, 'An Ancient Chinese Treatise on Alchemy, entitled *Ts'an T'ung Ch'i*, written by Wei Po Yang about 142 AD', *Isis*, 1932.

## Winthrop, John Junior
**New England alchemist and book collector; 1606–76**

John Winthrop Junior was the first Governor of Connecticut, and the son of the founder of the Massachusetts Bay Colony. He was America's first known astronomer of distinction.

He studied at Trinity College, Dublin, and from 1630 his accounts show that he was purchasing chemicals and **apparatus**. He started his well-known collection of alchemical books before emigrating from England to join his father in Massachusetts in 1631, and became famous in New England for his expert practice of chemical **medicine**. He was constantly in demand in his medical practice.

Winthrop kept up a vigorous contact with the **Hartlib** circle, who took a keen interest in **alchemy**. He built up volumes of correspondence with men of science and was the first colonial member of the Royal Society in London (he was charter member in 1663).

His valuable library contained Paracelsian works, and ten volumes purchased from **John Dee**'s remarkable library.

*See* R.S. Wilkinson's New England's Last Alchemists' in *Ambix*, 1962, and 'The Alchemical Library of John Winthrop Jr (1606–1676) and his Descendants in Colonial America' in *Ambix*, 1963.

# Z

## Zosimos of Panoplis
### c.300 AD

Where **Maria Prophetissa** may be called the founding mother of **alchemy**, Zosimos is certainly the father of the Hellenistic tradition. He seems to have been a polymath, writing works on **medicine**, history, agriculture and warfare as well as on chemistry and philosophy, reminding us of **Bolos of Mendes**. He was certainly a true philosopher, belonging to the Poimandres sect of the gnostics, and the tradition of alchemy after his death was completely dominated by **Gnosticism**, with its powerful mystical impulse towards realization beyond this dark world.

Zosimos and his sister Theosebeia composed an encyclopaedia of alchemy called *Cheirokmeta* in 28 books: the Greek alphabet has 24 letters, with four Coptic letters making 28, but the number may have astral or lunar significance. He was much interested in **apparatus**, and cites Maria Prophetissa as the expert on this, providing a detailed description of the *tribikos*.

Zosimos was immersed in the Hermetic **magic** of his time, being mainly preoccupied with the gnostic concepts of the first man (*anthropos*), his fall and ascent or **redemption** (*see* **Adam and Eve**). He does not seem to have been a Christian, though subsequent writers were gnostic Christians, but he corresponded with Origen on the Book of Susanna and also wrote on the genealogies of Christ in the Gospels.

With Zosimos we gain insight into the depths of mystical speculation, as well as the practical, laboratory orientation of the whole tradition. He believed explicitly in the **transmutation** of **metals**, referring to the four metals lead, copper, tin and silver. He launches a prolonged attack on those who seek 'opportune or timely tinctures', and who rely upon favourable 'daimones' (spiritual beings). For him, the philosopher must liberate himself from the shackles of good and bad fortune, which in Gnosticism are the product of the cycle of astrological time: it is the foolish alchemist who relies upon spirits and favourable planetary conjunctions.

In his *Alchemical Studies*, Jung provides an extensive account of the symbolism of the 'Visions' of Zosimos. These have a shamanistic quality, as the adept in a vision seems to be torn to pieces witnessing a strange priestly sacrifice. The themes of torture, death and rebirth here assert themselves, as throughout the tradition, and leave us in no doubt of connections with the ancient Mithraic and gnostic mysteries, revelations and rites.

In a long passage quoted by Jung, Zosimos also attests the importance of male and female principles in the universe, as active and receptive, sounding much like the Taoist alchemists of Chinese tradition (*see* **Chinese alchemy**).

*See also* illuminating material cited by Jack Lindsay, *The Origins of Alchemy in Greco-Roman Egypt*; Jung, *Collected Works*, Vol.13, pp.59-65.

# Bibliography

Alchemy is a vast subject, and this bibliography is intended as a guide to works which will easily provide the reader with the broadest perspectives. This *Dictionary* is intended to suggest the cultural importance of alchemy in the context of the history of science, magic and philosophy, and also ventures into the cultural implications of alchemy in various traditions. For this reason the works listed are mainly general in character: a bibliography of Chinese alchemy alone, for example, would occupy considerable space. (However, Joseph Needham's monumental works on *Science and Civilization in China* are furnished with a lavish bibliography, not only on Chinese, but also on European alchemy.)

I have included very few articles from the journal *Ambix*, but practically every article published in this important journal is relevant to the entries in this book.

Allen, Don C., *The Star-Crossed Renaissance* (Durham, North Carolina, 1941).

Ammann, P.J., 'The Musical Theory and Philosophy of Robert Fludd', *Journal of the Warburg and Courtauld Institutes*, XXX, 1967, 198–227.

Appleby, J.H., 'Arthur Dee and Johannes Banfi Hunyades', *Ambix*, 24, July 1977, 2.

Aquinas, Sir Thomas, *Aurora consurgens*, ed. Marie-Louise von Franz (Bollingen, London, 1966).

Ashmole, Elias, *Elias Ashmole (1617–1692): His autobiographical and historical notes, his correspondence, and other contemporary sources relating to his life and work*, ed. C.H. Josten (5 vols, Oxford, 1966).

Atwood, Mary Anne, *Hermetic Philosophy and Alchemy: A suggestive inquiry into 'The Hermetic Mystery'* (revised ed., Julian Press, New York, 1960).

Aubrey, John, *Brief Lives*, ed. A. Clark (2 vols, Clarendon Press, Oxford, 1898).

Bacon, Roger, *Opus Maius*, ed. J.H. Bridges (3 vols, Clarendon Press, Oxford, 1897).

—, *Opera quaedam hactenus inedita*, ed. J.S. Brewer (Vol. 1 includes *Opus tertium, Opus minus, Compendium philosophiae*, Longman, London).

—, *De retardatione accidentium senectutis cum aliis opusculis* (Clarendon Press, Oxford).

—, *The Mirror of Alchemy (Speculum alchimiae)*, tr. T.L. Davis, in *Journal of Chemical Education*, 8, 1945-53.

Berthelot, Marcelin, *Les origines de l'alchimie* (Steinheil, Paris, 1885).

—, *La chimie au moyen âge* (3 vols, Imprimerie Nationale, Paris, 1893).

—, *Collection des anciens alchimistes grecs* (3 vols, Steinheil, Paris, 1888).

Blau, J.L., *The Christian Interpretation of the Cabala in the Renaissance* (New York, 1944).

Boas, Marie, *Robert Boyle and Seventeenth-Century Chemistry* (Cambridge University Press, Cambridge, 1958).

Boerhaave, Hermann, *A New Method of Chemistry*, tr. Peter Shaw (2 vols, 2nd edition, Longman, London, 1741).

Burckhardt, Titus, *Alchemy: Science of the cosmos, science of the soul* (Stuart and Watkins, London, 1967).

Chardin, Teilhard de, *The Phenomenon of Man*.

—, *The Heart of Matter*.

Clulee, N.H., *John Dee's Natural Philosophy* (Routledge and Kegan Paul, London, 1988).

Crosland, M.P., *Historical Studies in the Language of Chemistry* (Harvard University Press, Boston, 1962).

Davis, Tenney L., 'An Ancient Chinese Treatise on Alchemy, entitled *Ts'an T'ung Ch'i*, written by Wei Po Yang about 142 AD', *Isis*, 18, 1932, 210-89.

Davis, W., *The Story of Copper* (1925).

Debus, Allen G., *The English Paracelsians* (Oldbourne, New York, 1965).

—, *The English Paracelsians* (Oldbourne, New York, 1966).

Dobbs, Betty Jo, *The Foundations of Newton's Alchemy or 'The Hunting of the Greene Lyon'* (Cambridge University Press, Cambridge, 1975).

Dunleavy, Gareth W., 'The Chaucer Ascription in Trinity College, Dublin MS D.2.8', *Ambix*, XIII, February 1965, 1, 2-21.

Duveen, D.L.: *Bibliotheca alchemica et chemica* (E. Weil, 1949).

Eliade, Mircea, *The Forge and the Crucible: The Origin and Structure of Alchemy* (Harper, 1971).

—, *Shamanism*, tr. W.R. Trask (Penguin, 1989).

Evans, R.J.W., *Rudolf II and his World: a study in intellectual history 1576-1612* (Clarendon Press, Oxford, 1973).

Fabricius, Johannes, *Alchemy* (The Aquarian Press, Wellingborough, 1989).

Ferguson, J., *Bibliotheca chemica* (2 vols, Maclehose, Glasgow, 1906).
—, *Bibliographical Notes on Histories of Inventions and Books of Secrets* (2 vols, Holland Press, London).
Festugière, André J., *La révélation d'Hermes Trismegiste* (3rd edition, Gabalda, Paris, 1944).
Forbes, R.J., *Metallurgy in Antiquity* (Leiden, 1950).
Franz, Marie-Louise von, 'The Idea of the Macro- and Microcosmos in the Light of Jungian Psychology', *Ambix*, XIII, 1965, 22–34.
—, *Alchemical Active Imagination* (Spring Publications Inc., US, 1979).
French, P.J., *John Dee: The world of an Elizabethan magus* (Routledge and Kegan Paul, London, 1972).
Gilchrist, Cherry, *Alchemy: The Great Work* (The Aquarian Press, Wellingborough, 1978).
Ginzburg, Carlo, *The Cheese and the Worms: The cosmos of a sixteenth-century miller* (Routledge and Kegan Paul, London, 1980).
Goodwin, J., *Robert Fludd: Hermetic philosopher and surveyor of two worlds* (Thames and Hudson, London, 1979).
Grossinger, R. (ed), *Alchemy* (California, 1979).
Hannaway, P., *The Chemists and the Word* (John Hopkins, 1975).
Holmyard, E.J., *The Works of Geber*, tr. R.Russel (1678) (Dent, London, 1928).
—, *Alchemy* (Penguin, London, 1957).
—, 'Medieval Arabic Pharmacology', *Proceedings of the Royal Society of Medicine*, 29, 1–10.
—, and Mandeville, D.C., *Avicennae de congelatione et conglutinationelapidum* (Guethner, Paris, 1927).
Hopkins, Arthur J., *Alchemy: Child of Greek philosophy* (Columbia University Press, New York, 1934).
—, 'A Study of the Kerotakis Process as given by Zosimos and Later Alchemical Writers', *Isis*, Vol. XXIV, November 1938, 79, 326–54.
Hung, Ko, *Nei P'ien* (tr. J.R. Ware, *Alchemy, Medicine and Religion in the China of 320 AD, Dover, 1981*).
*Jacobi, Jolande, Paracelsus, Selected Writings* (1951).
Jong, H.M.E. de, *Michael Maier's Atalanta Fugiens: Sources of an alchemical book of emblems* (E.J. Brill, Leiden, 1969).
Jonson, Ben, *The Alchemist*, ed. H.L. Mares (Methuen, 1958).
Josten, C.H., 'Truth's Golden Harrow', *Ambix*, 3, 1949.
—, 'William Backhouse of Swallowfield', *Ambix*, IV, December 1949, 1 and 2.
—, 'John Dee's *Monas Hieroglyphica*', *Ambix*, 12, 1964, pp.84–221.
Jung, C.G., *Collected Works* (20 vols, Routledge and Kegan Paul, London, 1979): *Aion* (Vol. 9); *Psychology and Alchemy* (Vol.12); *Alchemical Studies* (Vol.13).

—, *Mysterium Conjunctionis* (Routledge and Kegan Paul, London, 1963).

—, *C.G. Jung Speaking*, eds William McGuire and R.F.C. Hull (Paladin Books, 1967).

—, *The Psychology of the Transference* (Ark, 1983).

Jung, Emma (wife of C.G. Jung), *The Grail Legend* (Hodder and Stoughton, London, 1960).

Kibre, Pearl, *Studies in Medieval Science* (Hambledon Press, London, 1984).

Klossowski de Rola, Stanislas, *The Secret Art of Alchemy* (Thames and Hudson, 1973).

Lindsay, Jack, *The Origins of Alchemy in Greco-Roman Egypt* (F. Mueller, 1970).

Lu K'uan Yu, *Taoist Yoga* (Samuel Weiser, New York, 1970).

McIntosh, Christopher, *The Rosicrucians* (Crucible, Wellingborough, 1987).

McLean, Adam, *Alchemical Mandalas* (Magnum Opus series, 1976).

—, *Hermetic Journal*, No. 13, Autumn 1981.

Mahdihassan, S., 'Alchemy and its Connection with Astrology, Pharmacy, Magic and Metallurgy', *Janus*, XLVI, 1957, 81–103.

—, *Alchemy: A child of Chinese dualism* (Iqbal, Lahore, 1962).

—, 'Dualistic Symbolism in a Medieval Work on Pharmacy', *Janus*, LI, 1964, 49–61.

—, 'Significance of the Four Elements in Alchemy', *Janus*, LI, 1964, 303–13.

Maier, Michael, *Atalanta fugiens*, ed. L. Wuthrich (1964).

Manget, Jean-Jacques, *Bibliotheca chemica curiosa* (2 vols, Chouet, Geneva, 1702).

Multhauf, R.P., 'Medical Chemistry and ''the Paracelsians'' ', *Bulletin of the History of Medicine*, 24, 1954.

—, 'The Significance of Distillation in Renaissance Medical Chemistry', *Bulletin of the History of Medicine*, 30, 1956, 327–45.

—, *The Origins of Chemistry* (Oldbourne, New York, 1966).

Nasr, Seyyed Hossein, *Science and Civilization in Islam* (Harvard University Press, Boston, 1968).

—, *Man and Nature: The spiritual crisis of modern man* (Unwin, 1976).

—, *Islamic Cosmological Doctrines* (Thames and Hudson, London, 1978).

Needham, Joseph, *Shorter Science and Civilization in China* (Vol.2, Cambridge University Press, Cambridge, 1981).

—, *Science and Civilization in China*, Vol. V: Chemistry and technology. (This volume is divided into five substantial parts, all of which are concerned with early Chinese alchemy, with comparative material on western alchemy.) (Cambridge University Press, Cambridge, 1985).

—, and Ho Ping-Yu, 'Laboratory Equipment of Chinese Alchemy', *Ambix*, June 1959.

Pagel, Walter, *Paracelsus: An introduction to philosophical medicine in the era of the Renaissance* (S. Karger, Basle and New York, 1958).

—, *Joan Battista van Helmont: Reformer of science and medicine* (Cambridge University Press, Cambridge, 1982).

Paracelsus, *Paracelsus of the Secrets of Alchymy*, tr. R. Turner (London 1656).

Partington, J.R., 'Albertus Magnus on Alchemy', *Ambix*, I, May 1937, 3-20.

—, *A History of Chemistry* (4 vols, Macmillan, London, 1961-70).

Ray, P.C., *The History of Hindu Chemistry* (Indian Chemical Society, Calcutta, 1956).

Read, John, *Prelude to Chemistry* (Heinemann, London, 1937).

Regardie, Israel, *The Philosophers' Stone* (Rider, London).

Rickard, T.A., *Man and Metals: A history of mining in relation to the development of civilization* (2 vols, New York, 1932).

Rossi, Paolo, *Francis Bacon: From magic to science* (London, 1968).

Rowse, A.L., *The Case Books of Simon Forman: Sex and society in Shakespeare's age* (Weidenfeld and Nicolson, London, 1974).

Scot, Reginald, *The Discoverie of Witchcraft* (1586).

Scott, W., *Hermetica: The ancient Greek and Latin writings which contain religious or philosophical teachings ascribed to Hermes Trismegistus* (edited with translation and notes, 2 vols, Clarendon Press, Oxford, 1924).

*Secreta secretorum*, ed. R. Steele (Clarendon Press, Oxford, 1920).

Shepard, H.J., 'Gnosticism and Alchemy', *Ambix*, VI, 1957, 86-101.

Shumaker, *The Occult Sciences in the Renaissance* (Berkeley, 1972).

Singer, C., Holmyard, E.J., Hall, A.R. and Williams, T.I., *A History of Technology* (Oxford, 1956).

Stapleton, H.E., Azo, R.F., Hidayat Husain, M., and Lewis, G.L., 'Two Alchemical Treatises attributed to Avicenna', *Ambix*, X, June 1962, 41-82.

Steele, R., 'Practical Chemistry in the Twelfth Century: *Rasis de aluminibus et salibus*', *Isis* 12, 1929, pp.10- 46.

Stillman, John, *The Story of Alchemy and Early Chemistry* (Dover, 1924 and 1960).

*Tao te Ching*, tr. D.C. Lau (Penguin, 1963).

Taylor, Frank Sherwood, 'The Origins of Greek Alchemy', *Ambix*, I, May 1937, 30-47.

—, 'The Alchemical Works of Stephanos of Alexandria', *Ambix*, I,

1937, 116–39.

—, 'The Idea of the Quintessence; in Science Medicine and History', ed. E.A. Underwood, *Essays in Honour of Charles Singer* (Oxford University Press, Oxford, 1953, pp.247–65).

—, *The Alchemists: Founders of modern chemistry* (Collier Books, New York, 1962).

—, 'The Evolution of the Still', *Annals of Science*, 5, 185–202.

Thorndike, Lynn, *A History of Magic and Experimental Science up to the Seventeenth Century* (8 vols, Macmillan and Columbia University Press, New York, 1929–58).

—, 'Medieval Lapidaries', *Ambix*, February 1960.

Thymme, Thomas, *A light in darkness, which illumineth for all the Monas Hieroglyphica of the famous and profound Dr. John Dee*, ed. S.K. Heninger (New Bodleian Library, Oxford, 1963).

Vaughan, Thomas, *The Works of Thomas Vaughan*, ed. Alan Rudrum, Oxford, 1984).

Verrier, René, *Etudes sur Arnaud de Villeneuve: 1240–1311* (E.J. Brill, Leiden)

Waite, A.E., *Lives of the Alchemystical Philosophers* (London, 1888).

—, *Hermetic Papers*, ed. R.A. Gilbert (The Aquarian Press, Wellingborough, 1987).

Webster, C. , *The Great Instauration* (Duckworth).

Westfall, R., *Never at Rest* (Cambridge University Press, Cambridge, 1980).

Wilkinson, R.S., 'New England's Last Alchemists', *Ambix* X, October 1962, 3, 128–38.

—, 'The Alchemical Library of John Winthrop Jr (1606–1676) and his descendants in Colonial America', *Ambix* XI, February 1963, 1.

Willhelm, R., *The Secret of the Golden Flower: A Chinese book of life* (introduction by C.G. Jung).

Yates, F.A., *Giordano Bruno and the Hermetic Tradition* (Routledge and Kegan Paul, London, 1964).

—, *The Rosicrucian Enlightenment* (Routledge and Kegan Paul, London, 1972).

—, *The Occult Philosophy in the Elizabethan Age* (Routledge and Kegan Paul, London, 1979).

—, *The Art of Memory* (Ark, 1984).

Yeats, W.B., *Selected Criticism and Prose* (Pan, 1976).

Zosimos, 'Visions', manuscript text produced in translation by Jung, *Collected Works*, Vol. 13, pp.59–65.